Productivity and Publishing
Writing Processes for New Scholars and Researchers

Productivity and Publishing
Writing Processes for New Scholars and Researchers

Margaret-Mary Sulentic Dowell
Louisiana State University

Leah Katherine Saal
Loyola University Maryland

Cynthia F. DiCarlo
Louisiana State University

Tynisha D. Willingham
Mary Baldwin University

Los Angeles | London | New Delhi
Singapore | Washington DC | Melbourne

FOR INFORMATION:

SAGE Publications, Inc.
2455 Teller Road
Thousand Oaks, California 91320
E-mail: order@sagepub.com

SAGE Publications Ltd.
1 Oliver's Yard
55 City Road
London, EC1Y 1SP
United Kingdom

SAGE Publications India Pvt. Ltd.
B 1/I 1 Mohan Cooperative Industrial Area
Mathura Road, New Delhi 110 044
India

SAGE Publications Asia-Pacific Pte. Ltd.
18 Cross Street #10-10/11/12
China Square Central
Singapore 048423

Printed in the United States of America

ISBN 978-1-0718-1093-4

This book is printed on acid-free paper.

Acquisitions Editor: Leah Fargotstein
Product Associate: Yumna Samie
Production Editor: Vijayakumar
Copy Editor: Christobel Colleen Hopman
Typesetter: TNQ Technologies
Proofreader: Benny Willy Stephen
Indexer: TNQ Technologies
Cover Designer: Gail Buschman
Marketing Manager: Victoria Velasquez

SUSTAINABLE FORESTRY INITIATIVE

Certified Chain of Custody
At Least 10% Certified Forest Content
www.sfiprogram.org
SFI-01028

22 23 24 25 26 10 9 8 7 6 5 4 3 2 1

Brief Contents

Detailed Contents

Chapter 8 Beyond Impact Factor: Understanding Scholarly Metrics and Increasing Exposure (Invited Submission, Andrea Hebert & David Dunaway) 171

Preface

This text specifically targets doctoral students, newly-minted PhDs, and novice researchers aiming to write for publication. We hope this text helps readers understand the stated and unstated components specific to the publication process as well as those required for scholarly productivity more generally. Our primary audience for this book is education, psychology, and social science doctoral students enrolled in their coursework and matriculating through the dissertation process along with novice scholars and researchers from these disciplines. However, the contents of this text are useful for PhD students and novices from a variety of disciplines and fields that comprise the world of academia.

A challenge for every novice scholar and researcher is prioritizing their scholarly efforts and time. These challenges are embedded in graduate study and the rigors of carving out a position in academia. Yet, knowing and implementing flexible strategies for how to direct time and attention across the interrelated areas of research, teaching, service, and (possibly) administration is a skillset not often explicitly taught in doctoral programs or addressed in new faculty orientations. Balancing the need to be productive writers and scholars, in particular, with the other areas of the professorate is an art and science necessitating practice and a perspective toward continuous improvement.

As authors, teachers, scholars, and administrators, we arrive at this stance of valuing writing not only because we understand the nuances of faculty productivity but also because collectively and individually, each of us value the medium of writing as a way of knowing, as a means of promoting ideas, sharing research, and as a method of exercising our voices. To serve ourselves and our institutions well, PhD students, novice scholars, and even seasoned researchers need to assess and meet our distinct needs as writers and researchers. Scholarly academic writing demands can be intentionally ambiguous and are correspondingly fraught with complexity. In this text, we demystify academic writing processes, writing productivity, and publishing. We hope that this text can literally "teach" a novice scholar how to develop the discipline and skill to be productive.

Throughout this book, the authors explore writing publishing and productivity. To address this, the authors posit intentional spaces for productivity development as well as differentiated approaches toward publishing. We view productivity as beginning with the generation of an idea for research and the publishing process ending when a manuscript has been accepted and is scheduled for a publication date. As a result, each chapter has a specific focus and could serve as a stand-alone document around that focus. Yet chapters are also correlated and interconnected by the sequential procedures of productivity and subsequent publication.

Chapter 1 introduces strategic, targeted scholarly writing productivity supports specifically directed at doctoral students, newly-minted PhDs, and novice researchers, providing a means for both focusing and advancing individual interests and ideas regarding research. This chapter proceeds by offering strategies for translating those ideas and subsequent research findings into viable and successful publications. **Chapter 1** teaches how to develop a targeted research topic, increase understanding of how to craft problem statements and solution statements as initial writing activities, and improve ways to merge personal interests and passion with viable research topics and subsequent writing.

Chapter 2 provides readers with structures, methods, and simple, but effective, tools for establishing, articulating, and attaining goals and becoming more intentional in academic writing pursuits. Some of these structures explicitly taught in Chapter 2 include how to establish a writing routine, manage writing tasks, plan for publication opportunities, and increase weekly writing time.

Chapter 3 offers methods for ongoing practice, expert modeling and demonstrations, targeted guidance, specific feedback, and copious amounts of authentic, critical encouragement that are necessary to the development of writing productivity. Chapter 3's methods include how to write from a presentation, utilize technology for increased productivity, incorporate teaching or coursework into scholarship, and write solo.

Chapter 4 affords a structured framework for systematically producing a typical research-based journal article or research-based book chapter manuscript from start to finish. This chapter is, in many ways, the heart of the book and offers several suggestions including how to: schedule sufficient time to craft a complete journal article or book chapter, write engaging introductions, germane literature reviews, clear methods sections, cohesive results sections, compelling discussion sections, and adequate implications. Finally, the chapter suggests techniques and strategies for how to master the technical aspects of scholarly writing by addressing format, function, and form.

Chapter 5 explores options for determining "fit" for manuscripts and for minimizing outright rejection from editorial teams. Chapter 5 outlines how to: create a list of potential publication outlets/journals for a manuscript, curate the potential publications list to maximize fit, and cultivate relationships with editors and other publication professionals.

Chapter 6, an invited chapter, suggests methods for assisting authors as they navigate the editorial process for manuscripts submitted for publication in academic journals and academic publishing outlets. Dr. Renée Casbergue, Professor Emeritus, elucidates how to recognize the role of editors in the publication process, identify publication guidelines, query an editor, submit a manuscript, manage expectations on responses to manuscripts, and navigate co-authoring and publishing relationships with community partners and fellow researchers.

Chapter 7 stipulates the ways in which a novice scholar and researcher can become adept at revision, a constant that novices should expect and for which they should prepare. Utilizing a structured and systematic focus, the authors present the reconciliation chart as a tool for refining revision. This focus and corresponding tool helps authors understand how to: accept reviewers' comments as constructive criticism; trust editors' decision-making process; systematically and strategically addressing review comments, edits, and suggestions; acquire professional diplomacy when disagreeing with a reviewer or editor; and write succinct yet comprehensive resubmission letters.

Chapter 8, a second invited chapter, explores how the field of publishing metrics has evolved, how research impact is measured, and how research impact and research exposure are intertwined. This chapter introduces some of the most common metrics applied in publishing and productivity. Librarians, Andrea Hebert and David Dunaway, explain how to: understand citation metrics as a measure of research impact, identify the most common citation metrics used to measure research impact, explain the limitations of common citation metrics, calculate simple author-level metrics, identify some of the alternative measures of research impact and quality, and formulate a plan to increase the visibility of research.

Chapter 9 specifically addresses the logistic and stylistic choices, rewards, and potential concerns when collaborating with other researchers while designing and authoring research with an ultimate goal of publication. Chapter 9 focuses on how to: create networks of writing support through writing circles and accountability partners, cultivate relationships with potential collaborative partners for research, implement effective strategies for working within collaborative relationships, and navigate challenging situations in collaborative relationships.

Chapter 10 supports a novice's comprehensive thinking and strategic planning about their research and thinking in terms of leveraging efforts and opportunities. This *lagniappe*, or extra chapter, teaches readers strategies for how to: track, leverage, and maximize research impact, identify additional venues as potential outlets to leverage and maximize research impact, identify alternative outlets for research, and formulate a concrete plan to utilize various media outlets to increase the visibility of their research.

Chapter 11 focuses the readers' attention on creating and utilizing a research agenda and providing considerations regarding writing related to sustaining scholarly advancement or employment. In this closing chapter, we offer our perspectives on how to: create and utilize a cohesive research agenda, write for annual evaluation, write for promotion and/or tenure, and work both hard and smart toward your goals.

This book unpacks the ways a novice scholar and researcher actively engages in scholarly publication using a systematic and targeted approach. Our hope is that this text finds its way into doctoral programs and new faculty orientation programs in order to provide guidance and support to those who embark on this journey.

Best,
Margaret-Mary, Leah Katherine, Cyndi & Tynisha

Acknowledgments

Margaret-Mary Sulentic Dowell

Thank you to my coauthors, colleagues, and sister-friends, Leah Katherine, Cyndi, and Tynisha, for their deep commitment and unwavering dedication to writing this text. The epitome of a team, they cheered, cajoled, criticized, and celebrated as one, ever concerned about quality and the audience for this text, the doctoral students, newly-minted PhDs, and novice researchers who are on a journey to academia. I often wonder why I am so blessed to be in their company and so lucky to have been placed in their path in life; just know I am eternally grateful to each of you and for how you have shaped me as a scholar, writer, teacher, researcher, and learner. A heartfelt thanks to my husband, Tony Dowell, for his understanding during this project, for the encouragement he offered, for his interest in my work, and for the many nights and days he picked up the reins of our lives and rode on around me. I also want to thank the hundreds of graduate students who have touched my life in so many ways; this text is the result of what you have taught me about writing and scholarly productivity. Finally, I want to thank colleagues at Louisiana State University who supported this effort in little ways that meant a great deal.

Leah Katherine Saal

I am sincerely grateful for my mentors turned colleagues and coauthors on this journey. When the idea for this book began years ago, I was a doctoral candidate and novice scholar, eager to document all the information about publishing and productivity that my mentors (Margaret-Mary, Cyndi, and Tynisha) generously were sharing with me. From my experiences across academia, even then, I recognized that many fellow students and novice researchers didn't share in my good fortune. I knew that my experiences with this kind of transparency around the sometimes "unspoken" expectations of the professorate were more unique than they should have been. I am very grateful to have this opportunity to share what they have taught me and continue to teach me.

I also want to thank my friends and family, especially my husband, Anthony Zehyoue, for the continued support of not only this book but also my career as an academic. These processes and products are far from simple and completed with great persistence over many years across evolving contexts. From early morning coffee brewing to editing, my "framily" (the family I have and the family I chose) makes it happen. I love you BIG.

Finally, to all the students and community partners, former, current, and future, I hope this text serves you well, and I wish you great successes. Always write what you mean and mean what you write.

Cynthia Fontcuberta DiCarlo

I would like to thank my wonderfully dedicated coauthors for undertaking the journey of writing the text that we all wish we had as doctoral students, newly-minted PhDs, and novice researchers entering the academy. Throughout this project, I was continually amazed at your wisdom and felt fortunate to have such dedicated and determined multitasking women as colleagues.

Thanks to my family for entertaining themselves as I spent evenings and weekends in my home office writing, revising, and editing the multiple drafts of each chapter. Special thanks to my dad, who pretends that anything I write is the most interesting thing he has ever read.

This book is also dedicated to the many undergraduate and graduate students who I have had the privilege of accompanying on their journey. I hope that this text serves as a road map to guide those newly on this path and provides encouragement and support to those who read it.

Tynisha D. Willingham
First and foremost, I want to thank Margaret-Mary, Leah, and Cyndi. The crafting of this text is a demonstration of our commitment to the success of novice scholars entering higher education. We "talked" this book for almost a decade and now it has come to fruition. I am humbled to be able to work with three dynamic, compassionate, and brilliant women. When we embarked on this journey we could not have predicted writing through a pandemic, institutional changes, the welcoming of new life, and the departure of loved ones from this earthly realm.

I am grateful for my family and their continued support. To all my children, I hope that if you decide to pursue careers in academia this will be a text that you will turn to as you enter the academy. If you don't decide to pursue a career in academia, that is ok...just tell all your friends and colleagues about this text. I offer special acknowledgments to our editors for sticking with us through all of life's twists and turns. We did it...again.

Collective Acknowledgments

- -

The authors wish to collectively thank the SAGE team: senior acquisitions editor, Leah Fargotstein, who believed in us and our product; Liz Cruz, senior editorial assistant, who was so patient with our countless inquiries; and Yumna Samie, product associate, whose sharp eyes and capable assistance provided us with great visual options. You are all deeply appreciated.

SAGE and the authors would like to thank the reviewers listed below for their comments on the manuscript:

Margaret Adamek, Indiana University
Janelle Applequist, University of South Florida
Liz Burke, Saint Louis University
Kate Daniels, University of Cambridge
Octavio J. Esqueda, Biola University
Sydney Freeman, Jr., University of Idaho
Ahmed Ibrahim, Johns Hopkins University
Jennifer E. Lape, Chatham University
Travis Lewis, East Carolina University
Miriam Margala, University of Massachusetts Lowell
Sharon Erickson Nepstad, University of New Mexico
Evan Ortlieb, St. John's University
Heather E. Price, Marian University
Lisa Russell-Pinson, University of North Carolina at Charlotte
Kaye Shelton, Lamar University
Judith P. Siegel, New York University
Michael Sollitto, Texas A&M University–Corpus Christi

About the Authors

Margaret-Mary Sulentic Dowell, PhD, is Cecil "Pete" Taylor Endowed Professor of Literacy, Leadership, and Urban Education at Louisiana State University, Baton Rouge, USA. She is Director of the LSU Writing Project & Coordinator of the Educational Leadership PhD program in the School of Education. Her research agenda includes three strands focused on literacy in urban settings, specifically investigating the complexities of literacy leadership, examining service-learning as a pedagogical pathway to preparing preservice teachers to teach literacy in urban environments, and exploring ways to provide access to literature, writing, and the arts (arts integration) in urban environs. Sulentic Dowell has published widely, and she has been nationally recognized for scholarship and teaching; she was most recently recognized for her literacy advocacy for the "Light Up for Literacy" Award, Louisiana Endowment for the Humanities (2019). Sulentic Dowell is a career educator and fierce public education advocate, spending the majority of her 20-year public school teaching experience in the Waterloo, Iowa Community Schools, but also possessing experience in northern Minnesota and southern Mississippi. She most recently served public education as Assistant Superintendent, supervising 64 elementary campuses in the East Baton Rouge Parish School System in Louisiana (2002–2006).

Leah Katherine Saal, PhD, is an Associate Professor and Codirector of Literacy Graduate Programs at Loyola University Maryland. She teaches graduate courses in literacy education, educational research, and program evaluation. Saal is informed by her ongoing experiences teaching with and learning from families, adults, and communities in and out of school settings in urban areas. Saal's engaged scholarly agenda focuses on the intersection of literacy and social justice with a community literacy lens. Community literacy is fraught with complexities and encompassing of multiple and evolving dimensions of diversity, including home literacies, social class, (dis)ability, identity, and race. As a mixed methodologist, she uses quantitative and qualitative methods and a Freirean pedagogical stance to attempt to rigorously answer complex questions. Her research includes two dovetailing strands. In the first strand of her research, Saal focuses on the literacy skills and practices of adults and older students in and out of school settings. In the second strand of her research, she investigates the preparation and support of literacy educator-leaders to work for social justice.

Cynthia F. DiCarlo, PhD, holds the W.H. "Bill" LeBlanc LSU Alumni Association Departmental Endowed Professorship of Early Childhood Education and is the Executive Director of the Early Childhood Education Laboratory Preschool at Louisiana State University, Baton Rouge, Louisiana, USA. DiCarlo also serves as the Coordinator of the Early Childhood Education Teacher Education Program. DiCarlo's research focuses on interventions to improve outcomes for young children and clarification and innovations in recommended practices in early childhood. Prior to joining LSU in 2004, she was a Clinical Assistant Professor at LSU Health Sciences Center (New Orleans). DiCarlo has been recognized for her research, teaching, and service; her research on children's attention during whole group instruction received the 2012 Research Paper of the Year from the *Journal of Research in Childhood Education*; she was recognized for excellence in teaching receiving the Tiger Athletic Foundation Teaching Award (2010). Additionally, she has received recognition for her service, receiving the College of Human Sciences and Education Faculty Service Award (2016) and the Louisiana Champions of Service Volunteer of the Year: Plantation Region (2013). DiCarlo has incorporated her passion for research into the courses she teaches and her work in mentoring undergraduate and graduate students. Since its inception in 2014, she has mentored over 100 undergraduate students who have subsequently presented at LSU Discover Day, the university's undergraduate research initiative. She currently serves on the editorial boards for *Infants & Young Children* and for the *Journal of Teacher Action Research*.

Tynisha D. Willingham, PhD, is the Interim Provost and Chief Academic Officer at Mary Baldwin University and Dean for the College of Education. Prior to her arrival at Mary Baldwin, she served in various roles at St. Norbert College, in De Pere, Wisconsin, including Assistant Vice President for Academic Affairs, Assistant Academic Dean, and Chair of Curriculum and Program Development for Teacher Education. Willingham began her career as a Teach For America Corps member. She served as a classroom teacher and various administrative roles within K-12 teacher development. These experiences have informed and shaped her leadership focus, which is deeply grounded in relationship building and servant leadership. Willingham is an interdisciplinary literacy scholar. Her research focuses on working with the community to create change in classrooms to benefit the literacy development of BIPOC students. Her research is specific to literacy development within the context of teacher development, inclusive classroom culture, culturally relevant curriculum, service-learning, and literacy assessment and intervention. Employing qualitative methods, she explores the intersection of literacy practices in the classroom and teacher development. Willingham's research agenda is informed by her experiences as a teacher in urban and rural contexts. She is the author and coauthor of several books and journal articles. Willingham has a deep passion for teacher development. Her passion surfaces in how she leads organizations to use data to drive outcomes that ensure student success. She works closely with many school districts and has served on boards of education. She remains active in her local community to serve students.

About the Contributors

Renée Casbergue held the Vira Franklin and James R. Eagles professorship at Louisiana State University until she retired from the faculty in 2020. Over her academic career, she published scholarly articles and books primarily focused on literacy development and learning in early childhood. In addition to working with undergraduate teacher preparation programs, she directed the graduate literacy program and mentored masters and doctoral students. She served on numerous editorial boards and was a regular reviewer for both research and practitioner focused journals. She was coeditor for three volume years of Childhood Education, and served as editor of the *Journal of Research in Childhood Education*.

Andrea Hebert is an Associate Librarian at Louisiana State University, Baton Rouge, Louisiana, USA. She is the Human Sciences & Education Librarian and the liaison to the Schools of Education, Kinesiology, Leadership & Human Resource Development, Library & Information Science, Kinesiology, and Social Work. She has worked at LSU Libraries since 2013. Her research interests include the transition of graduate students into published researchers, the experiences of library and information science graduate students, and workplace mobbing and bullying in academic libraries. Hebert holds a BA in English and Latin from Louisiana State University, an MA in Latin from the University of Georgia, and an MLIS from Louisiana State University.

David Dunaway is an Associate Librarian at Louisiana State University, Baton Rouge, Louisiana, USA, where he is the Director of Open Scholarship & Affordable Learning and liaison to the Department of Chemistry. He has worked in the LSU Library for 10 years and has research interests in bibliometrics with a focus on research and researcher performance metrics. Dunaway holds a BS in Chemistry, a Master of Education, and a Master of Library and Information Science from Louisiana State University.

Introductory Chapter

Getting Started With Your Writing

Scholarly, academic writing can seem mystifying at times. Being a successful academic means that a new scholar becomes productive by translating ideas into research and research into publications. Publishing productivity may vary by institution. However, publications define a scholar's contributions to their field. This book can "teach" a young scholar how to develop the discipline and skill to be productive. The authors offer themselves as examples and have compiled strategies, activities, and concrete suggestions for increasing writing productivity.

The purpose of this chapter is to introduce strategic, targeted scholarly writing productivity supports specifically directed at doctoral students, newly minted PhDs, and novice researchers, providing a means for both focusing and advancing individual interests and ideas regarding research and translating those ideas and subsequent research findings into viable and successful publications. A great deal of preparation and intentional, strategic thinking is involved in realizing a successful career as an academic. In this chapter, readers will learn how to focus ideas for research and successive publication.

Learning Objectives

There are three learning objectives for this chapter:

1. Develop a targeted research topic.

2. Increase understanding of how to craft problem statements and solution statements as initial writing activities.

3. Improve ways to merge personal interests and passion with viable research topics and subsequent writing.

Premise of This Book

We came together to write this book out of experience and necessity. It is the guide we wished we had owned—in graduate school pursuing a PhD. This text is also the guidebook we immediately needed as we left the seemingly safe and familiar world of graduate school as doctoral candidates and embarked on our first jobs in academia as scholars. But, it is also the text we urgently need now as we advise and direct those students of our own who are pursuing a doctorate and readying themselves to launch into the professorate. As authors, we have varying degrees of expertise, and we possess distinct skill sets as they pertain to research, writing, publishing, and productivity. As scholars, we understand what success in academia demands, and we wrote this book to make that journey, not easier, but more accessible by demystifying the processes of productivity and publishing.

Source: iStock, smolaw11

We needed such a book although we were prepared as we initially entered academia. All four of us claim excellent preparation and mentorship—for writing up a PhD study. We learned from amazing scholars at several prestigious and well-recognized universities in the United States (US)—three are **research 1 institutions** and one is a well-known, urban, **regional institution**. We had exceptional professors and advisors. They counseled us well, advised us on classes that would develop and hone our research skills, held us accountable for our emerging scholarship, and provided us support and feedback—to write a dissertation. We can all remember being counseled to find a niche, to develop a **research agenda**, and to publish.

But what wasn't so clear sometimes while we were reading, researching, and writing a dissertation was how to craft a research agenda with coherence beyond our dissertation study and how to create a **research trajectory**. Culling articles from our dissertation was advice we all recall. But it was less clear, as we were awarded our doctoral degrees and started our first jobs in academia, how to merge our interests and passions with current issues in our respective fields and launch a career in academia. We were provided the requisite five-chapter formula for our dissertations, and one of us pushed the envelope (with encouragement) to seven chapters, but the advice about writing an article and finding a publication home for scholarly writing was generally absent. Encouragement was plentiful, but the nitty gritty details of moving from idea to manuscript was limited. Hereafter, we recount some specific examples of the advice we received and our responses and reflection about that advice.

Authorship advice and guidelines provided about negotiating order on publications that were coauthored were nebulous. Advice such as "the order of authorship follows effort" turned out to be vague and unhelpful. Recommendations were scarce and, oftentimes, ill-defined. Collaboration wasn't addressed sufficiently. Collectively, we all remember being prompted as graduate students to "find a **writing group**," as efficacious advice, but specifics about how writing groups function, or differing kinds of writing groups, were not forthcoming. For example, we needed sound advice, how to actually form a writing group, guidance on setting ground rules, information about how writing groups can function, and how to sustain the momentum when in a writing group.

There was a paucity of advice and information about how to handle **rejection** and how to either systematically **revise and resubmit** or seek a new publication venue. Limited guidance was provided about weaving our interests into conference proposals, grant proposals, or how to prepare a book proposal. Again, we were encouraged to do all of the above, but the finite steps and strategies to realize success often eluded, escaped, and at times, baffled us.

And, academia shifts. As academics, we have witnessed changes. One example of such a shift is the ever-increasing scrutiny around **metrics**. Within the last ten years, the use of citations as a measure of productivity has blossomed. With an eye toward quality and a rise in online and open-access publication outlets, institutions have put a greater focus on metrics. **Citation management software** attests to this increase. In tandem, **impact factors** and rankings for journals and publishing houses have become an entrenched aspect of evaluating scholars' productivity.

Authors' Message to Readers on How to Use This Book

As authors and scholars, we assume those who read this text will approach it from differing viewpoints and that readers will have different needs and interests in selecting this text. Our intention is for readers to use it as a pedagogical tool to increase productivity success and publishing savvy. We represent various levels of academic rank. At the time this was written, three of us have earned the rank of full professor, and one of us is an associate professor who recently earned tenure. Although we approached **tenure and promotion** differently and in different contexts, we share the experience as we were all assistant professors, faced with being productive and achieving success within our individual institutions' tenure and promotion processes. We wrote this book as a tool to help others learn from our paths to success. Chapters in this book spiral; they certainly build upon one another, yet they can also serve as stand-alone guides for achieving strategically targeted skill sets for increasing productivity and publishing.

In this text, readers will find eleven distinct chapters that provide useful knowledge about increasing publishing and productivity and a final chapter with additional writing activities, designed to stimulate publishing productivity. In many chapters, we attempt to clarify the academic writing and publishing processes through frank discussion and practical exercises that address chapter objectives. From creating writing and publishing goals (Chapter 1) and writing a journal or book chapter manuscript (Chapters 2–3), choosing an appropriate publishing outlet (Chapter 4), and moving the manuscript through the submission and revision process (Chapters 5–6) to promoting your work (Chapter 7) and leveraging your scholarship (Chapter 8), to finally examining institutional expectations and requirements for evaluation, promotion, and/or tenure in regard to writing, we hope this book helps the many striving academics who may be asking themselves "so, what do I do now?" The chapters of this book are presented as successive rungs of productivity in publishing. While it is not necessary to follow the chapters in the order they are presented within the text, we felt it was important to showcase the sequence and interconnectedness of the practices of academic writing. In making clear the practices, we believe we are demystifying the publication process.

With the end in mind—success as scholars matriculating through the rank, and scholars who negotiated the process—we want to start with how doctoral students, newly minted PhDs, and novice researchers can generate ideas for writing that are sourced from issues that they care about.

Generating Ideas for Writing

For some, but not all, doctoral candidates and beginning researchers and scholars, getting started with academic research, writing, and publishing feels overwhelming. Interest and passion can be used as a catalyst for generating ideas that can come to fruition as published pieces. We often joke about research and manuscripts as being comparable to relationships. How are they similar, readers might ask? In a relationship, if there is a sense of liking someone, it's easier to circumvent the pitfalls, challenges, and difficulties of what may be encountered in the life of a relationship.

The same holds true for researching and writing. A simple exercise can help to focus interests in a way that may be beneficial to the whole process. The premise is the same as the relationship example provided; if you have a genuine interest in an issue, you are more likely to persist when the work becomes tedious or difficult. In particular, selecting a dissertation topic feels daunting to many students. Some feel torn between investigating what they care about and have an interest in or trying to find a niche. A niche or specialty area often develops with practice and over time.

Source: iStock, fizkes

Activity 1.1 is a simple exercise to encourage readers to consider what interests them, and then seek out connections between interests and ideas for potential studies and subsequent publications based on research. The two-part process honors interests and allows for choice, with choice being a prime motivator when writing. If you are seeking a thesis or dissertation topic, or if you are searching for a new research idea, use the following activity to catalog your interests in a straightforward and uncomplicated manner.

Activity 1.1 Research Exercise

List four to five issues about which you are passionate:

-
-
-
-
-

Do any of them connect? How? Why?

Consider as a possible research possibility.

Moving From Idea to Manuscript

Once an individual has an idea of what they want to research and that topic aligns with their interests and, perhaps, passions, a simple writing exercise can assist with focusing that idea on a viable topic. Begin by listing the big question—what is happening? Or, what is the problem? Think: the problem is ... and a possible solution is ... This leads to writing a simple problem statement, keeping in mind what your research seeks to do is fill a gap that exists. The simple act of writing a statement can start the process of formulating thoughts and articulating ideas clearly.

Here is an example. *Teachers of elementary-aged students lack skill in assisting students with second language acquisition.* This is the problem statement. However, additional detail is still needed. Novice scholars can ask themselves where does the problem exist and within what population? And, what detail adds specificity to the problem? The problem statement can be further expanded by adding detail and specificity. When producing academic writing, all descriptors must be definitive. In the case of this example, precise description needs to be added as the problem statement is quite vague. Further description narrows the focus as in this extended example: *In South Louisiana, where public schools have experienced an increase of English Language Learners, teachers of elementary-aged students in first and second grade lack skill in assisting students with second language acquisition in the disciple specific area of English language arts.*

Next comes how to address this issue. For the sake of the example, solutions might be couched as a solution statement that adequately captures what can be conducted to address the issue: *Targeted, strategic professional development can increase teachers' awareness of strategies to teach second language learners and increase teaching capacity and skill.* Likewise, the solution statement needs refinement and additional specificity: *School-level leaders can provide targeted, strategic professional development in oral language acquisition that results in increasing first and second grade teachers' awareness of developmentally appropriate oral language strategies to teach second language learners while increasing teaching capacity.*

Now it is the reader's turn. Activity 1.2 requires readers to craft two statements, a problem statement and a solution statement. Begin with the responses rendered in Activity 1.1. Create a jot list of specific terms that address the ways in which your interest coalesced.

Activity 1.2 Writing Problem Statements and Solution Statements

Using the following simple formula, write an initial problem statement either on paper or while composing at the keyboard. This is a personal preference, so use the technique that fits your style. (1) The problem is…

After writing an initial draft, go back and revise adding detail and specifics. Read it out loud for flow and cohesion. What other details can you add to increase specificity and thus, narrow the topic? Continue to revise until you are satisfied with your problem statement.

Repeat this process with a solution statement. Again, create a jot list of specific terms that address the ways in which you intend to address the problem or issue. (2) The solution is …

Revise by adding additional detail and specifics. Read it out loud for flow and cohesion. Does the solution align with the problem statement? What other details can you add to increase specificity and narrow the solution? Continue to revise until you are satisfied with your solution statement.

Focusing Research on Passion and Pragmatics

Research should address pressing issues. Research should also involve an interest that can be sustained. All choices need to be grounded in the literature from related fields. The more definite descriptors are, the more targeted the literature review and the more focused the research and subsequent writing.

Working Hard But Smart While Maintaining a Passion for Research

Maximizing your time when writing and researching yields results. Typically, the more centered a study is on a precise statement of the problem and subsequent solution statement, the clearer the writing. And, from a productivity position, the more exacting a study's problem and solution statement, the more single-minded the work. Novice scholars and researchers can easily be distracted by interesting facets of a study. However, with practice, scholars learn to keep ideas germane to a central focus.

We return to the relationship analogy discussed earlier in this chapter. If earning a PhD, securing a job in academia, and being successful in publishing and

productivity was easy, more individuals would pursue these paths. Scholarly, academic writing is difficult, demanding, and emotionally and physically draining work. It requires discipline, focus, and wise and strategic use of time. Without discipline and the budgeting of time, focus can be hard to maintain. Choice, personal interest, and passion can be prime motivators when writing. The activity in this chapter can shape writing in productive ways.

SUMMARY

In this introductory chapter, an activity to assist with focusing interest was provided as a way to allow readers to take what they are passionate about and craft that passion and interest into working problem and solution statements. Setting the stage for productivity is important. Here, we make an important distinction: graduate students learn the research process and acquire the skill sets to conduct research and produce a successful thesis or dissertation. New faculty members (novice researchers and novice scholars) begin an academic journey as researchers that results in successful productivity and publications as defined by their institution. In Chapter 2, we will discuss ways to add discipline by learning how to set manageable goals. Setting goals and creating a submission schedule for your academic writing add structure to publishing and productivity and address demystifying the processes of writing inherent in publishing. Each chapter defines the key terms germane to that chapter. In addition, each chapter contains critical thinking questions designed to extend considerations of information presented therein as well as additional references and works cited for each chapter.

KEY TERMS

The following key terms are defined here. Key terms will be used throughout this book and applied uniformly.

Citation Management Software Citation management software are tools that permit researchers and writers to both organize and store scholarly resources and citational information. Software such as Mendeley© and Zotero© assist writers with a means to create reference lists or bibliographic lists of citations from stored items. Different citation software offers distinctive qualities, and writers need to decide which tool works best for individual needs.

Impact Factor This is an indicator used to rate a journal's impact by calculating the total number of times the articles in a journal were cited in the two years prior to the year that the impact factor is calculated, divided by the total number of articles published during that time.

Metrics Citation metrics are a measurement of the impact of research which can be considered when deciding where to publish.

Regional Institution A regional institution in the United States is an institution of higher learning (IHL) that is generally designed to provide regional programming with a designated geographical area within a state or region of the country.

Rejection In academic publishing terms, a rejection is a category of response that indicates a manuscript submitted for publication is either deemed not an appropriate fit for a journal or publication or is of low quality in terms of writing style or scholarship. A rejection equates to a decision by the editor(s) not to accept for further consideration.

Research Agenda A research agenda is considered a formalized plan of research that encapsulates explicit, detailed issues and ideas in any given field of study. A research agenda is fluid, yet provides a specific plan of action for a scholar and can be viewed as a driving design that helps a scholar to prioritize projects, publications, and possibly, publication venues in a formalized and articulated manner.

Research 1 Institutions Based on the Carnegie Classification of Institutions of Higher Education, this designation is based on an institution's level of research activity; a research 1 university denotes a university in the United States engages in the highest levels of research activity. As a subset of doctoral degree–granting institutions that conduct research, research 1 institutions are characterized as having conferred at least 20 research and/or scholarship doctorates and were awarded at least $5 million in total research expenditures. In 2020, the top four were: (1) Massachusetts Institute of Technology (MIT); (2) University of California at Los Angeles (UCLA) wherein as an example of high activity, every year since the 2009–2010 academic year, UCLA has averaged $1 billion in research funding; (3) Johns Hopkins University, founded in 1876 as the nation's first research university; and (4) Texas A & M University (TAMU) (https://carnegieclassifications.iu.edu/).

Research Trajectory This concept involves having a clear and discernable research identity as a scholar. Creating a research trajectory usually involves assuming a theoretical stance or adopting a theoretical framework from which research emanates. A research trajectory can be considered a kind of road map of what research you intend to accomplish and the products of that research—publications. Having a clear identity and crafting a research trajectory helps not only to find an eventual job in academia, as jobs are posted by position and need, but also, having a clear research trajectory allows other researchers with similar interests and research objectives to connect with each other. Typically, a research trajectory contains specific research questions or problems or lines of inquiry and usually involves methods of inquiry and research designs.

Revise and Resubmit In academic publishing terms, a revise and resubmit decision is a category of response that indicates a manuscript submitted for publication is either deemed an appropriate fit for a journal or publication or is of significant quality in terms of writing style or scholarship. A revise and resubmit signifies a decision by the editor(s) to request additional edits and major revision before potential acceptance is offered. However, a revise and resubmit is not a guarantee of publication. Consider a revise and resubmit decision an invitation to do more work for further consideration.

Tenure and Promotion Tenure and promotion is both a process and a product. The process is similar as a scholar moves up academic ranks—from assistant to associate to full professor. Institutions with tenure and promotion have particular documents that outline the process for new employees. Specifically, these documents provide common criteria and guidelines for tenure and promotion. Usually, tenure and promotion involve three categories: research (also called discovery and/or productivity by some institutions), teaching, and service. Typically, a faculty member is expected to have established an original, coherent, and meaningful research trajectory to earn tenure and promotion. Scholars are expected to provide evidence of research, teaching, and service. The type of institution usually dictates the percentage of a scholar's time devoted to these three categories. It is imperative to know your institution's policies and documents intimately; know where it is housed (e.g., Academic Affairs of the Provosts Office) and know the process at your institution.

Writing Group A writing group functions as a place where scholars produce writing in a dedicated space and allows for feedback and critique from members (Kelly, 2015). Writing groups provide scholars with constructive feedback as well as a social forum for academic writers to both connect and collaborate. Mechanisms for the frequency and duration of meetings and ground rules for functioning vary. There are no set rules, just guidelines that work for members. A writing group may form for a specific task or as a means of support for members who agree to come together to share and critique writing. Members can come from the same or dissimilar disciplines. Members of writing groups are equally responsible for reading and providing feedback. A writing group has no specific set number of members, although some scholars suggest a maximum of three (Curtis, 2011). A writing group can also provide a sense of accountability for members.

CRITICAL THINKING QUESTIONS———

1. What are current issues within my field of study?

    a. What are the problems that merit study within my field?

    b. What are possible solutions to these problems within my field?

2. How do my personal professional interests interface or intersect with issues prevalent within the field?

3. What tensions arise between and among different perspectives within my field?

4. What area of study should I capitalize on as I create a coherent research agenda and compile a research trajectory?

5. Is there a possible two- or three-prong approach to an issue or several related issues in my field that intersect and can provide facets of my research agenda?

6. With whom might I collaborate within my unit?

7. With whom might I collaborate across campus and beyond?

8. With whom might I form a writing group for support and accountability?

9. Who are my distant mentors or mentors-on-the-page whose work can help me frame the issues I am most interested in my field?

ADDITIONAL REFERENCES ——————————

http://www.theglobalarc.org/what-we-do/civically-engaged-research.

https://carnegieclassifications.iu.edu.

https://thewritepractice.com/writers-group/.

https://www.meetup.com/topics/writing/.

WORKS CITED ——————————————

Curtis, C. (2011, March 24). The Rules of writing group. *Chronicle of Higher Education.* Retrieved from https://www.chronicle.com/article/The-Rules-of-Writing-Group/126880

Diamond, R. M., & Adam, B. E. (1993). *Recognizing faculty work: Reward systems for the year 2000 (No. 81).* New York, NY: Jossey-Bass.

Kelly, A. (2015). Torch academic writing group blog. Retrieved from https://www.dralicekelly.com/academic-writing-group/

Setting Goals and a Submission Schedule for Your Academic Writing

Often, the best ideas can follow the path of the best intentions. While excellent in terms of purposes, really good ideas can easily fail to germinate and come to fruition. In this chapter, readers will learn structures, methods, and simple but effective tools for establishing, articulating, and attaining goals and becoming more intentional in their academic writing pursuits.

Learning Objectives

There are four learning objectives for this chapter:

1. Establishing a writing routine

2. Managing writing tasks

3. Plan for publication opportunities

4. Increase weekly writing time

One of the tools that some authors find helpful is a quick write. A quick write is a short, timed, typically 1–3 minute, writing activity which combines writing and thinking skills (Rief, 2002, p. 50). At the beginning of each chapter (except Chapter 8), readers will have the opportunity to engage in a quick write which is related to the chapter content. This allows the reader to actively reflect on their current practices, experiences, or knowledge on the topic at hand.

Quick Write # 1

In the first quick write, we want readers to focus on what might be their current writing routine, recognizing that there are many different forms of authoring. Think about the words *my authoring routine*, and pay attention to the images that come into your mind. Are you the kind of writer who must gather all your materials first and settle your working space before you write? Are you the kind of writer who must have the favorite coffee cup or "lucky glass" situated on your workspace before you write? Are you a writer whose routine includes working from the same home space or office space? Does your routine mean that you need to separate from home and work in a space with few distractions? Or, are you a coffee shop writer who prefers the background noise? Are you a slow, methodical writer and have adopted that style as your routine? Or, are you a binge writer that finds themself avoiding an assignment or deadline with trepidation, then cramming your writing into a small time-frame? Do you prefer to physically write in a notebook, journal, or paper pad first? Or, are you the kind of writer who simply opens your laptop and begins? What is your routine?

Source: iStock, Ivan Pantic

What comes to mind as you review the phrase *my authoring routine*? Notice the details of your mental image and think of the various descriptions we have provided. After collecting your thoughts for a minute or two, gather a timer and your preferred writing devices. Set the timer for two minutes. Next, start the two-minute timer and write or type everything that comes to mind while you think of the mental image of yourself as a writer and the prompt, *my authoring routine*, without stopping. After your two minutes of writing time is up, (1) be proud of what you wrote—words on a page are a cause for celebration, and (2) note themes or common ideas across your free write. What does the exercise tell you about yourself, about your authorship?

Establishing Writing Routines and Rituals

Significant effort goes into the many facets of authoring from idea generation, to organization, to revising, to editing, to one of the ultimate goals of academic writing—publication. Writing is a process that produces a product; improving the process improves the product. As the authors of this text, we take comfort in knowing that writers many times more successful than us, also struggle with the craft. Readers of this book should also take comfort that even highly successful writers struggle. However, the success enjoyed by high-volume writers comes with practice, discipline, workable routines, and personal rituals. We invite readers to briefly recall how their writing developed.

Many who read this book may recall writing in school settings, where formulas (think of the five-paragraph essay) were promoted. Readers of this text may also reflect upon learning about the classic strategy of The 5Ws—*who, what, where, when,* and *why* (and sometimes *how*) when writing about an event or a situation. In elementary, middle, and high school, students typically explore writing genres as they plow through required English classes, in hopes that they become well-rounded students, prepared for college and career.

During this time, one may remember the writing process as always starting with some form of prewriting, oftentimes a graphic organizer of some sort, an outline, or a thesis statement. Unknowingly, these are the early beginnings of learning how to establish routines and rituals to writing that are later refined and individualized. As a novice scholar, these routines are similar to those that the elementary or middle school teacher uses to encourage students to write such as: have a clear time to start and finish writing. Timers on phones or even some writing apps can help to achieve this simple goal.

Finding a sacred space to write is paramount. Sometimes a sacred space is an actual physical space that contributes to productivity. Some of us write in our offices—with the door shut. Some writers have the luxury of a dedicated or sacred space within their home that they can claim as theirs and use to spur productivity. Others of us rely on a public space. Some writers prefer the background noise that a local coffee shop affords. Some of us have established rituals such as assembling all needed materials, putting on a favorite playlist, using the same coffee cup or mug, and writing at the same personal place or maybe a favorite table in a public space that allows for productivity. For some, a sacred space is a frame of mind—a feeling of becoming inspired and capable of production. Other writers can write on demand; those individuals take their writing everywhere and can write something when the opportunity presents itself. Some writers have a favorite pen and use specific notepads to generate jot lists, outlines, and work through ideas. Other writers prefer to compose at the keyboard or dictate orally, maintaining electronic files.

We discuss these routines and possibilities, as writing is highly personal, and every writer needs to figure out what they need, where they write best, and when they are the most productive. Author, Stephen King, a prolific and successful writer and former high school English teacher, was not always the successful, recognized author he is today. But King developed a habit of daily writing. He tells readers that he attempts to write a few pages every day (around 1,500 words) and the words and pages mount (Lawson, 1979). As a PhD student, new scholar, or novice researcher, becoming a skilled writer is paramount to your success. Like King, beginning with a daily writing routine will produce writing; steady production leads to productivity.

There is a science to scholarly, academic writing, and whether you are producing a quantitative, qualitative, or mixed methods piece of scholarship, there are commonalities regarding anticipated elements and an expectation of rigor, relevance, and accuracy. Academic writing is an acquired skill—sometimes strenuous, often challenging and exciting, but also, precise and exacting work. While academic writing as a genre of writing is demanding, it can also be highly satisfying. Seeing scholarly ideas through to fruition in order to be shared among colleagues and the public can be highly motivational.

Like most research and scholarly endeavors, academic writing calls for skill sets that are developed and honed over time. No one is born an academic writer (Casanave, 2005), although some aspects of academic writing can appear to be acquired more easily for some writers. For example, some scholarly writers seem to never lack for topics and direction and have a constant stream of projects, presentations, and resultant publications. Others appear able to quickly call up the needed, necessary, and exact words they want to convey meaning and method. Some scholars give the impression that they are natural masters of the mechanical aspects of writing. Currently within the academy, platforms and digital demands also require a nuanced degree of technical skill and expertise. All aspects of academic authoring require development, attention to detail, and time.

By demystifying the academic writing processes for PhD candidates, new scholars, and novice researchers, striving writers can access, practice, and master the aspects of scholarly writing, and productivity can increase dramatically. One of the first steps to mastering academic writing is to become skilled at how to strategize writing and to acquire the discipline needed to see writing ideas and concepts through to fruition. While the eventual focus of academic writing is on the product—what gets accepted—concentrating on the elements of the process increases the quality of the product.

Reviewing Generating Ideas for Writing

In the introductory chapter, attention was given to generating ideas for writing. Here, a fuller discussion is provided. Regardless of how you select topics for research and writing, or what you decide upon, being able to establish and achieve writing goals increases publishing success.

Learning to Set Realistic Goals

Breaking work into realistic goals or chunks and accomplishing tasks in a systematic manner results in productivity. Tightly focused goals help writers gain traction and keep momentum moving forward. But, how do you accomplish this? Writing from a set of clear, concrete, and time-bound goals is more controllable and less unwieldy—making progress tangible and much more visible. As an example, instead of being overwhelmed by large tasks and goals, divide manuscripts into requisite parts—introduction to the issues being researched or discussed, a review of literature pertinent to the issue, study design, methods, including questions, setting, participants, data sources, analysis, findings or results, and implications. These elements are the commonly required parts of a research study and subsequent manuscript for publication.

Being productive and being able to track productivity is motivating, inspiring you to continue writing. Logging writing productivity can help a scholar to discover when you are actually most productive. Despite the often-repeated advice that novice scholars need large chunks of time to write, you can accomplish much by addressing smaller tasks and goals in smaller amounts of time. To do this, we have developed a few simple forms to keep authors focused, organized, and methodically writing from a goal-oriented approach.

The form itself is not important; it is simply a means to record what is needed to be accomplished and to visually record accomplishments as they occur. It can help you to more systematically manage writing projects and to develop a writing habit. Silva (2007) also suggests a similar kind of record-keeping, recording writing accomplishments by minutes spent and goals achieved using an excel file. It's not the form that matters, but the structured act of recording goals, tracking writing, and recognizing when you are productive that helps develop writing habits. In order to be productive, a scholarly writer has to budget time to produce writing.

Before you can set goals and establish a viable writing routine, it is helpful to inventory how you spend time writing and to examine the timeframes within a day and week where you could budget adequate time for writing. Scholars across academia rarely just focus on writing. Writing is a part of their scholarly lives whether an individual is a research professor, on the tenure track, or not. As authors, we are cognizant of the various types of faculty that reside at institutions as well as the ongoing changes to faculty academic ranks that various institutions are considering at this time within the academy. In a similar way, many graduate students are also working (full or part time) and many graduate students and scholars have robust personal lives that involve caring for family and loved ones. Habits developed in graduate school can contribute greatly to productivity. But, before an individual can set productive writing goals aligned to specific projects, identifying your habits and optimum times for authoring is essential. In other words, know thy writerly self.

Taking Inventory: Establishing a Writing Routine

Realizing that you have to discipline yourself, and that no one else is going to do that for you, is an important lesson. You are responsible for your writing productivity. You want to establish and maintain healthy writing habits that result in thoughtful writing. While emulating what works for others might seem like a good strategy, you need to know when your productivity is at its peak during the day, week, or month; what works for others may not work for you. Trying to cram several meaty goals into inappropriately small chunks of time isn't an optimal strategy. You also do not want to sit and stare at a blank page or screen, overwhelmed by a task that feels too large, unwieldy, or just plain unattainable. You want to be able to be thoughtful and reflective. Developing thoughtful research and writing habits that result in publication takes time.

The Logging Your Weeks Activity in this second chapter is a method that can be used to initially track writing productivity over the course of three weeks and identify possible writing times and/or times of greater productivity. Think of it as an inventory of how you spend your time. Tracking writing productivity over a three-week period allows scholars to identify days and times that are opportune, productive times to write. Tracking writing productivity over a three-week period also permits a reflective academic writer to make decisions about when they can write, what may be inhibiting them from setting a writing schedule, and be able to see what other activities consume their time and, possibly, to make any adjustments in order to schedule regular writing time.

For this four-step activity, first select an upcoming three-week period and record when you write. Do not just look for times when you have more open spaces in your calendar; rather, simply pick three weeks. Record date, day, time spent writing, and what you accomplished. Keep in mind that writing can also involve searching for sources, checking citations, addressing a Works Cited/ Reference section, or rereading what you have written. However, the majority of time ought to be spent drafting or revising writing. Also, some days are sacred days—nonnegotiable or off limits. For instance, you may not write on a particular day dedicated to other tasks.

Activity 2.1 Three-Week Writing Log Inventory

Week 1: (Month, date range, year)

Sunday, month date, year	Time from___to___.	Activity accomplished
Monday, month date, year	**Time from___to___.**	**Activity accomplished**
Tuesday, month date, year	**Time from___to___.**	**Activity accomplished**
Wednesday, month date, year	**Time from___to___.**	**Activity accomplished**

Thursday, month date, year	Time from___to___.	Activity accomplished

Friday, month date, year	Time from___to___.	Activity accomplished

Saturday, month date, year	Time from___to___.	Activity accomplished

Activity 2.1 Exemplar: Three-Week Writing Log Inventory

Here is an exemplar for a possible Week 1; it provides ideas about how you can actually track your writing. As a cautionary note, no one's log will look like another writer's log.

Sunday, month date, year	Time from___to___.	Activity accomplished
2/3/2020	6:00–8:00 a.m.	Identify additional citations for social skills manuscript

Sunday, month date, year	Time from___to___.	Activity accomplished
2/3/2020	8:00–9:00 a.m.	Compare in-text references to reference page and vice versa

Monday, month date, year	Time from___to___.	Activity accomplished
2/4/2020	8:00–9:00 a.m.	Create reconciliation chart for whole group instruction paper for conference call tomorrow.

Tuesday, month date, year	Time from___to___.	Activity accomplished
2/5/2020	8:00–8:30 a.m.	Conference call with Aaron on whole group instruction edits requested from journal. Divide tasks.
2/5/2020	9:30–11:00 a.m.	Address whole group instruction reviewer comments.

Wednesday, month date, year	Time from___to___.	Activity accomplished
2/6/2020	9:00–10:00 a.m.	Conference call with Ashley to develop IRB for active questioning study

(Continued)

(Continued)

Wednesday, month date, year	Time from___ to___.	Activity accomplished

Thursday, month date, year	Time from___ to___.	Activity accomplished
2/7/2020	4:30–6:00 a.m.	Generate outline/literature for active questioning study
2/7/2020	10:00 a.m.–12:00 p.m.	Address whole group instruction reviewer comments

Friday, month date, year	Time from___ to___.	Activity accomplished
2/8/2020	8:00–9:30 a.m.	Work on literature review for executive function project

Saturday, month date, year	Time from___ to___.	Activity accomplished
2/9/2020	7:00–9:30 a.m.	Write methods section Cut and paste citations into works cited Format tables for findings section Email Trina to read/edit the intro
2/9/2020	10:00–11:30 p.m.	Reread findings sections and draft conclusion and implications section

Second, scrutinize your productivity after one week. Pay attention to *when* you write. Question yourself as to *why* that time or day works well. Highlight those times as potential scheduled writing blocks. Examine what you are doing during writing time and where you are physically. For example, during the hour and half block time on Saturday, did you try to do the nondrafting or crafting tasks on the couch rather than at a desk? Did you have your email or social media up in the background or your volume up on your computer so that you heard every "ping?" These questions may seem like we are getting into unnecessary minutia. However, these small distractions can consume valuable minutes of productive writing time. How many actual paragraphs and/or pages you were able to complete? After analyzing the data you have, you are ready to complete the process for another consecutive week. Using the same Activity 2.1 Three-Week Writing Log Inventory Week 1, create a Week 2, noting the consecutive month, add a second week as a date range, and add the year).

Third, examine your productivity after Week 2. Again, as in Week 1, pay attention to *when* you write, and ask yourself *why* these times or days work well. Be critical of your routines. Once again, highlight those times as potential scheduled writing blocks. Examine each week side by side for times, days, and what you are doing during writing time. Record how many actual paragraphs/pages you were able to complete. Record patterns. It is in this week that you want to get in the weeds of when were good writing or crafting times versus revision times. You may want to note the difference in when you are more productive at tasks like formatting, checking references, following up with editors or coauthors, or even when to email or schedule calls. After completing this analysis, you are ready to complete the process for a final third consecutive week. Using the same Activity 2.1 Three-Week Writing Log Inventory Week 1, create a Week 3, again noting the consecutive month. From the exemplar, examining times spent writing and tasks accomplished, this scholar writes best during morning hours. Yet, the evening time is best for other tasks that contribute to being productive.

As a fourth and final step, you will complete your inventory of time spent writing. Now that you have logged your writing time by date, day, time of day, total hours spent writing and what you have accomplished for three consecutive weeks, it's time to analyze your writing patterns. After three weeks, examine all three weeks side by side carefully. Note patterns of productivity and down times. It is a good exercise to compare how much time you actually spend relative to your contract requirements to know if you are doing "enough." So, if you have 20% of your contract dedicated to scholarship, about 20% of your work week should consist of writing and other activities that lead into activities that will fall into that category for your setting. If you are teaching, go back and note those times as well in the margins on the form. Record on the weekly forms what other nonnegotiable or off-limits tasks you cannot reschedule.

Add your nonnegotiable or off-limits tasks to your writing log. For example, if you have children and you have to pick them up from school every afternoon, this is an example of a nonnegotiable. If you have a weekly or reoccurring commitment whether it is religious services, a yoga class on Saturdays, or a book group during the week, record these activities as well. You may have a family or committed relationship that places certain demands on your time or other nonnegotiable activities. By examining a span of three weeks, you can ascertain when you can realistically and consistently dedicate time to writing. Now, you are ready to establish a writing routine.

The idea of the Three-Week Writing Log Inventory is to systematically record *when you write* and to record *what you are writing*. Adding nonnegotiables and other activities that have systematically consumed your time allows a novice researcher and scholar to critically examine when a dedicated, regular writing schedule can be realistically implemented. You may even notice some tasks that you can shift to make better use of your time. Using this form can be the beginning of developing productive writing habits.

As a graduate student or affiliate faculty member, you may also have other forms of employment. As a novice researcher, new scholar, and/or newly appointed academic, many issues will consume your time. Acclimation to a new unit, or campus and even city or locale, teaching, related service, and advising, will all pull at you and consume your time. Serving as a reviewer for journals in your field, which we recommend, will consume your time. Writing itself will take many forms. You may have to plan more for some manuscripts, and planning is a necessary part of writing. Watching/listening to multimedia, reading and annotating articles, book chapters, reports of research, and books is a significant part of writing. Drafting and revising are part of writing. Checking that in-text citations are part of your reference section and that your reference section does not include works cited that don't appear in your text are part of writing. All of these components are time-consuming and should be considered when budgeting your time. Therefore, these tasks should also be documented as you are gleaning when you write best versus when you may engage in other tasks.

By examining when you have time to write and what might be consuming your time, you can set a realistic writing schedule and establish a writing routine that works for you. You may realize that you have to alter priorities. As a graduate student and doctoral candidate, Margaret-Mary, one of the authors of this text, also worked (taught) full time and had two children of her own, one in middle school and one in high school. She was also an avid softball player, so involved she earned a silver medal in the Iowa Games, an annual event for postcollegiate athletes. It was her release, she told herself. But, she had to prioritize. There may be activities in your life that are fulfilling, but time-consuming, that you may decide to curtail during different seasons of your academic life.

Margaret-Mary gave up softball, both a passion and a physical release for her and carved out writing time early each morning. She tracked her productivity (or lack thereof) and, by critically examining her writing output and nonnegotiables over a three-week period, was able to set a routine wherein she'd arise at 4:00 a.m., and write until she woke her children up at 6:00 a.m. each weekday morning and then began her workday. Initially, she scheduled these 10 hours of writing each week to take place only during the week.

Twenty years later, Margaret-Mary still maintains this early morning writing routine, generally adhering to this schedule three days per week, writing from 6:00 a.m. until noon on the days she does not teach. She writes other times as well, schedule permitting, but the early morning time slot works well for her and has become an established routine. The key to writing productivity is inventorying your productivity and other nonnegotiable activities and disciplining yourself to write when you have scheduled writing time. Careful consideration of your most productive times of day can lead to long-term productive writing habits. Your "found" time may be more or less, but guard it carefully and protect this new-found time for your writing goals. Finally, we encourage you to review this activity each semester or academic term, as commitments change, and your authoring schedule may need to adjust as well.

Managing Writing Tasks: Setting Reasonable Goals

Briefly, we have mentioned setting goals. In this section, a discussion of goal setting as an activity that allows writing to be managed is presented more fully. Begin by thinking of what you want to accomplish. Oftentimes, we have internal conversations with ourselves about large goals such as, "I need to complete Chapter 1." or "My introduction to this article needs to be completed." or "I need to write the literature review." While these are worthwhile goals, they lack specificity. A large goal can be overwhelming. Because such broad goals lack the steps to accomplishment, it may feel as if writing lacks direction. A basic outline, while a simple strategy, can provide direction with goals. What was a large task, such as a chapter or a literature review, now becomes a series of discreet tasks that are less overwhelming and more achievable. Commit to working in chunks; long sections of text can be intimidating with nothing but a blinking curser or blank page in front of you.

Try taking your large goal, for example an introduction, and break it into smaller, more manageable chunks via an outline. Consider your first item on your outline and create a short goal statement. Ask yourself: What am I trying to accomplish? Then consider, what time commitment have you set? Are your goals still too broad? Do you include manageable steps?

Activity # 2 Writing Goal Log is a simple charting method that allows writers to take a large, overarching goals, such as a Chapter 1 or literature review, and break it into smaller, manageable goals. Think of these goals as steps to accomplish the large, overarching goal.

Activity 2.2 Writing Goal Log

Large overarching goal		
Small goals	Task	Completed
1		
2		
3		
4		
5		
6		
7		
8		

Here we provide an exemplar to generate ideas about how this simple tool can be utilized.

Large overarching goal: Complete Solid Draft of Social Skills manuscript		
Small goals	Task	Completed
1 Literature review: Social Skills Project	Section: How social skills develop	12/13/2019
2 Literature review: Social Skills Project	Section: Impact of social skills on academics	12/17/2019
3 Literature review: Social Skills Project	Section: Kindergarten learning contexts	12/19/2019
4 Literature review: Social Skills Project	Methodology	12/27/2019
5 Literature review: Social Skills Project	Theoretical Framework	12/29/2019

Once you have completed your goal sheet, use it the next time you have a sizeable amount of time to write, for example, at least a two-hour block of time. Get yourself comfortable and situated; have everything you need to accomplish this goal. This means you need the head or physical space to write, the tools, such as your laptop, access to any articles, sticky notes, highlighters, etc., whatever you need when you write. Employ the **Pomedoro technique** (Cirillo, 2018): write for 25 minutes, reread what you've written, take a five-minute break, and write some more! If reading, do so actively; if reading electronically, use available tools to add comments and notables, if reading a hard copy, use sticky notes, a highlighter, and pen/pencil to note possible changes. Stop at intervals in review and also read for flow and cohesion. Take the time to revise often, and if you make changes in the document while reading, go back afterward and "make them real."

You will have times where you feel stuck, the words won't come, or you find yourself reading and rereading something over and over. When you hit a block, DO SOMETHING ELSE!! However, resist the urge to read email, scan social media, shop online, or engage in other behaviors that do not move writing forward. When you get stuck, commit to doing something useful. For example, read literature germane to this manuscript or another, proofread, check references, etc., but continue for that allotted timeframe (the example of two hours). Near the end of your time, stop and address components listed on the goal sheet provided as Activity # 2.2. Writing Goal Log. Assess what you accomplished and what next steps are needed. While at first this may seem cumbersome, accomplishing smaller goals leads to feelings of satisfaction. No matter how small the goal, once accomplished, you have gained traction. And traction is forward progress. Keep trying this method until it feels more natural and familiar. The act of time and tracking goals can become a habit as can the practice of breaking large goals into smaller goals.

Source: iStock

Plan for Publication Opportunities: Setting a Submission Schedule

It is often difficult to maintain busy schedules and remain productive in your writing. Trying to remember everything, including due dates, can be overwhelming. We suggest keeping a calendar and keeping it accurate and easily accessible. Being organized is vital to being productive. Treat your established writing time as a standing appointment with yourself to focus on writing. Resist the urge to schedule other events during this dedicated time. While you want to be a good faculty citizen or collegial graduate student, give up your established writing time only as a last resort. Consider using a three-semester schedule to track important dates and upcoming calls for manuscripts as suggested in Activity 2.3: Yearly Writing Log by Academic Semester.

During each month of each semester, track what is coming due. Be opportunistic and realistic. Literally, research is everywhere and chances to craft studies and publish them abound. Often, opportunities present themselves, especially in the form of special issues of journals or edited books in your field and subsequent calls for manuscripts. Keep the previous academic year's map and use it to make decisions about conferences to attend and deadlines to manage. As an aside, as you gain productivity and publications, keep up with updating your curriculum vitae (CV) for work in progress, published, etc. That is another way to track success at your own goals as well as make sure you are updated so when you arrive at your annual review or evaluation, it is all up to date. You can place a note on your calendar once a month for 45 minutes to update your CV. And, while you may not always need the 45 minutes at this monthly juncture, it is a reminder to yourself about being strategic, organized, and timely. Being strategic and thoughtful needs to be part of the fabric of your writing routines. Activity 2.3, the three-semester schedule, is a tool that can help you think strategically about what is due and coming due and allows you to determine if an opportunity is reasonable.

Activity 2.3 Yearly Writing Log by Academic Semesters: Increasing Weekly Writing Time

Systematically keeping track of what you need to do and what may present itself calls for organization. Start with what you know is an absolute. Each academic year, note start dates for each semester or quarter, when syllabi are due, when quarterly or annual evaluations are due, and holidays such as winter and spring break. Visit the academic calendars website at your institution and use that as your guide. Track any upcoming due dates for annual conferences and targeted manuscript submission. This allows you to make informed decisions about what can be reasonably accomplished and accomplished well. Look at the following blank yearly log. Begin where you are and add your most important dates. As your monthly log fills out, start to think about what else can be added in a manageable fashion. The simple act of logging a semester or quarter or entire year according to your academic calendar allows you to make informed decisions about what you can accomplish. Then examine the sample, created by one of our graduate students as a model.

Activity 2.3: Yearly Writing Log by Academic Year

August

September

October

November

December

January

February

March

April

May

June

July

August

August, 2019

September, 2019

Draft case study for special collections technical services reorganization project.

Review draft literature review for academic library spaces assessment.

October, 2019

Write outline for MSERA presentation about online-only practitioner-based graduate programs.

Group presentation for ELRC 7607
Complete all journals for ELRC 7607

"Collections as Data" grant submission by 10/31.

November, 2019

MSERA presentation on the 6th

ELRC 7601 final paper
ELRC 7601 group presentation. Read Demographics and the Demand for Higher Education.

Draft ELRC 7607 capstone proposal.

December, 2019

EDCI 7129 paper

ELRC 7607 capstone

January, 2020

Draft case study for special collections technical services reorganization project. Send draft to the journal *Library Collections, Acquisitions & Technical Services*.

Explore feasibility of quantitative study of library associate deans

> Review literature

> Determine institutional parameters—public R1?

> Draft questions

Submit proposal for Academic Library Advancement and Development Network (ALADN) conference by January 15th.

> Library fundraising since recession (HE fundraising since recession?)

> Manship school collaboration

February, 2020

Qualitative class assignments.
Strategic Planning class assignments.

March, 2020

Draft conference proposal for Association for the Study of Higher Education (ASHE) 2020.

April, 2020

ASHE 2020 proposal due mid-April

ALADN presentation?

May, 2020

Library associate deans project?

Summer 2020
June, 2020

Draft comprehensive exam questions
AERA proposal?

July, 2020
AERA proposals due
Finalize comprehensive exam questions.

August, 2020
Complete and submit comprehensive exam questions?

Each of these logs serves a purpose, and that is to help you establish or reestablish a writing routine and evaluate the routines you have in place. If you are currently a graduate student or a novice scholar, you may have some systems that have been working for you. We do not suggest getting rid of what works, but perhaps these activities can become additions to systems that can help you become more efficient. Or, perhaps, these structures will allow you to examine your time differently. Also, the authors have found recreating these routines using digital methods, such as using calendar apps or software, can also be helpful.

For example, Tynisha, another author of this text, prefers the use of an online calendar. Her writing times are set as appointment times and are reoccurring. Because of her various administrative obligations, online calendar appointments allow her to keep this space dedicated and this time reserved. This means, once she has time scheduled, this set aside time is off limits to any other activity. She also uses the notes function in the online calendar to link when journal articles are due, editor email addresses, and she may also create detailed to do list for how she wants to spend the time. Regardless of the approach you take, digital or not, creating and following a systematic, organized writing routine is what is paramount.

Systematically Tracking Calls for Journal Manuscripts

Monthly, we suggest that spending an hour or so searching for upcoming calls is time well spent. Put these hours on your calendar log or wherever you keep your time, so you will adhere to this activity which we have found can (and does) increase publishing productivity. Specifically, we often share calls and discuss coauthored feasibility with colleagues based on ongoing research. As a graduate student, new scholar and/or novice researcher, make it a point to form relationships with faculty whose interests are similar to or intersect with yours. Collegial relationships can flourish as you share calls and discuss research ideas. Invest time and energy to send one another manuscript calls, grant notices, and other academic announcements.

Consider extending this idea of sharing information to others with whom you work or other graduate students, but also, those who are not institutional colleagues. Many colleagues reciprocate; others do not. Regardless, cultivating this kind of collegiality and fostering collegial relationships pay dividends. Sometimes these informal networks expand, other times they shrink as exchanging information may only pertain to one or two additional colleagues. But, it is a productive habit to regularly spend time looking for calls and research possibilities. And, it is also good practice to share writing and research possibilities with colleagues. As you continue your writing productivity, be sure to add new projects and submissions to your CV (at least monthly) ☺.

SUMMARY

In this chapter, we provided some simple tools for writers to use to track productivity, record accomplished tasks, and map upcoming deadlines. These tools and the accompanying discussion provide organizational ideas, time management strategies, and formats that can be employed as is or amended to increase productivity and maximize effort. As we close, we return to the words of successful author, Stephen King, whom we referenced earlier in this chapter. King has published countless novels, many of which appeared on the *New York Times* Best Seller List. Shares King (2010), "The scariest moment is always just before you start. After that, things can only get better" (p. 269). The point of including this quotation? You have to reach that starting point. In the next chapter, an idea is presented for how to start a manuscript using an innovative presentation strategy. Avoiding the blank page strategy is designed to assist graduate students, new scholars and novice researchers jump-start a piece of writing.

KEY TERMS

Pomodoro Technique This is a *time management* method developed by Francesco Cirillo in the late 1980s. The technique uses a *timer* to break down work into intervals, traditionally 25 minutes in length, separated by short breaks. These intervals are named *pomodoros*, the plural in English of the Italian word *pomodoro* (tomato), after the tomato-shaped kitchen timer that Cirillo used as a university student.

CRITICAL THINKING QUESTIONS

1. When are your peak writing times? After completing the Writing Log Inventory, did you notice this pattern? How can you capitalize on this to maximize productivity?

2. Where could you "find" additional time that could be devoted to writing?

3. How can you reprioritize your current time commitments to schedule writing time on a regular basis?

4. Who in your network has similar interests to your line of research that may be a potential collaborator?

5. What community organizations address issues similar to your field of study? What relationships could you pursue for potential collaboration?

6. What journals do you currently read or have noted contain articles you have read and cited regularly?

7. What are considered the top three to five journals in your field?

ADDITIONAL REFERENCES AND RESOURCES ———————

National Writing Project. Retrieved from https://www.nwp.org/.

Shut Up and Write!. Retrieved from https://shutupwrite.com/.

Vanderkam, L. 168 Hours: Time Tracking Challenge. Retrieved from https://lauravan derkam.com/2017/09/welcome-168-hours-time-tracking-challenge/.

WORKS CITED ———————

Casanave, C. P. (2005). *Writing games: Multicultural case studies of academic literacy practices in higher education.* Boca Raton, FL: Routledge.

Cirillo, F. (2018). *The pomodoro technique.* New York, NY: Currency.

King, S. (2010). *On writing: A memoir of the craft* (p. 269). New York, NY: Pocket.

Lawson (1979). Behind the best sellers: Stephen King. Retrieved from https://archive. nytimes.com/www.nytimes.com/books/97/03/09/lifetimes/kin-v-behind.html

Rief, L. (2002). Quick-writes: Leads to literacy. *Voices from the Middle,* 10(1), 50.

Silva, J. (2007). *How to write a lot: A practical guide to productive academic writing.* Washington, DC: American Psychological Association.

Avoiding the Blank Page

Starting From What You Know

Writing takes time to develop, implement, and refine. Writing scholars agree that developing the craft of writing as embedded scholarly productivity requires a great deal of ongoing practice, expert modeling and demonstrations, targeted guidance, specific feedback, and copious amounts of authentic, critical encouragement (Atwell, 1998; Bickmore, Bickmore & Sulentic Dowell, 2013; Calkins, 1991, 1994; Graves, 1983, 1995, 2004; Hillocks, 1986; Murray, 2001; Ray, 2001). Graves (1995) posits, "if students had one good teacher of writing in their entire career ... they could be successful writers" (p. 14). The authors of this text maintain that not only does this statement hold true for PK-12 writing, it is particularly germane to the writing required of PhD students, novice researchers, and new scholars.

Learning Objectives

There are four learning objectives for this chapter:

1. Writing from a presentation

2. Utilizing technology

3. Making the most of your teaching (or coursework)

4. Managing writing solo

Quick Write # 2

In the second quick write, we supply an image. Take a few minutes and examine it.

Have you ever felt the way this writer looks? We have! As you view the image provided and the phrase "*I can't write because...*" focus on the image. See what comes to mind as you review the phrase "*I can't write because...*" and notice the details of the image you selected.

Source: iStock

After thinking of when you have been stuck and cannot write productively, gather a timer or your watch or phone and your preferred writing devices. Set the timer for three minutes. Next, start the three-minute timer and write down or type everything that comes to mind while looking at this image and the two prompts without stopping. After your three minutes of writing time is up: (1) celebrate what you wrote, words on a page are always a cause for delight; and (2) note themes or common ideas across your free write. What does the exercise tell you about yourself, about your authorship, about the reasons you supply for why you have struggled to write?

Many PhD students, novice researchers, and new scholars similarly find writing to be a daunting task, waiting for that inspirational, perfectly crafted sentence to come to mind before they begin. Good writing takes practice; the only way you get better at writing is to WRITE! Like any other acquired skill, writing skill improves with repetition, rehearsal, and revision. As we have already stated in the previous chapter, to become skilled at writing, you need to practice writing. This chapter will describe how those new to writing can use existing skills and activities they are already doing or have done to scaffold the writing process and avoid the blank page. This starts with what many PhD students, novice researchers, and new scholars already know: how to build a professional, scholarly presentation.

In Chapter 2, the focus was on establishing a writing routine, acquiring writing discipline, and identifying publication goals. In this chapter, we present ideas to give you a jump start on your writing, helping you to avoid the dreaded blank page.

Much of what is written here was developed through one of the authors of this text—Cyndi's experiences—in navigating a writing path that fits within the context of her teaching, research, and service responsibilities. As a former classroom teacher and current teacher educator, she has always been committed to translating research into practice, and she makes an effort to have a companion practitioner article for *each* research study she completes. However, she had difficulty in deviating from the predictable format of the research study—identifying an issue, crafting a literature review, and developing a method section, replete with subjects or participants, setting, data sources, and analysis, and writing up results. When left to her own organizational strategies, she struggled with how to organize her writing and particularly, determining which ideas came first.

As both a behaviorist and educator, she began to develop rubrics and strategies to avoid having to start from nothing. For Cyndi, and perhaps many other new scholars like her, editing was always much easier than starting from scratch. And so, began the process of identifying "writing shortcuts," or concrete ways to capture the essence of a scholarly publication through the process of preparing presentations for research conferences. Cyndi would share these presentations with her undergraduate and graduate students and with new faculty as a way to help her organize her thinking about research by describing it to others, to elicit feedback, and to serve the purpose of the research presentation operating as a catalyst to initiate her writing. This strategy propelled her to actually start on the writing process.

Creating a Presentation to Help Formulate a Manuscript

While many graduate students, novice researchers, and new scholars find writing overwhelming, and often, intimidating, most have experience with presentations. They have had the experience conducting class research projects, pilot research projects, perhaps a master's thesis, and for many, they have proposed and conducted, or began to conduct, their first major research study—the dissertation. This simple strategy can be employed by novice writers and used to jump-start the authoring process. The modest and straightforward strategy is to create a presentation from their completed research that includes requisite sections.

This approach may appear overly simple, but it is highly effective. Consider the following questions to guide you:

- How would you explain your research issue to a new colleague?

- How would you describe your research design in a succinct amount of time?

- How would you deliver the findings in a way that conveys your idea clearly and sequentially?

- What would you discuss with others about your implications for research?

These questions can aid in the development and organization of your presentation. Keep it simple by listing only one to two major ideas per slide. Also, keep in mind that typical presentations are presented within a 15–20 minutes timeframe, so strive to keep essential presentation information at a basic, yet comprehensive, minimum. As an aside, if you are a doctoral/thesis candidate, when you present your prospectus/proposal, you will likely not have more than 20 minutes. A good rule to follow is maintaining a 10-slide threshold.

Once you have the slides created, review for flow. Ask yourself: Do you begin with an issue? Do you include a succinct problem statement? Do you propose a solution that directly addresses the problem? Have you included slides that capture your literature review sufficiently yet succinctly? Are your study methods detailed yet brief enough for the slideshow presentation format? Within your methods slide(s) have you adequately included setting, participants/subjects, data sources and analysis? Do you end with your findings? And finally, what are the implications as well as possible future research directions?

Now that you have all information captured in the slideshow presentation format, rehearse through the presentation a few times, practicing it out loud. Time yourself carefully. Using this presentation format allows you to reorganize problematic sections that you can adjust to help the information flow cohesively. The important part initially is to capture your thoughts and record them within a slideshow presentation format. This provides structure to your work and a model for setting up your research and subsequent publication. In practice, every time you present research, you should be thinking of where to submit the study presentation as a publication. Your next step would be to review your targeted journal or call for manuscripts which can provide additional structure to inform the outline of your presentation.

Delivering the Presentation

An additional step that is extremely helpful is creating an audio presentation from this slideshow presentation. Within most slideshow presentation software programs, you can select "record slide show" in the "slide show" tab of the toolbar. This will allow you to record what you present within each slide. This additional step is beneficial because, during the presentation process, while engaging with the content, we are often more descriptive verbally than we may be when writing things down. For example, even as we write this chapter, we are using this same process to check on the thoroughness of covering the topic and adding detail.

Typically, humans acquire four different vocabularies. Our most robust vocabulary and literacy ability is often our listening vocabulary, then speaking, then reading, and finally writing. It is not that writing vocabulary is more difficult, but it requires a different type of metacognitive engagement (Krashen, 1989). Therefore, utilizing the voice over feature when engaging in the construction of a slideshow presentation puts you ahead in terms of your writing. This provides not just the framework for the publication but even some of the powerful aural/oral vocabulary that may convey your thoughts in a cohesive yet concise way.

Source: iStock

Utilizing Audience Feedback: Listening to Questions and Comments

Create or find an opportunity to present your slideshow presentation to colleagues and solicit feedback. If your colleagues are not local, upload your presentation to an online source where others can access, such as DropBox, Google drive, or even a private YouTube channel. If you are a doctoral candidate or PhD student, present to other students in your program as a way to garner response and commentary. If your program of study has an annual student conference, submit a proposal and present there. As you present, pay close attention to questions from the audience and ask specific questions geared for generating feedback like: Was there anything that was unclear or needed further detail? What suggestions do the audience have to make your presentation more well defined? Pay particular attention to comments that imply a lack of clarity or cohesion.

Also, review and examine your recorded commentary and explanations. What additional information did you state as you orally presented that was not captured in the slides? What questions prompted a response from you that clarified or exemplified your information, making it more comprehensible? What additional details made the presentation more logical? These additional details can bring the content to life for your audience—making the writing more relevant and accessible for the reader.

To ensure that you include information noted by your colleagues and/or peers as areas that warrant additional consideration, and to be sure to include any additional information that you added as you presented that was not a part of your original slide show, you will need to systematically record notes to adequately capture this information. If physically writing down notes as you present feels cumbersome, you can even use the voice memo function on your cell phone or computer to record the conversation between yourself and your colleagues while answering questions about your presentation. Many times, when describing technical information, we verbalize very clearly, then subsequently, we have trouble phrasing the same idea when expressing those thoughts in writing. Using a voice recorder allows you to listen to the discussion and capture the phrasing used to exemplify a point. This is not extra, tedious work; this is an exercise that gets you to optimal productivity and can increase opportunities for publication.

Activity 3.1 Step 1—Transitioning a Slideshow Presentation to an Initial Manuscript Draft

The steps from presentation to draft can be simplified by adhering to the following formula. Within the slideshow presentation software, select the "outline view" within the "view" tab of the toolbar to create an outline that can be cut and pasted into a word processing document. The following illustrates how to access this function.

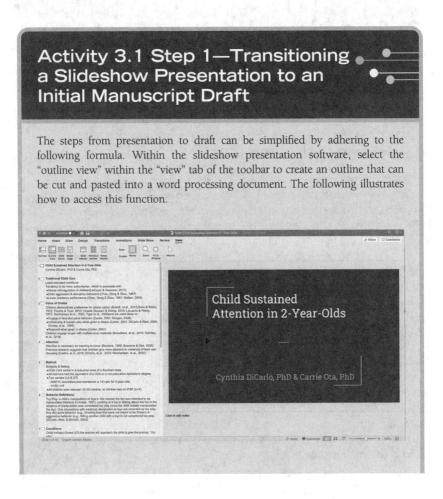

Begin with the title slide. First, open up a new word processing document and title it the same as your title slide—this is your **working title**. Now, listen to your presentation as you type into your word processing document to create your initial draft of your manuscript. Ask yourself how you introduce your topic, define the issue, and present a possible solution. The next two slides identify the issue and solution. In your word processing document, use the subheadings of *Issue* and *Solution* as you gather your thoughts and begin to write.

Activity 3.2 Step 2—Framing Your Issue Using a Slideshow Presentation

Method

___

Subjects & Setting

- Child Care center in a suburban area of a Southern state
- All teachers had the equivalent of a CDA or a non-education bachelor's degree.
- Two centers (LA & UT)
  - NAEYC Accredited and maintained a 1:6 ratio for 2-year-olds
  - n=36; n=9
- All children were between 24 and 35 months; no children had an IFSP

As you listen, pause, and add in thoughts about how you discuss this issue during a presentation. Talk it through as you type your thoughts. As with any manuscript, how you frame your issue is really important. Stop to reread what you have written. Then, continue adding text about your issue. Once you feel comfortable that you have explained your issue with sufficient detail for your audience, move on to how your research presents a solution to the issue posed. Be as specific and detailed as possible about how your research addresses the issue. Each of the five bullet points below can be extended into viable statement or even a few paragraphs. This process assists you in building a draft as you listen to your presentation and type into your word processing document to create your initial draft.

Theoretical Framework

- Quality, well-prepared teachers are the key factor in student achievement (Darling-Hammond, 2010).
- Quality teachers are prepared with connected coursework, carefully-crafted field work, and a capstone student teaching expirence with a quality mentor.
- Highly competent, proficient teacher to effectively mentor a novice teacher.

Love Purple
LIVE GOLD

Some fields and disciplines require a **theoretical framework**; others do not. According to Whetten (1989), a theoretical framework provides an understanding of why a researcher or researchers initiated an investigative journey, or what theoretical direction researchers are considering. For many scholars and researchers, a perspective exists that as researchers, "we cannot understand or interpret research findings without some theoretical lens." (Casanave & Li, 2015, p. 105). A theoretical framework grounds research and in essence, "map[s] out the conceptual landscape of a topic" (Whetten, 1989, p. 490). Many scholarly proposals require writers to demonstrate an explicit and sound theoretical framework that undergirds the research and is congruent with appropriate research methods/analyses. If you have included a theoretical framework, insert that information next. This exemplar study included a literature review on traditional childcare. In a study examining the dispositions of 108 host teachers who work with a student teacher for an entire semester, a theoretical framework was used. In this case, the work of Linda Darling-Hammond (2010) regarding coherent teacher preparation programming was the framework. Thus, in this example, if you are citing a theoretical framework, then, in your word processing document, you would discuss the theoretical framework at this juncture. *Theoretical Framework* would be your subheading in your initial draft word processing document. This following slide is actually a bit wordy; however, what is in the slide can be transferred directly to the initial word processing document as a wonderful starting point.

In the notes feature of the Theoretical Framework slide, the authors had written the following two bullet points, taken directly from Darling-Hammond's 2010 study.

- **Quality teachers are prepared with connected coursework, carefully crafted field work, and a capstone student teaching experience with a quality mentor.**

- **In essence, it takes a highly competent, proficient teacher to effectively mentor a novice teacher.**

Behavior Definitions

Toy Play- a child's manipulation of toys in the manner the toy was intended to be manipulated (Martens & Hiralall, 1997). Looking at a toy or talking about the toy in the absence of manipulation was considered toy play (once the child initially manipulated the toy). Only interactions with materials designated as toys are recorded as toy play. Any disruptive behavior (e.g., throwing toys that were not meant to be a thrown) or aggressive behavior (e.g., hitting another child with a toy) is not considered toy play (DiCarlo, et al., 2003; 2016)

Incorporating citations into your manuscript lends credibility to your topic and is required by all scholarly **citation styles** employed by journals. Understanding how to cite or paraphrase appropriately for each citation style is necessary. Authors must take care to understand which citation style is required by your discipline or target journal. We advise incorporating the appropriate citation style during the writing process for maximum efficiency and productivity. We also recommend purchasing, reading, and notating the style guide considered authoritative for your field. **Online citation style guides are inaccurate and/or incomplete as the style guides themselves are protected by copyright.** Having your own copy (perhaps even tabbed with frequently used sections ☺) will save you time and ensure accuracy in your initial drafts as you move toward submitting your manuscript.

As a general rule, you should cite research that was published in the last five years, as recommended practices can change, based on new research. This is not a hard and fast rule and does not apply to seminal work, for example, early research in a given area, or when citing research methods or methods of analysis. Sometimes it can be confusing for novice writers to know when to cite. You can ask yourself the following questions to decide:

- Did you think of it? If not, cite it.

- Is it original? If not, cite it.

- Is it common or considered **reified knowledge**? If it is not, cite it.

Another point of confusion comes from knowing when you should cite versus when a direct quote is necessary. Direct quotes should be used when including very specific information such as statistics or numeric information or when introducing novel terms or definitions or when something the author has stated absolutely exemplifies a point in the discussion. Often in academic writing using the American Psychological Association Style 7th edition, we see direct quotations following a phrase such as, "According to Author," or "Based on the work of Author." Citations only require the author(s) name and year, while direct quotes additionally require the page number (or for online sources, the paragraph number, as per the *American Psychological Association Style Manual*) (APA, 2020, pp. 270–274). Again, to ensure the correct treatment of citations, be sure to check your field's authoritative citation style for your disciplinary standard and your target publication's requirements.

Activity 3.4 Step 4—Converting Your Slideshow Presentation Literature Review to Text

As you continue through your slideshow presentation, you will repeat this process for your slides on the literature review for your initial draft. When sharing this information within a presentation, the literature is frequently compacted and presented in a quick, efficient style. When writing, you need to extend these ideas, concepts, and information fully. In a dissertation or thesis study, a writer should completely and comprehensively address all literature germane to the study, mostly confirming similar studies but also disconfirming related studies. In a journal, article, or book chapter, that review of literature information needs to be comprehensive, but this review of literature also needs to be succinctly addressed. The following slide, from the mentor teacher study, indicates the review of pertinent literature that informed the study. In this exemplar, once again, the information listed in the slide would be fully explained in that initial draft word document created from the slideshow presentation. This section would simply be labeled as Literature Review. Do not spend time now trying to create interesting, provocative titles and subtitles; the purpose of this exercise is to take what you have created in the slideshow presentation and create a corresponding word processing document that will function as your initial draft of an article.

Issues of Mentoring

- **Matching & Selection**
  (Ambrosetti, 2014; Block and Grady, 1998; DePaul, 2000; Huling-Austin, 1992; Killburg, 2002; Newton et al., 1994)
- **Emotional Support**
  (Newton et al., 1994)
- **Communication & Coaching**
  (Newton et al., 1994; Boreen et al., 2000; Kinlaw, 1999)
- **Time**
  (Ganser et al., 1998; Guyton & McIntyre, 1990; Arends, 1998; Latham, Gitomer & Ziomek, 1999; Turner, 1998)
- **Change & Conflict**
  (Kilburg, 2002)

LOVE PURPLE
LIVE GOLD

In this Literature Review section, note that there were five issues. Each one of these—Matching and Selection, Emotional Support, Communication and Coaching, Time, and Change and Conflict—would then become subheadings within the Word document.

Four additional sections would follow. The next section would be Study Methods, followed by Findings, then Implications, and finally, Discussion. Following the process of viewing your presentation, mentally (or verbally) talking through each of these headings, and writing what you are thinking or stating aloud, you can easily convert your slideshow presentation into your initial draft of a publication.

This slideshow presentation-to-initial draft exercise is but one way to capitalize on work completed in order to draft a piece for publication. As authors, we all live by this rule: every presentation should be converted into at least one publication. Yet, there are other ways to avoid the blank page and begin drafting. Every writer needs to develop his or her preferred method and perfect it—with practice. Another method that many writers use is the time-honored method of outlining.

Outlining as a Strategy to Avoid the Blank Page

As you begin a manuscript, an outline can be an important and timesaving step. First, map an outline of what you want to write about in the introduction, what topics—possible theoretical frameworks—whose research—what scholars—you want to discuss in the literature review, and how you plan to organize the existing scholarship in an area. Then, outline how you would structure and segment a methods section, followed by an outline of how you intend to present and address major findings, and finally, record how you will communicate implications. As an example of how this method can be multifaceted, at the thesis or dissertation stage, a tight outline can often become a table of contents as well as structure you want to use as you draft.

In the next few pages, we detail other ways that writers can capitalize and maximize ongoing efforts, become more productive, and realize more publications.

Keeping Your Writing Moving

When conducting meetings with writing partners, it is a great strategy to make use of your smart phone's voice recorder, in order to capture discussion during your meetings. Oftentimes, when discussing ideas, someone will explain a concept in a unique or succinct way and someone will say, "That sounded great! What did you say, again?" and sometimes, it is hard to recapture. Recording creative conversations allows for the flow of conversation to be accessed at a later date and then **mined as discourse** for writing. Next steps can be discussed with timelines, keeping everyone on the same page and keeping the flow of writing moving. A "to do" list with due dates before the next writing group meeting can be very motivating. This strategy can be combined with the use of dictation software.

Whenever Cyndi, one of the authors, meets with graduate students on their research or writing projects, she uses this strategy and requests that students send a follow-up email, detailing what was decided at the meeting and the tasks each person will do before the next meeting. When she receives the email from the graduate student, it is a chance to clarify any point of discussion or task that may not be accurate or complete. She then saves this email to the student's file on her computer by date, and reviews these notes prior to their next meeting.

Source: iStock

Activity 3.5 Capturing the Essence of a Writing Meeting With Follow-Up Email

From: Sally Smith
September 7, 2019
To: Cynthia DiCarlo

Discussed:

TO BE DONE THIS WEEK:

- *Create operational definitions for Positive and Negative Climate indicators on the CLASS observation sheet*

- *Reworking the interval data sheet from TMA to replace with Positive and Negative behaviors as well as a No Opportunity option*

ROUGH PLAN FOR METHODS:

- *Observing three teachers at the preschool for at least five to seven baseline points (to acquire stability)*

- *Interviewing to determine what mindfulness practices they already implement before implementing the intervention.*

- *Give a protocol of what to do throughout each day and create a checklist to account for fidelity data.*

- *After a week of implementing mindfulness, begin collecting data again (while also collecting fidelity data each week to be sure, they are completing the protocol)*

** Methods need to be approved before collecting data. Strong methods chapter needed.
I think this is all we discussed. If I left anything off, please let me know!
Thanks so much for your help! I always feel better after we meet ☺

Sally Smith
Peer Lead Teacher
ABC School

While capturing conversations as a way of being strategic with communication can help move writing along, another option that the authors of this text frequently use is the expanding technology of dictation software. This technology is likely to change and develop, but, at this point in time, we are referring to what is currently available.

Activity 3.6 Dictation Software as a Method to Help You Work More Efficiently

There are several speech-to-text dictation software applications that can assist you in your writing journey. While using a presentation can help you organize your thoughts, you can also use a presentation to get a jump start on writing an article using dictation software. Some current applications include Google Docs Voice Typing (Google, 2020), Dragon Professional Individual (Nuance, 2020), Braina Pro (2020), Speechnotes (2020), e-Speaking (n.d.), Voice Finger (2020), Apple Dictation (2020), Windows Voice Recognition (Microsoft, 2019), or Otter (2020). While there is a nominal charge for some of these services/software, the time you save is immeasurable, and most companies offer a trial period, so you can try out the features of each. As a caution, while we cannot predict how technology will advance, we recognize it will.

Before beginning your presentation, open the speech-to-text application and hit "record" as you begin your presentation. Be sure to either turn off the software or obtain consent from audience participants prior to the question and answer segment of your presentation. One of the authors, Cyndi, has used this strategy when writing an article on collecting data within an undergraduate course. The resulting manuscript did require some editing, but this strategy gave her, the author, a head start on the writing process and again, avoided the blank page. The authors of this text do not endorse any specific software, just the practice of utilizing it in the manner describe herein.

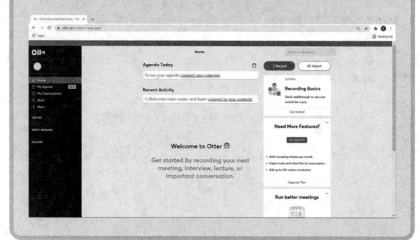

Activity 3.7 Questioning as a Writing Strategy

When working with collaborators, questioning can yield rich descriptions and jump-start the writing process. When considering your writing topic, think about the questions you could craft for your collaborator, then set up an in-person meeting, open your dictation software, and start your conversation. You can later change your questions to headings within your manuscript. If your collaborators are not available for in-person meetings, you can make use of video conferencing. Below is an outline used to help supervisors include classroom teachers in developing practice articles. In the field of teacher education, there is often a differentiation between **practitioner articles** and research articles. Practitioner articles are focused on the development of pedagogical or clinical practice. The sample questions included here demonstrate the types of questions that could be asked to use an interview format when talking with the teacher about their experiences with a research project. This interview was captured using Otter© and is in the process of being edited for submission to a practitioner journal. Not all fields have a practitioner element, but we have found this tool helpful for that end.

In Cyndi's role as Executive Director of a laboratory preschool, she is charged with disseminating research-based practices to the field of early childhood teacher education. This particular exemplar is germane to that field.

Teacher Practice Articles

Include our teachers in writing through strategic questioning, targeting the practitioner publications, below.

The process.
Identify a teacher who has strength in a particular content/topic area. Compose several questions that would provide sufficient background for a reader to understand/replicate essential elements for the reader.
You will read the questions to the teacher and type in the responses (or email them the questions and get them to type in). You will change the questions to shorter headings and edit, adding references as needed.

Example – Video self-reflection

- How did you feel when you first heard you would now be evaluated using the CLASS tool?
- What were your thoughts when you were asked to participate in a video project where you would record yourself teaching and self-evaluate using the CLASS tool?
- How did you feel when you started receiving the voice over feedback from your Associate Director?
- Did this change the way that you interacted with other teachers, particularly those involved in the study?
- How did this effect the way you viewed yourself as a teacher?
- Has this impacted your teaching? How?
- What would you suggest to other teachers regarding this process?

In addition to using Otter© or other dictation software with questioning, you can also utilize teleconferencing options to "mine" interviews that can become a rich source of writing to contribute to your productivity and publishing agenda.

Activity 3.8 Maximizing Video Conferencing by Recording a Call With Transcription

Another technological tool that can assist in the writing process is video conferencing software with transcription. When conducting interviews or focus groups, make use of the transcription tool on recorded video conferencing software (e.g., LogMeIn, 2020; ZDNet, 2020; Zoom, 2020; GoToMeeting). Please note that this feature is usually only available in upgraded (read: not free) versions of video conferencing. Conduct your virtual meeting using video conferencing using the "record" feature. After the meeting is completed, the recorded version will include a transcription of the conference, ripe for analysis. If you already have a video conference recorded, you can always use a transcription service (e.g., Rev, n.d.); Transcription Hub, 2020; WayWithWords, 2020). The cost is nominal for the time and effort you will save in transcribing. We suggest first reviewing these transcripts for accuracy and making the appropriate edits. However, after edits, you can "mine" this discourse for inclusion in your writing.

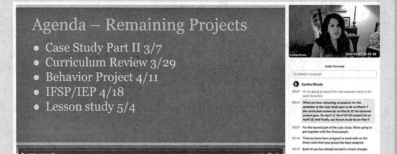

In the next section of this chapter, we offer yet additional ways to work harder and smarter. In other words, these are ways that we make every effort to take what we are doing or have done and find ways to publish it. For graduate students who have completed mini-studies or advanced studies within their advanced coursework, these are ways to again, maximize effort.

Utilizing Pilot Studies and Mini-Studies

Within the course of many graduate programs, doctoral students are encouraged to engage in **pilot studies**. For example, you might be enrolled in a qualitative course that discusses the five traditions of qualitative research. Perhaps, as a graduate student, you are given the option to create a pilot study that is a case study, an ethnography, or autoethnography, as part of the course requirement. Typically, such pilot studies are couched within a semester-long course and may be the culminating activity of such a course. Or, you might be enrolled in a quantitative course that focuses on creating surveys, and your professor might assign a project to create a survey, an activity that allows graduate students to understand how survey questions are actually created, the issues with "outlier questions," and the subsequent discovery of questions that are initially poorly phrased or don't match/load with the concept assessed. With careful planning with your major advisor, these course assignments can serve as a focus of study and further your research and publications. These "pilot" studies, sometimes referred to as "mini-studies," can also be viewed as a rich source of material that can be parlayed into a viable publication.

One example was a doctoral student, working with one of the authors of this text, in Curriculum and Instruction, and enrolled in an Intervention Research course. Part of the course requirement was to conduct a single subject, multiple baseline design research project. The graduate student elected to use a social story intervention to complete this course assignment. Over the course of the semester, the student designed the intervention, implemented the intervention, and was required to analyze the results. Working with her course professor, the graduate student crafted the assignment into a manuscript and submitted the manuscript for publication. The initial decision from the editor was a Revise & Resubmit decision, which we will cover in more detail in a subsequent chapter. Prior to her graduation, this graduate student was able to attend to all reviewers' suggestions and resubmit her initial manuscript, which was published before her graduation. This is just one small example of how graduate students, novice researchers, and new scholars can maximize the tremendous amount of effort that they expend in graduate coursework and convert a pilot study or mini-study into a viable publication.

As a cautionary tale, graduate students, in particular, should be very careful to communicate clearly and openly with both their major professor and the professor who assigned such a course requirement. In this particular case, the professor of record for the Intervention Research course was not a member of the student's committee. The student was very careful to communicate with her major professor about her proposed course research and subsequent publication plan. The major professor recognized the amount of work the course professor invested in the student, and according to university policy, did not want to be a **ghost or guest author**. In academia, it is always wise, and suggested, to adhere to the APA (2020) or other citation style guidelines for suggestions on authorship and to make sure that you understand all of the issues involved in authorship. Whether you are a graduate student or advising graduate students in their research, these issues and concerns should be learned and taught clearly and explicitly to prevent confusion and corresponding ethical concerns. As an aside, most universities have created policies surrounding authorship, such as Louisiana State University policy (2018), below.

II. DEFINITIONS

Publication: as used in this policy is meant generically, representing as inclusively as possible any publicly shared academic or creative work, including any manner of report, paper, manuscript, article, electronic publication, discovered or derived dataset, artistic creation, or other research manifestation.

Author: an individual who has made significant intellectual contributions to a publication (see section IV.A.1 Attribution of Authorship).

Conflict of interest: any real or perceived interference of a person orentity's interests with the interests of another person or entity, where potential bias may occur due to current, past, or contemplated personal or professional relationships.

Covered Individual: LSU faculty and all individuals engaged in any form of research and/or creative or scholarly work at, in collaboration with, or on behalf of LSU, including any person paid by, under the control of, or affiliated with LSU.

Relevant Information: that information having any tendency to make the existence of any fact that is of consequence to the resolution of the dispute more probable or less probable than it would be without the information.

Translating Research-to-Practice/Policy (and Building Your Vita)

As scholars, we first and foremost must focus on the development of our research agendas. However, even in the midst of our research endeavors, we can easily increase our publication record by additionally developing **practice articles** or policy recommendations from our research.

When translating research-to-practice, we should focus on the practical applications of what we have found through our research—what should practitioners' in your field do in light of what the research study has found? How should they go about this? These ideas can be conveyed through taking your original research article and quickly modifying it to get a practitioner draft. For example, for an intervention research study, first take the most essential background information from your literature review, and then take the intervention section from your method and the clinical implications section from your discussion. These sections will serve as a starting point for your draft. Be sure to look over the guidelines for your targeted practice journal or publication outlet as a guide for formatting; then develop your slideshow presentation. Using this strategy can help graduate students in fields with clinical or practitioner areas (education, social work, therapy, etc.) to get a minimum of two publications from their thesis or dissertation.

This same practice could be replicated for those in areas without clinical practice by applying their research results to policy conversations. For example, consider how policy makers or those charged with implementing policy in your field may "take up" your findings. Where does your field engage with policy makers? Are there specific journals or venues that would be interested in these pieces? Taking time to locate these and write a piece for publication related to your original research gains you both traction in your area through an additional publication. However, for both practitioner/practice or policy-based publications, it is important to determine how these are viewed (or counted) by your academic field and current/perspective institution.

Incorporating Writing into Your Teaching

You can also incorporate writing into your teaching and include graduate students in the process. This involves careful planning but can be beneficial for your writing agenda and also your students. One of the authors of this text, Cyndi, completed a project that was developed into a text on case method of instruction (Snyder & McWilliam, 2003), which emerged from her use of this method within her teaching. This assignment began by using prewritten case studies and having students discuss and answer questions about the cases. When new recommendations for professional practice came out, Cyndi and her coauthor decided to have students use a rubric to develop and refine their own cases. In order to develop this rubric, a literature review was conducted to incorporate recommended practices in case method of instruction. The case studies developed by the graduate students reflect the new recommendations from the professional organization and are illustrative of best practice. With editing and a review of case method of instruction, they had a good start on a text that could benefit others working with undergraduates in their teaching about recommended practices in special education. In subsequent semesters, rather than asking graduate students to create new case studies, graduate students reviewed previous cases for inclusion in the proposed text. This yields not only a book for the course instructors, Cyndi and her coauthor, but book chapter credit for the contributing graduate students. In this instance, incorporating writing into teaching generated a very timely book proposal and subsequent book publication.

Mining Graduate Coursework Assignments

Faculty can help graduate students in the publication process by tailoring course rubrics to align with author guidelines for practitioner or action research publication outlets. In graduate courses the authors of this text teach, we embed calls for proposals and author guidelines into all courses to help facilitate products for graduate students. We use the semester map found in Chapter 1, Activity 1.3 as well as embedding calls within a syllabus. In a recent course that Cyndi taught, for example, students focused the first half of the semester amassing information from early childhood standards, environmental tools, child assessments/developmental inventories, and recent peer-reviewed research studies. All of this was a precursor for students in order to be prepared to collect their own data. The information was utilized in a variety of ways including to: submit for small foundation grants, develop conference proposals, webinars, podcasts, and write practitioner publication (selected from a list of several early childhood practitioner journals). Within the context of the course, the students were also taught many of the writing strategies presented in this chapter. This maximizes students' time and can lead to professional products that should make them more marketable upon graduation. The same flow can be used by new faculty and novice scholars to maximize their efforts.

SUMMARY

Writing is a skill to be learned like any other skill. Mastering the art of writing requires practice, time, and patience. Following the above-mentioned steps can provide a roadmap for graduate students, novice researchers, and new scholars who may feel initially overwhelmed by the writing and publication process or simply not know how to begin. Using previously mastered skills, such as presentations or outlining, can help graduate students, novice researchers, and new scholars work through their preliminary hesitation in writing in order to avoid the blank page.

KEY TERMS

Citation Style This is a formal set of descriptions that outline and guide the information necessary for a citation, how information is ordered, as well as abbreviations, capitalization, punctuation, and spacing among other conventions. There are several citation styles, but common ones include: American Psychological Association (APA) style typically used by the social sciences, Modern Language Association (MLA) style typically used by the humanities, and Chicago/Turabian style frequently used by history, business, and fine arts. Each publication venue can choose their own citation style. Most fit within their disciplinary expectations, but there are exceptions.

Ghost or Guest Authorship These terms refer to the practice of adding authors to publications who do not contribute to the manuscript in meaningful ways. For example, according to APA (2020), "[a]authorship credit should reflect the individual's contribution to the study. An author is considered anyone involved with initial research design, data collection and analysis, manuscript drafting, or final approval" (p. 2). Guidance on authorship should be reviewed for each citation style.

Mining Discourse This concept pertains to the mindful process of maximizing all efforts expended as a researcher and writer. The examples provided in this chapter illustrate how typical endeavors can be utilized and converted to viable publications.

Pilot Study Also called a "mini-study," pilot studies are typically conducted during the course of graduate work in research coursework. Pilot studies are primarily learning opportunities for research methods for graduate students. However, with planning, the efforts can be maximized and converted to a publishable manuscript.

Practitioner Article This term, which can be used interchangeably with the term "practice" article, is germane to fields of study that involve field work, clinical work, internships, or capstone experiences that result in licensure or certification. The purpose of these articles is to bridge the research-to-practice gap. While the genesis of these articles is research, the focus of these articles is the practical application of the research to the field.

Reified Knowledge Also called common knowledge, reified knowledge is information that is something that many or most people know or possess. Reified knowledge is in the public domain, or a widely known date. For example, London is the capital of the United Kingdom. Reified knowledge can also be information or knowledge of a fact or event that has become so commonly known that it has lost its original relevance. For instance, Mount Vesuvius erupted in AD 79 is an example of reified knowledge.

Theoretical Framework For some disciplines, providing a theoretical framework is a mandatory practice when conducting research and completing a manuscript. A theoretical framework is the overarching theory that undergirds the foundational issue(s) that inspires an entire research study and leads to subsequent publication. A theoretical framework is the foundation that supports the need for a research study and provides an established basis for a research publication.

Working Title Often when we write academically, we need to do so expediently. This means we create a draft publication that we recognize will undergo many revisions before it is ready for submission to either a dissertation committee or to a publishing outlet. As the name implies, a working title is a kind of place marker. It indicates the essence of a study yet lacks refinement.

CRITICAL THINKING QUESTIONS ─────────

- What research projects have I recently completed that could be developed into research articles?

- What conference presentations have I prepared in the recent past that could be developed into a practice article?

- Which focus groups or interviews could I conduct using technology in order to "mine" the transcript data?

- What novel practices am I using with collaborators that could be turned into an article through interviewing?

- In which courses might I incorporate student writing that might yield a publishable product both for the instructor and the graduate student?

- How can I model these practices for my graduate students in order to help them be more productive and yield publications?

ADDITIONAL REFERENCES AND RESOURCES

Apple Dictation (2020). Apple support: Use voice control on your Mac. Retrieved from www.support.apple.com/en-us/HT210539

Berkeley Graduate Division (2020). *Academic misconduct: Cheating, plagiarism, and other forms.* Berkeley Graduate Division Graduate Student Instructor Teaching & Resource Center. Retrieved from https://gsi.berkeley.edu/gsi-guide-contents/academic-misconduct-intro/

Berkeley Graduate Division (2020). *Preventing plagiarism.* Berkeley Graduate Division Graduate Student Instructor Teaching & Resource Center. Retrieved from https://gsi.berkeley.edu/gsi-guide-contents/academic-misconduct-intro/plagiarism/prevent-plagiarism/

Berkeley Graduate Division (2020). *Paraphrasing exercise.* Berkeley Graduate Division Graduate Student Instructor Teaching & Resource Center. Retrieved from https://gsi.berkeley.edu/gsi-guide-contents/academic-misconduct-intro/plagiarism/paraphrase-exercise/

Berkeley Graduate Division (2020). *The art of paraphrasing.* Berkeley Graduate Division Graduate Student Instructor Teaching & Resource Center. Retrieved from https://gsi.berkeley.edu/gsi-guide-contents/academic-misconduct-intro/plagiarism/art-of-paraphrasing/

Braina Pro (2020). Braina Pro: Speech recognition software. Retrieved from www.brainasoft.com

e-Speaking (n.d.) e-Speaking: Voice recognition software. Retrieved from https://e-speaking.com/

Google (2020). Type with your voice. Google Docs Editor Help. Retrieved from https://support.google.com/docs/answer/4492226?hl=en

LogMeIn (2020). GoToMeeting. Retrieved from www.gotomeeting.com

Microsoft (2019, April 22). Use voice recognition in Windows 10. Retrieved from https://support.microsoft.com/en-us/help/4027176/windows-10-use-voice-recognition

Nuance (2020). Dragon Professional speech recognition. Retrieved from www.nuance.com/Dragon-Pro/Individual

Otter (2020). Otter voice meeting notes. Retrieved from Otter.ai

Rev (n.d.). Rev: Transcribe audio to text. Retrieved from https://www.rev.com/

Speechnotes (2020). Speechnotes: Speech to text online notepad. Retrieved from https://speechnotes.co/

Transcription Hub (2020). Transcription Hub: Services on the cloud. Retrieved from https://www.transcriptionhub.com/

University of Queensland (n.d.). *Three minute thesis.* St Lucia, QLD: The University of Queensland. Retrieved from https://threeminutethesis.uq.edu.au/

Voice Finger (2020). Voice finger. Retrieved from https://download.cnet.com/Voice-Finger/3000-7239_4-75118688.html

WayWithWords (2020). WayWithWords. Retrieved from https://waywithwords.net/?gclid=Cj0KCQjwmdzzBRC7ARIsANdqRRk7ltBZTpa9xl5H2AVXr0EPCaQqZRLHFDhxjDr5b79VrKAhTOfsNRMaAlhkEALw_wcB

ZDNet (2020). ZDNet: All the essential tools for telecommuting. Retrieved from https://www.zdnet.com/

Zoom (2020). Zoom: Video-first unified communications platform. Retrieved from https://zoom.us/ent?zcid=2582

WORKS CITED

American Psychological Association (2020). *Publication manual of the American psychological association* (7th ed.). Washington, DC: American Psychological Association.

American Psychological Association (2020). *Publication practices & responsible authorship*. Washington, DC: American Psychological Association. Retrieved from https://www.apa.org/research/responsible/publication/

Atwell, M. (1998). *In the middle: New understandings about writing reading and learning* (2nd ed.). Portsmouth, NH: Heinemann. Retrieved from http://collegequarterly.ca/2003-vol06-num01-fall/banbury_janz_mcdermott.htmlO

Bickmore, D., Bickmore, S., & Sulentic Dowell, M.-M. (2013, January). Initiating a writing revolution in your school. *Principal Leadership Magazine*, 13(5), 34–38.

Calkins, L. (1991). *Living between the lines*. Portsmouth, NH: Heinemann.

Calkins, L. (1994). *The art of teaching writing*. Portsmouth, NH: Heinemann.

Casanave, C. P., & Li, Y. (2015). Novices' struggles with conceptual and theoretical framing in writing dissertations and papers for publication. *Publications*, 3(2), 104–119.

Darling-Hammond, L. (2010). Teacher education and the American future. *Journal of Teacher Education*, 61(1–2), 35–47.

Ertmer, P. A., & Russell, J. D. (1995). Using case studies to enhance instructional design education. *Educational Technology*, 35(4), 23–31.

Graves, D. (1983). *Writing: Teachers and children at work*. Portsmouth, NH: Heinemann.

Graves, D. (1995). *A fresh look at writing*. Portsmouth, NH: Heinemann.

Graves, D. (2004). What I've learned from teachers of writing. *Language Arts*, 82, 88–94.

Hillocks, G. (1986). *Research on written composition: New directions for teaching*. Urbana, IL: ERIC Clearinghouse on Reading and Communication Skills and the National Conference on Research in English. (ERIC Document Reproduction Service No. ED265552)

Krashen, S. (1989). We acquire vocabulary and spelling by reading: Additional evidence for the input hypothesis. *The Modern Language Journal*, 73(4), 440–464.

Louisiana State Univeristy (2018). *Authorship guidelines and dispute resolution (Policy Statement 27)*. Baton Rouge, LA: Louisiana State University. Retrieved from https://www.lsu.edu/policies/ps/ps_27.pdf

Murray, D. (2001). *A writer teaches writing*. Portsmouth, NH: Heinemann.

Ray, K. W. (2001). *The writing workshop: Working through the hard parts (and they're all hard parts)*. Urbana, IL: National Council of Teachers of English.

Snyder, P., & McWilliam, P. J. (2003). Using case method of instruction effectively in early intervention personnel preparation. *Infants and Young Children*, 16(4), 284–295.

Whetten, D. (1989). What constitutes a theoretical contribution? *Academy of Management Review*, 14(4), 490–495.

Writing the Journal Article Step-By-Step

Purpose of Chapter

This lengthy chapter provides a structured framework for systematically producing a typical research-based journal and/or research-based book chapter manuscript from start to finish. Think of this chapter as a structured process for producing a publishable manuscript. Requisite parts are included and attention paid to common challenges, pitfalls, and areas that can impede productivity and publication. Both quantitative and qualitative research design specifications are included.

Learning Objectives

There are multiple learning objectives for this chapter. They are:

1. Scheduling time to craft a journal article or book chapter to fruition

2. Writing an engaging introduction

3. Writing a germane literature review using **seminal** and **current references**

4. Writing a clear method section

5. Writing a cohesive results section

6. Writing a compelling discussion section

7. Adequately addressing implications

8. Mastering the technical aspects of scholarly writing by addressing format, function, and form

In the previous chapter, Chapter 3, we presented a major strategy that can be used to expand research data into a visual presentation, with the overall intent of then using the presentation as a springboard to a full article. Also, in the previous chapter, the time-honored practice of outlining was suggested as a viable method of both organizing thinking and as a way to save time by noting what you want to include in a manuscript. Both methods generate productivity. Writers need to use strategies that work best for them, the strategies that minimize unproductive behaviors and lead to fruitful and prolific writing habits. In this chapter, we briefly return to both the visual presentation combined with outlining as a means of addressing and capturing the requisite, necessary, and expected parts of a manuscript.

Systematically approaching the publication process means a researcher and writer becomes more productive and realizes more publications. Think of publishing as a three-part process. Part one involves the study itself, gathering and analyzing data. Part two is writing up the results of that research in an acceptable scholarly format, and part three is submitting your piece to a suitable and appropriate outlet for your research. Beginning with the necessary, requisite parts of a manuscript are essential, expected, and obligatory when reporting the results of research.

Quick Write # 3

This third quick write is a technical quick write that is more structured, mechanical, or conventional in nature and less generative. Begin this quick write by recording the following six terms. For the purposes of this quick write, we are being intentionally prescriptive to both illustrate a message of structure and provide readers with a document that can actually be used as a template, hence, the more narrow and rigid format of this particular quick write exercise. The six terms are: **Introduction, Literature Review, Method, Results, Discussion,** and **Implications**. Please follow this procedure:

1. open up a word processing document on your device,

2. record each term, centered and bolded, next,

3. hit "enter" on your keyboard, then,

4. insert a **page break** as you are typing so that the six terms are listed as if they are **level one headings**. This will move each to the top of a page. We recognize that many writers want to begin with a paper copy, so if you are physically writing, center the terms and skip approximately three to six lines after each term. Once you record them, if any term sounds a bit unfamiliar, you could read ahead to the end of this chapter and peruse the definitions of these terms, then return. Think of these sections of a manuscript as a universal blueprint for producing a journal article or book chapter. The blueprint then becomes a metaphor for the structure of a scholarly piece of writing. These sections are foundational pieces—necessary aspects of the blueprint. If you have physically written these terms and sections, we really want you to now go back to step 1 and enter into a word processing document what you recorded on paper.

Your study could be a longitudinal secondary data analysis, a quasi-experimental intervention pre-post design, or a case study. Or, your study might be single case design, a systematic review of literature and historical documents about a topic, or a secondary analysis of data research. Perhaps, your intended manuscript may be a recommended practice piece culled from a literature review, or an issues-based theoretical piece.

At the end of the day, for most research designs in the social sciences, following the blueprint gets you to a technically well-written piece with requisite parts that are expected and make sense to readers, who are the editor(s) and reviewers that will be your initial primary audience. The latter examples (recommended practice piece or an issues-based theoretical piece) may not contain either *method* or *results* sections, but the blueprint provides structure and allows a researcher-writer to provide a purpose for the manuscript, discuss what is relevant within a field, and offer results, and/or implications.

And, as we are referring to expected pieces of a manuscript, we want to extend that quick write. Before the *introduction* section, we want you to add these terms: **Title page** first and then, **Abstract**. Again, if you are creating an electronic document, please follow this procedure:

1. compose the new term and

2. hit "enter" on your keyboard.

These two sections, along with a possible list of **keywords**, tables, figures, and table of contents, are what is commonly referred to as **front matter**, especially in a thesis or dissertation, but the two terms also apply to manuscripts parts or sections. Front matter pieces are often uploaded to electronic platforms for blinded peer review as separate documents, whether you are submitting a manuscript to a publisher for consideration or submitting a conference proposal to a professional organization. Keywords in a journal manuscript typically are placed on the cover page, near the bottom.

After the *implications* section, we want you to add these terms, what we, as authors, refer to as **back matter**. Following the same procedure, add these terms: **Reference section (also called Works Cited)** and **Appendices**.

1. compose the new term and

2. hit "enter" on your keyboard.

Now you have set up what can function as a standard template for producing a manuscript that can be submitted for peer review for a potential journal article or book chapter. Included at the end of this chapter is an actual template of a standard research-based article or book chapter.

The remaining bulk of this chapter provides a step-by-step process for producing a publishable manuscript. First, engage in the following activity to begin your article or book chapter in earnest. This activity combines the two techniques discussed in the previous chapter, Chapter 2, by merging a visual presentation with strong outlining as a combined springboard strategy to a full article.

Activity 4.1 Maximizing a Research Presentation by Converting to an Article/Chapter Format

In Quick Write # 3, the authors of this text asked readers to create a basic working template; if you crafted a template physically, again, either convert it to a word processing document or proceed toward the end of this chapter and copy the exemplar called, *Manuscript template for a research-based journal article or book chapter*. The goal of this exercise is to create a rather quick, working draft from the template which is created from the visual presentation, capturing your thinking and previous work. Next, open up the visual presentation you created in Chapter 2 or an existing visual presentation you have created. Set the template you created and the visual presentation side by side on your desktop. Now, you are ready to complete this exercise. You are going to copy and paste content from your slide deck into the template, specifically copying and pasting your presentation topic into your *cover page* as the manuscript title. We recommend you skip the *abstract* at this point, but, as you should have it as its own separate page, skip it and proceed to your *introduction* section. Here, add your problem statement or statement of the problem and any details surrounding your topic as well as any solution you proposed by copying from the visual presentation and pasting into the template document. As you are working quickly, it is acceptable to use bullet points or an outline format.

Next, copy any slides that pertain to a literature review into your *literature review* section. Typically, a presentation is streamlined or abbreviated, so you will need to expand what you captured in slides to include a much fuller or complete review of literature. If those review sections or subtopics come to mind as you are copying and pasting, add them. If not, you can address them as you work through developing manuscript drafts. In Chapter 2, readers were encouraged to include setting, participants/subjects, data sources and analysis in visual presentation slides about method. Copy and paste this slide deck information into the *method* section. Follow with your findings by copying and pasting any results that you included in slides into the *results* section. Some information may also be placed into your discussion section. Don't spend a lot of time making big decisions here and get bogged down in the process. The objective is to transfer your ideas and work from the visual presentation into the manuscript template.

Next to last, what are the implications as well as possible future research directions that you addressed in your presentation? Add these to your *implications* section by copying and pasting. Finally, go back to your literature review section, copy it entirely, and paste it into you *references (works cited)* section. Working quickly, delete all text but the actual citations you are left with, including dates. Justify the left margin, and hit enter after each individual citation; then, reorder this list of citations, using the sort function on your laptop of computer or device. For example, to sort a list alphabetically in Word, quickly complete the following: (1) highlight the list of references you have cited, (2) Go to Home > Sort, (3) Set Sort by to Paragraphs and Text option, (4) Choose Ascending (A to Z), and (5) Select OK. This gets you a working draft of your *references (works cited)* section. Now, you have a working first draft of your manuscript. The remainder of this chapter addresses considerations for each section.

Scheduling Your Journal Article

Writing a manuscript is a significant investment of time. Whether you are writing an issues manuscript or a research-based article or chapter, you will need to budget the time necessary to work through successive drafts, polish it, and make it as complete and error free as possible. How long, you might ask, will this process take from start to submission? That depends on what else you have to accomplish in your professional and private life, but to be clear, writing a journal article or book chapter is not an effortless endeavor. In order for this to be manageable, we provide a practical structure that can be implemented. Belcher (2019) suggests in her field-tested workbook that an article (or we add, book chapter) can be written in 12 weeks. As the authors of this text, we agree that 12 weeks is an estimated, feasible timeframe that is reasonable, if you are disciplined, set realistic goals, and steadily work toward completing them. Simply put, you must budget this time consistently in order to accomplish the goal of completing a publishable manuscript.

Source: iStock

Given the other demands on your time and how much you can and are willing to dedicate to this task, the 12-week timeframe is both realistic and achievable. However, the drafting may take longer, depending on if you are working solo or as part of a collaborative team, and in some cases, it may actually take less time. Scheduling regular writing intervals will render this undertaking doable. The degree to which writing a manuscript is attainable and achievable depends on an individual's adherence to sufficiently addressing the requisite sections of a manuscript, and the ability to craft a manuscript that is coherent, deemed appropriate for a journal's audience or a book's overall concept, and is publishable. With the 12-week timeframe in mind, also consider that the submission process involves manuscripts undergoing a review process, which likely results in revision, and that manuscripts are published based on editors' decisions and preset publication timelines. Productivity begins with creating a manuscript and publishing ends when a manuscript has been accepted and is scheduled for a publication date. Rounds of review and editing components can add several months, at a minimum, to the timeframe. The discipline discussed in Chapter 1 is implemented here as scholars anticipate the time, effort, and skill needed to take an idea from germination to fruition, from idea to manuscript.

Writing the Introduction: Introducing the Issue, Topic, and Considering Audience

An introduction to a manuscript or chapter involves thoughtful decisions about how to introduce or frame the issue or topic as well as careful consideration of an intended audience and purpose for writing. Nearly four decades before this writing text was being written, seminal writing researchers, Graves and Hansen (1983) discussed the dual notions of audience and purpose among young children's writing, especially when given choices about what they decide to write. In essence, we write for distinct purposes, and we write for specific audiences. The same concepts hold true for adult writers. As author, you get to determine your purpose for writing a piece as well as self-selecting your topics. Essentially, as author, you also decide your audience as you both craft your manuscript and determine the best publication outlet. However, you need to be explicit about your topic and carefully consider your purpose. Overall, an introduction should *engage* readers and encourage, persuade, and provoke readers—your audience—to continue reading.

Usually, academic writers enjoy the freedom of selecting their topics for writing. In fact, the authors of this text strongly believe in choice as a prime motivator. In the Introductory chapter of this text, Activity 1 was an exercise in connecting writers in exploring the interplay between personal interest and ideas for potential studies and subsequent publications based on research. Consider including a statement or explanation of interest that also points to why the manuscript is important and to whom the article or chapter is intended. Briefly, we return to the blueprint metaphor.

Part of an introduction is to engage the readers in the importance of a topic. Extending the blueprint metaphor, an introduction should accomplish three distinct functions: (1) explain why a topic is important, (2) establish a purpose, and (3) address the need for research and subsequent writing about the research as a rationale for the manuscript. As every manuscript needs a precisely stated, overt purpose statement, such statements typically bridge to a need for the research and manuscript.

For many scholars, the work of Swales (1990) is considered foundational in terms of providing insight into the importance of introduction. Swales offers readers and researchers a model, Create a Research Space (CARS). Swales's CARS model involves three primary elements which Swales refers to as moves: Move 1, establishing a territory; Move 2, establishing a niche; and Move 3, occupying the niche. With each move, there are steps that delineate a process of creating an introduction to a research article, and by extension, a book chapter. Numerous researchers have applied, critiqued, and adapted the CARS model ranging from Feak, Swales, Irwin, and Swales (2011) who extended the CARS model to writing introductions across genres to Yasin and Qamariah (2014), who applied a critique to students whose first language is not English.

Clear Purpose Statements

Introductions include a purpose statement that conveys both what a manuscript entails as well as why it is being written. Think of a purpose statement as a declaration of what the manuscript will address but written in a persuasive and convincing manner. You will describe what you are doing and why in your purpose statement. Your purpose statement should be both explicit and precise in terms of what you are intending, not general, ambiguous, or vague; it should also be compelling. Include either the word *purpose* or use the word *intent*. Your purpose statement should also be succinct, no more than one or two sentences.

Activity 4.2 Reading and Writing Purpose Statements

For this activity, reopen draft 1 of your manuscript. Do you have a purpose statement specifically written in your introduction? If so, reread it and revise it to refine what your intent is for this research. If you do not have a clearly articulated purpose statement, move to the next step of this exercise.

Locate and open up a published article that you have read and cited in the past or in this presentation, outline, or working manuscript. Locate the purpose statement. Note where it is located within the document. Read it several times and ask yourself if it is clear what the article is claiming to do? Circle the words in the purpose statement that signal to you that this text is the purpose statement. If you have a purpose statement written within your introduction, compare yours to the published manuscript's purpose statement. Circle what words you used in your statement to signal your purpose to your audience. Are they strong and clear?

Revise your statement until you are satisfied that your purpose statement clarifies explicitly what your intentions are for this manuscript. Be sure to include the phrasing, *The purpose of this study…* (*or investigation or exploration or manuscript*) or a similar phrasing like, *The intent of this study…* (*or investigation or exploration or manuscript*).

Establishing Need

In addition to a clear and compelling purpose statement, a statement of need further clarifies the purpose of a manuscript and is a powerful mechanism to convey the significance of a topic. Establishing need illustrates why any particular topic is timely and why publication about the topic is warranted, necessary, and justified. One way to establish a clear need is to provide data or a specific data point that indicates the need, and in a sense, influences the reader to consider the purpose of the manuscript as necessary in the current context of the research trajectory.

Activity 4.3 Reading and Writing Need Statements

For this brief activity, again, reopen draft 1 of your manuscript. Locate your purpose statement specifically written in your introduction. Briefly reread the purpose statement. Now compose a need statement that supports and extends your purpose. This may involve additional context or additional data. Read your purpose statement with your need statement together. Are they interconnected? Does the need statement clearly expand or extend thinking presented in the purpose statement? Does it articulate why your manuscript is relevant to the current academic conversation, why it is timely? Reread and revise until you are satisfied that both work cohesively and in tandem with your need statement corroborating your purpose statement and aligns with what your goals are for this manuscript.

If you have been adhering to these activities, you should have a solid draft 1 of your manuscript. You have at least a page, maybe more of an introduction. If you began with what you had as a visual presentation, and you have added a purpose statement and a need statement, you are well on your way to completing an introduction to a manuscript about your topic. Most writers will share that engaging readers early, or using a hook within the first few paragraphs, activates readers' interest in your topic. Now, it is time to get serious about completing a provisional introduction. Whether you are crafting a journal article for publication or a book chapter as this chapter implies, or you are writing a Chapter 1 of a dissertation or thesis study, the principles in this chapter are the requisite parts of a manuscript. In the next activity, you will be taught to complete an introduction.

Activity 4.4 Fleshing Out an Introduction

The activity is the start of the heavy lift, but if you keep working through the activities, step by step, you will accomplish solid writing. Try to budget at least 45 minutes for this 3.4 activity. Begin by reopening draft 1 of your manuscript. Your task is to fully introduce your topic, combining your purpose statement with your need statement. Read what you have, then ask yourself what else needs to be captured in your introduction. Create a list or outline of what you want to say, then expand the list into coherent sentences. Write freely from your list of what you want to include. Imagine you are writing for someone who is not familiar with your topic. Try to write for at least 15 minutes, then stop and reread what you have written. Are you noticing any "holes" or "gaps" in your argument? Are you writing clearly? Continue writing, then pausing to read, then returning to writing for two more 15-minute periods.

An introduction sets the tone for your entire manuscript. The function, to explicitly describe your topic, needs to clearly present your purpose and adequately address the need for your research and manuscript, while appealing to readers. Overall, an introduction should captivate readers and inspire, convince, and prompt readers to continue reading. In many discipline and fields, an introduction also ends with an overarching research question that indicates what the author really wants to know about the topic. A well-written literature review sustains the issues presented in an introduction, reinforcing both purpose and need. In order for an introduction to an article or chapter, or any manuscript for that matter, to be considered complete, it needs to be backed up; your central tenets, your purpose, and need have to be supported with a coherent, connected literature review. This holds true for a thesis, dissertation study, journal article, book chapter, or any piece of scholarly writing.

Writing the Literature Review

Begin your review of literature by first describing how you conducted your search including keywords and phrases used to locate literature, search engines accessed, and years of the search that were included. In a journal article or book chapter, this should be accomplished concisely and in a crisp manner, yet comprehensively. In a dissertation, this should be expanded to include a comprehensive list of terms and perhaps, a list of key journals that included scholarship pertaining to your topic. Systematically describe what you did and how you accomplished your literature review. These statements, while brief, should convey what you did in terms of where you searched and what terms were used.

Great literature reviews are highly organized. Organization stems from thinking deeply about how you will order and arrange the information you want to present. In a review of literature, that thinking encompasses careful consideration of decisions about the sequence and arrangement of ideas. Organization of a literature review also includes how a writer links separate sections of a discussion. Using an outline to sequence sections of a literature review is an initial necessary step.

Activity 4.5 Organizing a Literature Review

For this activity, copy and paste your slides from your visual presentation into a separate Word document. Using an outline format, look at the major sections, and left-justify those key sections. Question what are the big ideas and concepts? What presents a logical sequence or order of ideas and concepts? Next, determine what subsections should be addressed within each main section, and, underneath major sections, indent (tab) those subsections. Review your list by talking through your organization, reading it aloud, or, if you prefer, use the read-aloud speech function on your computer to listen and consider your order. Determine if it is logical, sequential, and comprehensive.

Confirming Need and Situating Research Through a Literature Review

Before you delve into the literature that surrounds your issue, confirm; don't just restate the need for your research succinctly. Next, situate your research within a context that strengthens your purpose or argument and reaffirms the need for your study. Well-written literature reviews extend your central argument. A review of literature should thoroughly explore an issue and provide additional support for why research is important. This means that you strive to use **current literature**, preferably within the last five years, but also, include classic, seminal pieces that represent defining phases and stages of a field, to support your central argument.

Why Descriptors Are Important

Well-selected descriptors indicate to your audience the scope of your literature review and by default, what your research accomplishes. Descriptors create the borders and margins of your literature review and provide the perimeters or limits of your entire study. Descriptors also allow other researchers to access your study and publications. As academic publishing advances as a practice, providing access

Activity 4.6 Reading and Writing Descriptors

For this very brief activity, once again, reopen draft 1 of your manuscript. Go to your title page. As you submit a manuscript for consideration, an editor will ask you to provide five to seven keywords. At the bottom left hand corner, enter the words, "Keywords:" and think for a minute about this manuscript. What is the topic? It may be one word or two words (or phrases). Enter that after the colon. Next ask yourself, what field does it address? Enter that next. Then, thinking about the major areas of your literature review, what areas did you capture as keywords? Enter that information. You might also question who might be interested in this manuscript, in other words, who is your audience? Enter that information. Finally, what is your study design? Enter that as well. Now, you are ready to return to your review of literature and make sure it is expansive and comprehensive yet succinct enough for an article or book chapter. Begin to write each section and subsection. This is especially true if condensing a literature review from a completed dissertation or thesis. In the next section, we offer a discussion regarding the need to synthesize reviews. This brief exercise illustrates writing's recursiveness.

to your work to other researchers becomes increasingly important. As a graduate student, new scholar, or novice researcher, the degree to which other scholars can access and subsequently cite your research contributes to your success. While Chapter 7 is a deep dive into metrics and how this practice is evolving within academic publishing, it's important to note the efficacy of carefully selected descriptors.

Descriptors are synonymous with what publishers routinely request as **keywords**. Typically, articles and book chapters display key terms and phrases on a published manuscript's title page. Key terms and phrases announce what to expect within a publication, defining both the restrictions and limitations as well as the extent of the publication. Descriptors are vital to a successful publication.

Synthesizing Your Reviews

The efficacy of using an outline can be illustrated by examining the literature that supports a research study and its intent. A tightly organized outline can add cohesion and clarity to a discussion of the literature from a field or perhaps multiple fields that surround an issue and substantiate a manuscript's central purpose or argument. There should be an order and flow to the discussion you are providing. An outline can also keep a writer on track regarding what to include and what to exclude. Organizing and discussing similar studies together is more impactful than writing a scattered review that lacks consistency, interconnected-ness, and precision. Consider that most articles call for 5,000–10,000 words. Oftentimes, calls for articles (and chapters) provide a page limit that includes references and appendices, tables, and figures. Divide that number in half, whether it is a word count or page limit. The first third to a half should be devoted to your introduction and literature review, and the latter two-thirds to a half to your method, results, discussion, and implications. We would recommend reviewing a few sample articles from journals you are citing in the paper to determine which percentage most closely fits the expectations of your publication outlets and discipline. However, always strive for a balance within the manuscript—as a literature review should do justice to the studies being reviewed. This balance ultimately depends on the publication outlet as well as the discipline.

One quick note, in terms of overall productivity as well as ensuring reliability, validity, relevance, and timeliness of your research, literature reviews should be written as you are planning and developing your study. The information and themes you find within should inform your choice of methodology, data collection, and analysis a-priori—a fancy research word for the process of theoretical deduction prior to formal empirical observation. Further, if you are doing the kind of research that requires an **IRB**, this information is typically required to apply for approval from your institution or research site. If you wait to write your review post-study, you may find that your topic is not relevant nor timely or that you use methods the field no longer considers valid or reliable.

Regardless of when you choose to sit down to write your formal review, prior to beginning research or when you write the manuscript up for publication, there are two main ways to structure a literature review. In the first, each seminal or related study is reviewed separately. Each study reviewed should contain accurate detail about the participants or subjects. A thorough description of the setting including when a study was conducted as well as where it occurred should also be included. A brief description of the study design, data sources, and analysis should also be incorporated into the literature review of that particular study. The remainder of the literature review of a specific study should contain a discussion of results. Ideally, for each study reviewed, this should be accomplished in one to two paragraphs. Providing this level of detail allows readers to compare the literature being reviewed to the current study you are presenting.

The second way to structure a literature review is to group similar studies together—or categorize the studies in your review. These may be addressed by themes addressed in the research, method used, or periods/timeframes of the research. Most importantly, whatever theme you choose to follow, synthesize findings from study to study, indicating how they are similar and thus comparable, and how they are dissimilar, yet related. Justify your rationale. In Leah Katherine's research classes, she plays a simple sort game where each study to be included in the review is written on an index card or word processing document. Then, she challenges the students to sort them and come up with categories across the sorts they select and take notes on these choices. Next, she has them re-sort at least two more times completing the same process with increasing levels of nuance. Usually, by the end of the sorting exercise, the themes or categories of the review emerge along with their rationale. Finally, she has the students create a literature map which visually outlines how they choose to group the studies. Students are able to use the map to write the review as well as revisit when they write up their discussion.

Well-Placed Headings and Subheadings

Think of headings and subheadings as markers within a manuscript. Headings and subheadings systematically separate sections of a manuscript to guide readers. Headings and subheadings that are derived from a tightly focused and well-organized outline can greatly authenticate the purpose of a manuscript. We have been interchangeably using purpose and argument, but we want readers to pause for a minute and consider that when a writer crafts a manuscript for publication, they are, in essence, convincing readers of a stance—their argument—which is intermingled with their purpose. Headings alert readers to large concepts and ideas and convey by their placement that a major section of a literature review is being presented. In tandem, subheadings signal to a reader that a related section, connected to but somewhat distinct and subordinate from a major heading, is being presented.

In essence, both headings and subheadings inform and notify readers what will come next. When used judiciously and advantageously, headings and subheadings offer writers the opportunity to group similar studies together for consideration and to organize a literature review for optimal impact. A well-written and well-organized literature review builds substantial momentum for an issue, supports a purpose and argument, and creates a sense of confidence about the research that is being presented. Well-placed headings and subheadings are tools that, when used optimally, assist a scholar to guide readers to the current study—prepared to consume and contextualize the new research in the milieu of the field.

Guiding the Readers With Transitions

A review of literature can feel tedious at times. Sometimes they read laboriously, and well, to be perfectly honest, they can be boring. But reviews of literature can also read effortlessly, informatively, and be highly engaging. What and how a scholar crafts a review of literature can be appealing and spark an interest in readers. One way to craft a seamless review of literature is to pay close attention to transitions. Transitions guide readers. Transitions alone won't work, but transitions can aid in the organization of the writing and improve flow. Previously, we provided a short discussion of the importance of organization of ideas within your manuscript. While organization involves the sequencing of ideas and concepts, organization also addresses how a writer connects different sections of a discussion. Transitions are not a replacement for effective organization, but transitions can clarify your organization and result in a literature review that is easier to read and follow. There are three types of transitions to consider: transitions between sections, transitions between paragraphs, as well as transitions within paragraphs. All three types come into play within a literature review. The differences may seem subtle, but the distinctions are important.

Transitions between sections of a manuscript. When considering longer works, or longer sections of a manuscript such as the literature review, it is crucial to include *transitional paragraphs between sections* that provide a summarization for the reader regarding the information just presented and to specifically connect the importance or weight of this information to the content that will be presented in the in the next section. Transitional paragraphs between sections provide connectivity and continuity. For instance, writers might summarize a section succinctly and then explicitly provide readers with an indication of what they will be reading next.

Transitions between paragraphs. If tightly organized, so that paragraphs are arranged logically and sequentially so that the content of one paragraph lucidly connects to the next paragraph, *transitions between paragraphs* will emphasize an existing relationship by summarizing the previous paragraph and indicating the gist of the content of the succeeding paragraph. Transitions between paragraphs are a simple writing convention or device that could be a word or two that indicates the relationship. Examples include: however, for example, for instance, similarly, and/or in tandem. Transitions between paragraphs can also be a phrase, or a sentence, that again signals the relationship or connection between paragraphs. The placement of transitions between paragraphs can occur at the end of one paragraph, at the beginning of the second paragraph, or, in some cases when the writer wants to convey the significance of the relationship that connects the two paragraphs, in both places.

Transitions within paragraphs. Similar to transitions between sections and paragraphs, *transitions within paragraphs* function as signals to the reader by helping readers to anticipate what information is coming before they read it. As with all transitions, transitions within paragraphs highlight connectivity and relationships between concepts, ideas, or assertions being made by the author.

Power Words and Weak Verbs

As authors, we have advocated for strong transitions and clear organization throughout a literature review; varying your word choice as you review others' work is also sound writing practice. Because literature reviews can be dense at times, varying how you refer to research makes reading a literature review easier to read. Pay attention to the next literature review you read and note how often certain words such as *stated, said, wrote, found*, etc. Below is what we call our starter list of power verbs. We invite readers to use them versus the monotony of reusing the same tired verbs repeatedly. This list is presented in present tense; verbs can be changed to past tense easily (Table 4.1).

Table 4.1 Scholarly Power Verbs	
Articulates	**Highlights**
Attests/is an attestation to	Illustrates/is illustrative of/is an illustration of
Characteristic of	Indicates/is indicative of
Connotes	Is evidence of/evidences
Conveys	Portrays/is a portrayal of
Delineates	Posits
Denotes	Postulates
Depicts	Reflects/is a reflection of
Designates	Represents/is a representation of
Emblematic	Shows
Emphasize(s)	Signifies
Exemplify/Exemplifies	Symbolizes
Exhibitive of	Underscores

In tandem with this list of power verbs, we point to the work of Frels, Onwuegbuzie, and Slate (2010). In a delightful article, these three researchers and prolific, productive writers, discuss the function of verbs and the carefully selected, deliberate use of verbs in scholarly writing. Frels et al's (2010) examination of inaccurate, disproportionate, and weak verbs is a revealing treatise on the power of words, particularly verbs, when conveying an idea, a concept, or a finding in academic writing. The typology they offer in their article is a strongly recommended read for graduate students, new scholars, or novice researchers. We encourage you to pay particular attention to their Tables 1, 2, and 3, which contain excellent active scholarly verbs.

Reestablishing Need

Once you are satisfied with the order and progression of your literature review, consider a way to tie your literature back to your expressed need. Reestablishing need exemplifies why a topic is appropriate and why publication about the topic is needed. Returning to your need can bring closure to a review of literature and ending your review by reaffirming the need for your topic and research provides an extra measure of clarity and cohesion. Once you are satisfied with your literature review, it's time to write your method section.

Writing a Method Section

A method section is the soul of a research article. Think of it as the essence of your writing. The need to be clear and exacting is paramount. You have expended a great deal of effort on an introduction and literature review; now you want to present your research in the most cogent possible manner. Whether your study is a replication, replicable, or very unique, you want readers to be able to ascertain what you did from choosing your research question(s), to understanding why you selected a particular design, setting, participants or subjects, instrumentation, and analyses. Readers need to clearly understand your process. And readers need to be reminded of your overarching research question; thus, restating it in your methods section not only reminds readers of your topic's importance, but can also provide an opening to your subquestions. A sound research section often carries an article, and for some of us, that is the section where we go first when reviewing research.

Theoretical Framework/ Epistemological Stance

Theoretical framework and/or epistemological stance refer to a researcher's perspective. Within the academy and between disciplines and fields, debate to the efficacy of including a theoretical framework exists. As an example, among the four authors of this text, three of us were trained at three different universities, all of which required a theoretical framework as part of dissertations; one of us was trained at a fourth university that did not. Many proposals require a theoretical section, and they can be included as an introduction to a literature review or a methodology section. So, what is a theoretical framework? A theoretical framework is a research device that provides an undergirding stance for research, offers a broad depiction of the interconnected relationships in a research study, and functions as a scaffold for the work. With a manuscript, a theoretical framework section is typical. An epistemological stance differs from a theoretical framework in that this stance motivates how a scholar selects a research topic as well as the methodology and method you use. For an extensive discussion of epistemology and ensuing method, Koro-Ljungberg, Yendol-Hoppey, Jude Smith, and Hayes (2009) offer a solid discussion of the interplay between epistemology and method. "The authors argue that efforts should be made to make the research process, epistemologies, values, methodological decision points, and argumentative logic open, accessible, and visible for audiences" (p. 687). In addition, Casanave and Li (2015) provide a rich discussion of potential struggles that novices encounter when considering conceptual and theoretical frames in both dissertations and publications.

Labeling and Defining Research Design

Most crucially, within a method section, a writer must clearly label and define the selected research design with citational authority. Whether a design is quantitative or qualitative, both paradigms and traditions have achieved legitimacy within academic research practices. This is a writing text, not a research text, so building knowledge about research method is not a main focus of this book. Methods have developed from the make-up of particular disciplines and have given rise to specific perspectives (Lincoln, Lyman, & Guba, 2011). The design should be stated explicitly within the first paragraph of a method section. For example, if considering a case study (Stake, 2013; Yin, 2018) and depending on the kind of case study, including analysis, whom a scholar cites is important. This type of citation should be attached to any design discussion. In another example, if a researcher is reporting on a mixed-method design, they must be specific like, "concurrent exploratory mixed model design" (Tashakkori & Tedlie, 2003). Notice again, the citation is needed to fully and accurately describe the design.

In addition, the appropriateness of the method employed should be discussed succinctly but comprehensively, allowing readers to conclude that given the issue and/or problem, it is appropriately aligned to the research question. This is significant. For example, as authors, writers, and scholars, we have read many published manuscripts (and dissertations) that simply claim to be using a qualitative design. This umbrella term can refer to any number of methods, offers a limited description, and is not appropriate. A research design is the actual method and procedures used in both collecting data and analyzing data in order to answer a research question. A clearly written design statement distinctly defines the study type and plainly identifies the research problem and research question it is addressing. Following this statement, both data collection method and an analysis plan are explicated.

Activity 4.7 Identifying Research Method

For this activity, again, reopen your draft 1, and if you did not complete the visual presentation, open a blank word document. If you are the latter, you will be combining with the other activities you completed in this section. You are going to be working through a description of your research method section. Record your research design. Cite it accurately in text (and add the citations to your *reference* section). Then, write a sentence or two describing why the design you selected is an appropriate method to answer your research question. Save this as draft 2; you are at the half-way point of your manuscript. Keep this draft open as you read further in this chapter. Save your work. Now, you are ready to continue writing up your method section.

Designating Setting

Where is your research situated? Return to your method section document or section of your document and describe your setting fully. Talk it through, record if you need to, jot down notes, then expand those notes. At this point, use real names, places, and institutions. In a minute, you will rename them and label them as **pseudonyms**. Read it aloud. Have you adequately captured the essence of your setting? If your setting is physical, close your eyes and picture it mentally, then reread what you have written. Do you need to add additional details, expand descriptions, and expound on any details? Have you addressed the cultural or sociopolitical context of your setting? What other aspects of the context of your setting are pertinent to your study? Have you addressed those sufficiently? Now, go back and revise, employing the strategy of assigning pseudonyms.

Describing Subjects—Portraying Participants

Distinct and explicit research paradigms specifications need to be appropriately adhered to and adequately addressed when reporting research. Both paradigms (qualitative and quantitative) have their own rigor and terminology. Lincoln, Lynham, and Guba (2011) provide a discussion of paradigms as well as shift that has occurred within academic research within the past 20 years within the qualitative tradition. Terminology is important when discussing subjects or participants in a research article. Here, general guidance is provided for both quantitative and qualitative traditions. The tradition within the quantitative research paradigm typically uses the term *subjects* when referring to persons who participated in a research study. Conversely, within the qualitative paradigm, researchers use the term *participants* to portray individuals involved in the research study. You will need to describe how you selected your participants/subjects and/or chose your sample. Who did you include, decide not to include, and why? This is another area that requires citation. For example, if your study uses purposive sampling, you will need to describe what type, like "extreme or deviant case sampling" (Palinkas et al., 2015). Again, in your manuscript, you will need to describe and defend why this selection/inclusion technique is appropriate for and aligned with your research question and study design. Additional relevant information about those in your study, such as age, gender/identity, home language, race/ethnicity, culture, and developmental information, is typically included to provide general characteristics.

Returning to your working draft 2 document, describe your subjects/participants fully. Include the number and any pertinent demographic information. Include information that is relevant. Will you include gender? Will you include race and/or ethnicity? Are the ages of subjects/participants to be reported? Is experience an important factor? It may be helpful at this point to create a quick table that helps you visualize and describe subjects/participants cogently. Table 4.2 is a template that can be used to organize subjects/participants. While experience and years in position are listed as a possible category in the template in Table 4.2, readers are encouraged to replace those headings with what factors are appropriate or germane to their study. Readers should consider what demographic information is significant and should be included. What do articles you have cited in your own literature review include in their descriptions?

Table 4.2   Using a Table to Organize Study Subjects/Participants

Total number	Gender	Race	Age	Experience	Years in current position

Try filling out the table and then write from it, supplying full and rich descriptions in your draft 2 of your manuscript document. Next, return to articles you have cited in your literature review; do they include tables about participants/subjects in addition to written descriptions? Consider including a similar table within your manuscript—it will assist editors and reviewers.

Reread what you have written and revise anything that needs to be expanded, or that seems extraneous. The strategy of reading writing aloud forces a writer to really pay attention to the details of their writing; when you read aloud, you notice missing pieces of information that make your descriptions deep and expansive, and thus, understandable to readers of your work. While you want your descriptions to be full, you also want to be economical in your writing. Descriptions of subjects/participants are important, but these should be a balanced portion of your method section. Now that you have a working draft of your section on subjects/participants, it's time to describe your data sources.

Defining Data Sources and Data Collection

Previously, a method section was described as the heart and soul of a research article. Data are the essence of any study. Data, a somewhat quantitative term, refers to the statistics and units of information that are collected directly by the researcher. Denzin and Lincoln (2008) advocate for the use of the term for empirical materials when specifically conducting qualitative data. Typically, the design of a study dictates the potential data sources to be collected or empirical materials gathered. Studies can have primary and secondary data sources. Data can be procured (as is often the case for secondary analysis of large datasets) or collected by the researcher once or at intervals over time. These decisions are determined by the research question and design as well as the scope of a research study. In your working draft, describe your data sources or empirical materials. Use this series of questions to describe data sources/empirical materials:

- What are your data sources or empirical materials? Examples include a set of statistics, survey responses, observations, various types of interviews, reflections, artifacts, documents.

- How did you ethically acquire access to the dataset, if it was procured?

- What is considered your primary data source/empirical material?

- Why is it primary?

- Did you collect data/empirical material at intervals or all at once?

- How did you collect the data?

- How did you ensure validity and reliability? Or How did you ensure trustworthiness?

- How did your choice of collection method impact the data you ultimately collected?

- If including the data as separate variables for the purpose of statistical analysis, how will the data be coded as independent, dependent, control, etc.?

In the data collection section, the researchers should carefully describe the procedures for data collection including any tools (researcher created or purchased, digital or paper based) which were also used to assist in this process.

Similar to most sections in the method, these choices must be articulated and grounded in your chosen research question, design, and backed with appropriate citation. Therefore, generating an outline list may be a helpful first step as you draft this section of your method section. Or, if you have a visual presentation slide, this can be the genesis of this significant section of a method section. From an outline list or visual slide, fuller descriptions can be written that describe what are being gathered as data or empirical materials. This is rigorous writing activity, and it takes patience to achieve precision in your discussion of data sources or empirical materials.

Employing the *Pomodoro Technique* presented in Chapter 1, write freely from your list or slide of what you want to discuss. Try to write for at least 25 minutes, then stop and take a brief break; stand up, stretch, walk a flight of steps or complete a quick household activity, then resume by rereading what you have written. Are you noticing any "holes" or "lapses" or noticeable "gaps" in your discussion? Are you describing precisely and clearly? Continue writing, then pausing to read, then returning to writing for an additional 25-minute period. This kind of practiced writing is going to further develop your writing stamina and writing skill.

Communicating Data Analysis Clearly

While the data and/or empirical materials a researcher collects are perhaps one of the most significant aspects, or the core of any study, how a researcher *interprets* that information is equally important. Analysis is the process of converting raw data and inferring results. Analysis is, in a sense, the procedures used to uncover the story behind that raw data. Analysis procedures are aligned to a study's research question, design, and what is collected. Therefore, discussion of analysis needs to be meaningful, grounded in the research question, design, and backed with citation. For example, in a quantitative, specific single case research design, you would describe how you "graphed the data collected daily over 60 days and completed a visual analysis every five days (Lane & Gast, 2013) in order to drive decision making." In qualitative example, you may describe how you analyzed the data for a phenomenological study using the "constant comparative method" (Glaser, 1965). For research involving complex statistical analysis, be sure to include information about how you selected a statistical program, input the data, cleaned and accounted for missing data, and which tests you chose for analysis and why.

For each of these examples, and any data analysis method, the articulation of the method or analysis frame should be more fully explained to describe any analysis tools which were also used to assist in this process—for example, name any software (researcher designed or commercially designed) used to assist in your analysis. For example, did you create a spreadsheet for code-counts across themes? Did you use a specific software to analyze video-based data? Describe it all. Also, remember that for each type of data collected, you will have to describe the analysis method. If they are similar, say so. If they utilize different method, you need to clearly articulate the connection between each.

If this recommendation around clarity, grounding in design, and providing citation sound familiar, it is the same for all parts of the method section. Each section must articulate how the components of the method fit with one another and assist you in, you guessed it, answering your research question. This aspect of unanimity reassures reviewers, editors, and readers that study itself was designed, executed, and evaluated with care. Alignment and grounding across sections is one of the first assurances of validity/trustworthiness and reliability/generalizability, which will all be further articulated below.

Writing up analysis is also a demanding writing activity, requiring both practice and patience to achieve accuracy and a degree of meticulousness in your discussion of analysis. And again, we suggest writers utilize the *Pomodoro Technique* discussed in Chapter 1. Return to your working draft 2 document and write freely from your list or slide of what you want to discuss. Set a timer to write for 25 solid minutes, then pause and take a brief break, no more than five minutes. After five minutes, resume by rereading what you have written. Are you noticing any "holes" or "lapses" in your discussion? Are you describing precisely and clearly? Could someone follow your analysis procedure? Resume writing, then pausing to read, then returning to writing for an additional 25-minute period if you are not satisfied. If you are pleased with what you have produced, save your work. Persisting with this sustained kind of writing practice is going to continue to develop your writing stamina and writing skill. Two additional considerations are presented next. Not all studies require researcher positioning or situatedness. And again, the research question and aligned study design will dictate if such a section is warranted.

Situatedness: Addressing the Researcher's Positionality

Within the qualitative tradition, a discussion of situatedness or positionality, a part of qualitative research ethics, is needed in many manuscripts that describe certain kinds of studies. If you are a nurse examining some practice of nursing, you need to describe your relationship to the study, setting, and participants. If you taught for 15 years and you are investigating pedagogical practices, as the researcher, you need to discuss your experience and perspective. When a researcher is connected, even tangentially to a research site or to participants through the study topic, your position needs to be disclosed. Spradley (2016) explores this positionality in his notions of participant-observer.

Evaluating the Study

In the final section of method, the researchers must articulate how they assured that the study is worthy of inclusion in the scholarly tome. Like all other aspects of the method section, this must be done with clarity, grounding in design, and providing citation. Similar to the discussion of participants/subjects, the terminology and procedures for evaluating the design and execution of the study depend on the methodology selected.

In a qualitative study, the researcher will need to articulate what constitutes this study as a trustworthy scientific study which Towne and Shavelson (2002) describe as one which:

> Must allow direct, empirical investigation of an important question, account for the context in which the study is carried out, align with a conceptual framework, reflect careful and thorough reasoning, and disclose result to encourage debate in the scientific community. (p. 6)

To assure trustworthiness, the researcher should describe their strategies for ensuring credibility and rigor. Again, these strategies must be described in detail and grounded with a citation. For example, a researcher may describe the use of triangulation, member checking through participant validation, using a critical friend or community of practice, soliciting an external auditor, or several of these strategies to ascertain the accuracy of their findings. This final step allows reviewers, editors, and readers to determine if your study can be useful for others or have applicability in other situations.

In a quantitative study, the researcher must also explain how they insured validity, or accuracy, and reliability, or replicability/stability, of the results. This can be done in multiple ways, depending on the design and analysis technique chosen. The beginning of establishing validity and reliability in manuscripts for most quantitative studies starts with a complete description of how the data were treated. This component is typically included in the data collection and analysis section as described above. In this section, further details on the investigation of statistical error and corresponding power should be included. Effect sizes should always be reported. A discussion of effect sizes allow fellow researchers to understand the strength of the results, and, along with the other contextual factors of the study, determine the extent to which the study's results are generalizable, or applicable, to other situations/populations.

Findings/Results

The findings or results section is the zenith of your research study. Writing the findings/results in a way that is in keeping with your research choices and decisions is important. In a qualitative study, the next section, where the researcher presents information about the answers to their research question, is called findings. In a quantitative study, this same section is named results. So, how you write/report findings/results will be driven by, you guessed it, your research question, design, and chosen analysis method. This alignment is paramount.

Within the qualitative paradigm, there is a great variation across the genre of writing which makes up the findings section. This genre of writing is dictated by the specific qualitative design chosen. For example, perhaps your findings are a series of themes derived from a cross-case analysis, multicase designed study. Then, the author will first need to describe the findings of each case and contextualize using exemplars from the data. As a second level of findings, the researcher will also articulate the findings of cross-case analysis including themes, exemplars of themes from the data, and a description of the quintain. In contrast, for a narrative or autoethnographic study, the findings may consist of a composite sketch or a full narrative.

As you write your findings, consider what additional components will assist your readers in understanding your results. Would the addition of tables or figures assist in the explication of the findings? Longer embedded exemplars in the form of transcripts? Many of these decisions revert back to our central question of research design, but, as authors, we encourage you to consider how you can represent the information in more than a written narrative—where appropriate. As we are unable to give you specifics about what to write and how to write your qualitative results section, we instead offer this activity to scaffold your understandings of the demands of the writing task.

Activity 4.8 Explore the Genre Features and Characteristics of a Qualitative Results Section

For qualitative findings in particular, given the large disparity across the genres for the different methods, we recommend beginning by reviewing several (at least five) published studies which employ your specific research method and treat them as mentor texts that can guide and inform. As you read and review, note the genre features—specifically the elements included and the language characteristics. By noting and studying the specific elements, language characteristics, and graphical features commonly present in your selected genre, you are better able to apprentice yourself into the craft of writing an effective outline and corresponding full results section. We hope that the chart below may assist you in this task. We encourage you to chart your responses to the prompt, "Does your genre include?"

Genre Elements Present	Genre Language characteristics	Graphical Features
Narratives	Connotative language	Photographs/realistic illustrations
Vignettes	Denotative language	Researcher-generated Figures

Code/Theme counts	Specialized or technical vocabulary	Headings
Theme descriptions	Repetition	Flowcharts
Sequential/ Ordinal descriptions	Detailed descriptions	Timelines
	Temporal/causal transitions	Tables
	Type of clause and sentence structure	Labels/captions
	1st, 2nd, or 3rd person language	Lists Charts

Across the quantitative paradigm, there is less variation of the genre of writing for the results section. Quantitative studies may organize their results section by research question. Regardless of if the study utilizes descriptive or inferential analysis or both of them, the writer should present the corresponding results in tables, figures, and detailed written description. As scholars ourselves, we would recommend the construction of the requisite tables and figures first. Not only does the formatting of these result section components take time, but the tables and figures can also serve as a visual outline of your writing for this section. In the write up, be sure to include detailed descriptions, incorporating the numeric output, of the results of each statistical test and reference (in text) the relevant components of the corresponding tables. In your descriptions, remember to use the precise language and the technical vocabulary of quantitative design and corresponding analysis techniques.

New Considerations: Alternative Data Displays

Traditional data visualization, or representing information in the form of charts, graphs, tables, and maps, has been a part of the print-based publishing industry for years. Increasingly however, data visualization is taking on new forms as publication outlets are offering authors opportunities to display their findings/results as what many term **alternative data displays**. This is particularly the case for digital outlets with increased multimedia capability. Innovative publishers are encouraging the use of video, photography, an interactive dashboard or infographic, and even an entire digital media page among other strategies for representing the findings of a study. For example, Leah Katherine has utilized video-based alternative data displays to represent the findings in a published phenomenological study. As this is a developing area in the publishing community, we recommend that you further explore how and what kind of alternative data displays are burgeoning in your field and which publishers are making use of these devices.

Source: iStock

Discussion

There are two main components found in most discussion sections. Authors must (1) explain and situate their findings/results within previous research or theoretical literature, and also (2) provide details about any potential limitations to the study. While there is more consistency in the writing style of a discussion section across different study designs, as was discussed in the previous section, we always recommend reviewing a few discussion sections in related publications specific to your research method and design prior to moving forward.

Situating Findings/Results in Current Literature
••

Findings should always be compared to what was presented in the literature review section. Returning to the literature with findings and comparing the findings to literature strengthens an overall article or book chapter by situating it within the field. This type of comparison is expected within the discussion.

Discussion sections should be comprehensive and fully explore and situate all findings/results of your study.

Limitations and Delimitations

No academic manuscript is complete without a section on the limitations of your study. Limitations emanate from your research question and corresponding design and method decisions. Limitations are often beyond a researcher's control but directly impact the study. Again, we recommend reviewing a few articles you have cited and are familiar with to locate where the limitations section is placed. Frequently, this is a subsection of the discussion, which is why we included it here. However, the authors have also noted studies where the limitations were listed as part of the method section. In writing the limitations, the author should consider the weaknesses of the study that may have impacted the results or its usefulness/replicability. Limitations should note any challenges or problems with the research design, data collection, data analysis, and findings/results. They should also contextualize how these limitations impacted the study, its findings/results, or the implications for the research moving forward. Specifics on limitations to studies are again drawn from the choices of study design. For example, a small effect size is one type of limitation common to quantitative research studies which has specific implications. Another example may be an interrupted timeline for data collection in an ethnographic study due to a pandemic. As these two examples illustrate, in this section, it is important to contextualize limitations caused by problems within the study and problems bracketing the study.

The delimitations of a study are the elements and characteristics that come from limitations regarding the boundaries of a study and refer to the deliberate decisions made by a researcher to either include or exclude some element or elements. So, delimitations stem from the deliberate choices that researchers make. Examples include questions, choice of theoretical perspective(s), the design selected, and participants. Delimitations should be overtly discussed.

Implications

Implications propose how the findings/results of the study could be significant for research, policy, and practice. You could consider the implications of the conclusions that you have drawn from your findings/results and explanation of how they may be applied. A well-designed social science study is ripe for all three sets of implications, and we encourage you to spend some time in reflection considering each of the areas below prior to attempting to write them. Importantly, the implications sections should also substantiate and be reasonably based on the study design to avoid the overgeneralization of results/findings. For each of the following sections, authors typically compose one paragraph per implication/recommendation.

Research Implications/Recommendations

In this section, you are speaking to fellow and sister researchers, most of whom study your same topic and are in your field or a similarly related field. As you reflect on the questions that follow, we want you to consider how to "continue the conversation" about the practice of research and the specific findings of your study. Typically, in this section, you want to address considerations for how other researchers may do their job and recommendations for future research directions.

For example, when reflecting on your study, are there nuances of the research method itself that may be helpful to share to others who use it? Did you showcase new uses of the method that others may want to try with new populations or in new contexts? Did you create or employ a new method of study or analysis that hasn't been used before in your discipline or field but may have use with new populations or new contexts? What are the implications of these or any other innovations you made through your research? Did you address a gap in the literature? Based on your answers to the questions above and where your discussion section positions your current study in the larger academic conversation, you are also able to make concrete recommendations about where the research should go next.

Policy Implications/Recommendations

Implications and recommendations for policy involve discussing what your findings/results might mean in the context of the specific policies, guidelines, and regulations which guide or evaluate your field of study. To write this section, we ask you to consider and possibly enumerate the specific policies that your discipline uses to guide both research and practice. What might your findings/results signal for what is included in this policy, excluded? Are there any changes to the current policies, guidelines, and regulations you would recommend? You need to ground those recommendations in the results/findings of your study.

Practice Implications/Recommendations

Implications and recommendations for practice involve discussing what your findings/results might mean for individuals who work as practitioners or clinicians in your field of study. To write this section, we ask you to consider what people do and the types of careers/jobs in your field. What might your findings/results signal for their work? How could your findings/results impact or effect practice? You may also discuss here recommendations about method of sharing or disseminating your findings to practitioners. Your area of study and discipline will typically dictate how research is shared with practitioners. Typical recommendations for practice may include opportunities for one-time or ongoing professional learning, a specific change in a method of practice, or a change in how practices are regulated/evaluated in your area.

Works Cited—References: Correspondence Between In-Text Citations and Works Cited—Reference Section

Anything you cite, whether a direct quote or a summarization and paraphrasing of someone else's work, that appears in the body of your manuscript or in-text, also must be listed in the **works cited-reference** section. Conversely, if you list a reference, it must also occur in-text. While this is a very mechanical aspect of writing, it also conveys the level of detail you have applied to the manuscript and is important. It is also a very easy aspect to check for accuracy. A writer can begin with the references and search for each author in-text, or a scholar can print out the reference section, and read through the manuscript, checking each reference as s/he locates them in the manuscript. Once you read through the entire manuscript, you should have physically checked each citation listed in the reference list.

Appropriate and Adequate Citational Authority

Throughout your manuscript, appropriate citing is required. Simply put, if you are borrowing concepts, knowledge, information, or ideas from someone, cite them. If you are using their exact words, cite appropriately with included page numbers. With the advent of iThenticate© and other software that examines a piece and determines authenticity and indicates when frequently phrases are replicated, it is to every researchers' benefit to cite appropriately and ethically in first drafts to ensure accuracy.

Tables, Figures, and Appendices

There is no hard, fast rule as to where writers place tables and figures. Every citation style and publication venue has its own rules regarding how to include tables and figures. Some citation styles and publication venues require tables and figures to be included where they are discussed within a manuscript. Others want them at the end of a manuscript after a reference section. Still others ask that tables and figures be uploaded as separate documents from the manuscript itself. It is a scholar's job to seek out this information and place these sections appropriate to manuscript preparation guidelines. Appendices are always listed last, after a reference section.

Final Practice Opportunity

Putting all the sections of a manuscript together involves effort. We return to the idea of balancing a manuscript presented previously. Earlier in this chapter, we discussed this concept of balancing a manuscript into two major parts, the introduction and literature review as part one, and the method, results, discussion, and implications as the second part. This is an estimated concept, not an absolute or exact model. However, once the requisite parts are created, it is time for a scholarly writer to put all the sections together and address coherence. Finally, it is time to look at the technical aspects of a manuscript.

Exercise 4.9 Combining Sections of a Manuscript

In this final exercise of this lengthy chapter, your task is to reread and review every section generated as draft 2. This is a cohesion-flow kind of exercise, and this exercise is also a bit technical in nature. By now, readers will have grasped the concept that crafting a journal article, book chapter manuscript, a proposal, a final dissertation, or thesis is a blend of generating thoughts, applying knowledge, and composing written text and technical expertise. This exercise will take at least an hour, so budget this time, locate a suitable location, and open up draft 2 of your manuscript.

Begin by opening your saved draft 2. Read carefully but with a sense of detachment. We grow close to our writing. Often when reading a piece, some writers tend to anticipate a section, and in that anticipation, skip over parts of it. After all, we may reason that we wrote it, so we may assume we know what it states. Read the entire piece, word for word, sentence by sentence, and section by section. As you read and note any issue that needs addressing, either quickly make that correction or generate a comment that reminds you of what needs to be done. Continue working through the entire document until you reach the end. You have only budgeted an hour, so avoid the tendency to revise heavily. Don't stop to open a browser and look something up. Keep focused on reading for cohesion. When you do reach the end, **paginate** your manuscript. Format for margin specifications. Make sure your manuscript is double spaced. Take a deep breath, and save your manuscript as draft 3. If readers have followed the exercises in this chapter, they have a viable manuscript. No doubt, it will need revising, expansion, and checking.

Ending With the Beginning: Creating Titles and Writing Abstracts

Often scholars begin with a working title, and as the study progresses, they fine tune that title. As authors, we often think of titles the same way we do an individual's name. Titular meaning is important in that titles situate and identify a manuscript, and a title is used to locate scholarship. We suggest you begin with a working title, then let that marinate as you work through a study and an eventual write up. Consider sharing your title with a colleague for feedback.

Abstracts are often approached as the last piece we add to a manuscript. While institutions vary in terms of the total word count of a dissertation's abstract, and journals do the same, a good rule of thumb is to keep an abstract between 200 and 250 words. Waiting until you have completed a study and publication allows a scholar to think clearly about which elements of the current study should be included in the abstract. You want to include a brief statement about the topic (or research question) as well as why it is important. You want to include a statement about the design including the setting as well as subjects or participants, and you want to briefly describe data sources. Think of this information as the first half of the abstract that serves to introduce your study. The remaining half should present brief findings and implications, and circle back to the importance of the topic and study. Typically, this is the only area of the manuscript where citational authority is not expected.

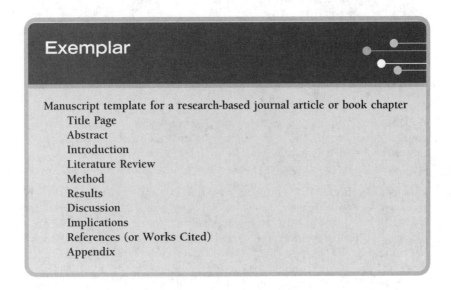

Exemplar

Manuscript template for a research-based journal article or book chapter
    Title Page
    Abstract
    Introduction
    Literature Review
    Method
    Results
    Discussion
    Implications
    References (or Works Cited)
    Appendix

SUMMARY

In this extensive chapter, a step-by-step process was provided for how to write a publishable manuscript. Each section of a manuscript was detailed in order to provide scholars with a blueprint of how a manuscript can be sequentially created. While publication venues have specific manuscript guidelines that typically focus on mechanical issues such as font size, six sections are recognized as be requisite: Introduction, Literature Review, Method, Results, Discussion, and Implications.

KEY TERMS

Abstract This section is an overview of the work, which provides a brief description of each section within the work, generally no more than 250 words. Should include up to four keywords that represent the work.

Alternative Data Displays Ways of displaying data can be accomplished traditionally, or as technology continues to evolve, in innovative ways. The issue of alternative data displays has been discussed since at least the late 1990s as differing ways to display data emerged.

Appendices These are materials referenced within the work that provide additional detail. These should be labeled using alphabet letters sequentially in the order that they appear in the manuscript.

Back Matter Typically, a term that is used in theses and dissertations, but also applies to manuscript, this term refers to all materials that are placed after a manuscript's text and usually consists of the references or works cited and appendices. In some journals and books, this also includes any tables and figures.

Citational Authority This term, borrowed from the practice of law, refers to the citation of authorities and is the law practice of citing case law when writing a law brief or legal response or legal opinion. In academic writing, citational authority is the source(s) that supports your discussion. Citational authority could refer to a key concept or practice, or it could refer to a method or a kind of analysis, or any concept, practice, or method that is not commonly understood. Providing appropriate citational authority adds depth and richness to academic writing and allows readers to investigate further; citational authority assists the reader in his/her own research.

Current Literature or References Manuscripts should reflect the most current thinking in a field; this term generally refers to scholarly references (peer-reviewed) published in the last five years, although this can vary by field.

Discussion This section of a manuscript is the interpretation of your results, situated in the current literature germane to your study.

Front Matter Typically, a term that is used in theses and dissertations, this consists of the title page, abstract, list of tables, list of figures, and table of contents. It may also include acknowledgments and dedications.

Implications Typically, a final section of a manuscript, these are recommendations for the field, based on the results of your current study.

Introduction An introduction states the purpose of a manuscript and provides an overview of the topic being addressed. An introduction may also briefly include the literature surrounding your topic of interest in a study and establishes the gap in the literature that your current study addresses.

IRB This acronym is derived from the Institutional Review Board. This board or committee oversees the protection of human subjects of research and reviews the method a researcher intends to safeguard, confirm, and certify that it is ethical. The use of the acronym has morphed into it being used as a noun.

Keywords These are words and phrases that are descriptors for your work and signify to your audience the scope of what your research accomplishes. Think of keywords as signposts that create the boundaries and limitations of your entire study.

Level One Heading Headings help to organize your writing, and they provide a hierarchical organization. Depending on the citation styles, APA, MLA, Chicago/Turabian style, or whatever a particular institution and/or journal and editor is requiring, headings serve the purpose to guide readers in a logical sequence. In this text, we are adhering to APA, thus a level one heading is a major section as indicated by its placement as centered on a page.

Literature Review A review of literature is a synthesis of scholarly sources in a topic area that provides current knowledge and helps to identify gaps in the topic area.

Method This section of a manuscript describes how the research was conducted to include the subjects, setting, research design, data collection, reliability, and data analysis. Research method varies depending on the type of research method.

Page Break This term refers to a function in a word processing program that creates an end to a page, ensuring that the next section appears on a separate page.

Paginate This term is simply dividing a document into separate pages.

Pseudonyms A common research and writing convention, these are the created or false names given to protect the identity of an individual, and institution or entity, or setting/location.

Reference Section (Also Called Works Cited) This is a comprehensive list of all sources cited within the manuscript; these are formatted according to a style manual specific to a field of study (e.g., APA, Harvard, MLA, Chicago).

Results The specific findings of a research study that are presented according to your research questions using analyses specific to your research question(s) are the results.

Seminal References Some important references are original scholarly works in a given topic area or field of study.

Title Page This is the cover page of a manuscript that includes the authors names and affiliations; format varies depending on the style manual used (e.g., APA, MLA, Chicago).

Works Cited (Also Called References) This is a list of all sources cited within the manuscript; these are formatted according to a style manual specific to a field of study (e.g., APA, Harvard, MLA, Chicago).

CRITICAL THINKING QUESTIONS

- As you prepared your manuscript for publication, what was the easiest section to compose, the most challenging? Why?

- As you prepared your manuscript for publication, what was the most challenging section to compose? Why?

- How is the process of writing a manuscript similar to your previous academic writing?

- How is the process of writing a manuscript different than your previous academic writing?

ADDITIONAL REFERENCES AND RESOURCES

Arbuthnot, K. (2009). The effects of stereotype threat on standardized mathematics test performance and cognitive processing. *Harvard Educational Review*, 79(3), 448–473.

Arbuthnot, K. (Ed.) (2017). *Global perspectives on educational testing: Examining fairness, high-stakes and policy reform*. Bingley: Emerald Group Publishing.

Cooper, R. (2009). Decoding coding via the coding manual for qualitative researchers by Johnny Saldaña. *The Qualitative Report*, 14(4), 245–248. Milles, M. B., Huberman, M. A., & Saldana, J. (1984). Qualitative data analysis.

Eisner, E. W. (1997). The promise and perils of alternative forms of data representation. *Educational Researcher*, 26(6), 4–10.

Kratochwill, T. R., Hitchcock, J., Horner, R. H., Levin, J. R., Odom, S. L., Rindskopf, D. M., & Shadish, W. R. (2010). Single-case designs technical documentation. Retrieved from What Works Clearinghouse website http://ies.ed.gov/ncee/wwc/pdf/wwc_scd.pdf. http://www.ithenticate.com/about

Lane, J. D., & Gast, D. L. (2013). Visual analysis in single case experimental design studies: Brief review and guidelines. *Neuropsychological Rehabilitation*, 3–4, 445–463.

Onwuegbuzie, A. J., Frels, R. K., & Hwang, E. (2016). Mapping Saldana's coding methods onto the literature review process. *Journal of Educational Issues*, 2(1), 130–150.

Paris, D., & Winn, M. T. (Eds.) (2014). *Humanizing research: Decolonizing qualitative inquiry with youth and communities*. Thousand Oaks, CA: SAGE.

Ridder, H. G. (2014). *Book review: Qualitative data analysis*. A Methods Sourcebook.

Ritchie, J., Lewis, J., Nicholls, C. M., & Ormston, R. (Eds.) (2013). *Qualitative research practice: A guide for social science students and researchers*. Thousand Oaks, CA: SAGE.

Saal, L. K., & Minson, C. W. (2017). Working to learn together: Engaged scholarship addressing long-term unemployment. *Adult Learning*, 28(4), 167–170.

Saldaña, J. (2008). Analyzing longitudinal qualitative observational data. In *Handbook of longitudinal research: Design, measurement, and analysis*, 297–311. Netherlands: Elsevier.

Saldaña, J. (2011). *Fundamentals of qualitative research*. Oxford, UK: Oxford University Press.

Saldaña, J. (2015). *The coding manual for qualitative researchers*. Thousand Oaks, CA; SAGE.

Skolasky, R. L. (2016). Considerations in writing about single-case experimental design studies. *Cognitive and Behavioral Neurology*, 29(4), 169–173. Retrieved from http://www.dissertationrecipes.com/

Stoecker, R. (2013). *Research methods for community change: A project-based approach*. Thousand Oaks, CA: SAGE.

Viera, A. J., & Garrett, J. M. (2005). Understanding interobserver agreement: The Kappa statistic. *Family Medicine*, 37(5), 360–363.

WORKS CITED

Belcher, W. L. (2019). *Writing your journal article in twelve weeks: A guide to academic publishing success*. Chicago, IL: University of Chicago Press.

Boyer, E. (1996). The scholarship of engagement. *Journal of Public Outreach*, 1(1), 11–21.

Casanave, C. P., & Li, Y. (2015). Novices' struggles with conceptual and theoretical framing in writing dissertations and papers for publication. *Publications*, 3(2), 104–119.

Denzin, N. K., & Lincoln, Y. S. (2008). *Collecting and interpreting qualitative materials* (Vol. 3). Thousand Oaks, CA: SAGE.

Feak, C. B., Swales, J. M., Irwin, V. V., & Swales, J. M. (2011). *Creating contexts: Writing introductions across genres*. Ann Arbor, MI: University of Michigan Press.

Frels, R., Onwuegbuzie, A., & Slate, J. R. (2010). Editorial: A typology of verbs for scholarly writing. *Research in the Schools*, 17(1), xx–xxxi.

Glaser, B. G. (1965). The constant comparative method of qualitative analysis. *Social Problems*, 12(4), 436–445.

Graves, D., & Hansen, J. (1983). The author's chair. *Language Arts*, 60(2), 176–183.

Howard, J. (2007). Is it engaged scholarship? Retrieved from http://kdp0l43vw6z2dlw 631ififc5.wpengine.netdna-cdn.com/wp-content/uploads/2009/04/is-it-engaged-schol-arship-3-ps-assessment1.pdf

Koro-Ljungberg, M., Yendol-Hoppey, D., Jude Smith, J., & Hayes, S. (2009). (E)pis-temological awareness, instantiation of methods, and uninformed methodological ambiguity in qualitative research projects. *Educational Researcher*, 38(9), 687–699.

Lincoln, Y. S., Lynham, S. A., & Guba, E. G. (2011). Paradigmatic controversies, con-tradictions, and emerging confluences, revisited. *The Sage Handbook of Qualitative Research*, 4, 97–128.

Palinkas, L. A., Horwitz, S. M., Green, C. A., Wisdom, J. P., Duan, N., & Hoagwood, K. (2015). Purposeful sampling for qualitative data collection and analysis in mixed method implementation research. *Administration and Policy in Mental Health and Mental Health Services Research*, 42(5), 533–544.

Spradley, J. P. (2016). *Participant observation*. Long Grove, IL: Waveland Press.

Stake, R. E. (2013). *Multiple case study analysis*. Guilford Press.

Swales, J. (1990). Create a research space. CARS) model of research introductions. In Wardle, E., & Downs, D. (Eds.), *Writing about writing: A college reader*. Boston, MA: Bedford/St. Martin's.

Tashakkori, A., & Tedlie, C. (Eds.) (2003). *Handbook of mixed methods in social and behaviors research*. Thousand Oaks, CA: SAGE.

Towne, L., & Shavelson, R. J. (2002). *Scientific research in education*. Atlanta, GA: National Academy Press Publications Sales Office.

Yasin, B., & Qamariah, H. (2014). The application of Swales' model in writing a research article introduction. *Studies in English Language and Education*, 1(1), 29–41.

Yin, R. K. (2018). *Case study research and applications*. Thousand Oaks, CA: SAGE.

Selecting an Appropriate Publishing Outlet

Publishing is time-consuming and involves considerable effort. If this is beginning to sound redundant, it is simply because we want and need to emphasize this point. You can maximize your time and effort, and be efficient and more productive, if you acquire solid skills and solid time management. This chapter provides options for determining "fit" and for minimizing outright rejection from editorial teams.

Learning Objectives

There are three learning objectives for this chapter. They are listed below. Graduate students, novice researchers, and new scholars will learn to:

1. Create a list of potential publication outlets/journals for a manuscript

2. Curate the potential publications list to maximize fit

3. Cultivate relationships with editors and other publication professionals

The intent of this chapter is to offer strategic considerations and thoughtful approaches for optimal publishing opportunity. In this chapter, a quick write activity is provided to help you to begin to create a list of journals to investigate. Next, an explanation regarding how to critically analyze each journal (or specific manuscript call) to better curate your list and better determine fit for your manuscript is offered. Finally, recommendations and reflections from our perspectives as editors for several publications is afforded. We hope our insider knowledge furthers and supports your publishing and productivity goals.

Many PhD students, novice researchers, and new scholars feel daunted by the possibility of finding a home for their beautifully-crafted and personally-significant manuscript. Additionally, releasing your manuscript (and ideas) into the public space can be both anxiety inducing and just plain scary. As authors of this text, we want to acknowledge that many scholars have very real feelings of trepidation around rejection—which can be paralyzing. More widely-accepted journals in most fields have acceptance rates that are typically less than 25%, which means that 75% or more of the submissions they receive are not ultimately published. So, yes, rejection is statistically very likely to happen to you at some point in the publication process. It has, of course, happened to each of us, as individual authors and as members of writing teams.

However, the submission and review process is an excellent opportunity to receive meaningful feedback on your ideas and refine your thinking and writing. Getting your manuscript through to the peer review process is an accomplishment in itself. When any manuscript is submitted to a publication outlet, typically, the editors of journals, or their highly trained assistants, conduct an initial "desk review." In this first round of review, the editor(s) decides whether each individual submission "fits" within the parameters they have set for the journal. "Fit" can be a nebulous and highly subjective term. Ultimately, our goal in this chapter is to teach you how to analyze your manuscript in the same way these editors will. In this way, you can not only better prepare your manuscript for review but also better determine which journals or publication outlets are a better "fit" for the focus of your scholarship. Remember, your goal in this initial submission step is to get the editor(s) to send your manuscript "off their desk" or "out of their inbox" and out to your peers for review.

Creating an Initial List of Journals to Investigate

Spending time to create an initial (or master) list of journals to investigate is not only worth your time prior to submitting your first manuscript, it is also a timesaving strategy long term. Once you spend some time compiling an initial list of potential outlets, you will be able to continue to expand and amend this list and draw from it as a valuable resource as your career progresses and evolves.

Each of the authors of this text has one or more versions of the list we are recommending you write. Typically, we have one for each strand (or topic area) of our research. For example, Leah Katherine, one of the authors, systematically publishes across multiple (although related) fields. Therefore, she has three lists of journals (along with key details) for the areas of her research—literacy, adult education, and engaged scholarship. Each list contains key details which she keeps updated. Therefore, when she starts to think about where a particular piece of writing should be submitted, she is able to take out these lists to begin the thinking around the notion of "fit."

When drafting your list of journals, consideration should also be given to audience—is your topic best suited for a **generalist journal** (Early Childhood Education) which may be more competitive, but yield a higher impact factor, or **specialty journal** (Technology) which may be more targeted in order to reach your intended audience and help shape the future in a particular field? To illustrate, an article on the use of technology with young children may be a novel application of technology with this population, but not necessarily a novel technology for researchers who focus on technology use in general. Finally, some journals are explicitly **interdisciplinary journals** which strive to publish articles from across multiple disciplines and cater to a wider variety of fields. Often, these journals focus on a specialized area of scholarship, like the *International Journal of Research on Service-Learning and Community Engagement,* or a specific kind of research, like *International Journal of Qualitative Methods.* The goal of these journals is to bring together scholars from a wide array of fields who study one area or approach studies using the same tools and publish this research.

Quick Write # 4

In order to jumpstart this process, we offer you a simple quick write activity as both a motivator and as a place to begin your search for publication outlets. Set a timer for five minutes and take out your preferred writing tools. For the next five minutes, we want you to complete a strategy known as list, group, label (Taba, 1967). To begin, brainstorm a list of every academic journal/periodical name you can remember reading as part of your research training. List everything you can remember, even pieces of titles or other identifying information you can recall. They don't need to be exclusively in your topic area (include both generalists and specialty journals), they just need to be names of outlets with which you have some familiarity. At the end of your five-minute quick write, spend the next several minutes grouping these titles into categories by topic, methodology, or audience, and give each category a name or label. Once you have some initial categories identified, use a search engine to confirm your list of titles. Spend some time searching for those titles you could not quite identify by official name or recall completely during your quick write. Make sure to capture the full and accurate name of the periodicals/journals you have identified.

Using Reference Lists and Keywords

While the Quick Write activity above is one way to start a list of potentially appropriate journal articles, you can also begin this process by using what you have—a partially completed manuscript which you have created by working through activities presented in the preceding three chapters. If you already have a partially completed manuscript, we would encourage you to use your reference list from that draft to identify journals and other publication outlets you cited in the paper. Particularly note any publications that have been cited more than once. Typically, journals and other publications have a specific focus and scope, and, by using the list you have, you can identify outlets which already publish work directly related to your scholarship.

Similarly, you can also use the keywords you created for your manuscript as an avenue to identify more possible places for you to submit your work. Use your keywords to perform a series of "keyword/subject search" academic searches in your research/scholarly databases. Again, this process assists you in making note of the journals and publication outlets that publish work directly related to your own. As you complete your keyword searching, pay close attention to journals that are repeated for particular keywords, and, especially, journals which are listed across keywords. Journals that appear across multiple keyword searches are more likely to have a stronger or tighter fit to your particular manuscript.

Using Your Institutionally-Assigned Reference Librarian

Source: iStock

Another resource you can use to create (or find) a list of journals which may be interested in your manuscript is to seek assistance from your institutionally-assigned reference librarian. For most higher education institutions, academic disciplines are divided up across the staff of reference librarians. In this way, each discipline has a point of contact who has specialized knowledge and skills in searching for domain/genre specific knowledge sources and repositories. All of the authors of this text have wonderful relationships with our assigned reference librarian and value and solicit their expertise often—for teaching and research; they are frequent guest scholars in our courses. In fact, we invited two of them to write a chapter for this textbook (see Chapter 8) because of their expertise with metrics. Your institutionally-assigned reference librarian is a valued writing resource. Seek them out and establish a solid working relationship early in your career at your institution (or upon reading this chapter).

Typically, your assigned reference librarian is able to help you identify a list of journals which publish in your discipline, area, or scope. In fact, some of this work may have also already been done. Many institutional reference librarians have curated a set of digital research references and links organized by discipline on the library's website. These amazing professionals can also help you to set up alerts and notifications for new research published in your area or specific field of study. This is another time-saving tip to keep your manuscript updated with the current research conversation that surrounds your topic as you work through the publication process as well as work on new pieces.

As a matter of course, if you have not yet done so, we recommend that all PhD students, novice researchers, or new scholars make an appointment to introduce yourself and your academic pursuits to your designated librarian. If you don't know or can't find who this person is, contact your institutional library and ask to speak to any reference librarian. They will generally be very happy you called and will be able to assist you or point you to the correct person.

In tandem with accessing your institutionally-assigned reference librarian, major publishing houses, such as SAGE, also maintain lists of journals. These lists can typically be accessed through the publishing house's website under the "journals" tab. On the SAGE webpage, there is a tab for journals where premier journals are listed by year as well. You can browse journals by disciplines and like most publishing houses; SAGE maintains an alphabetized list of journals. Finally, SAGE, Taylor and Francis, and Wiley, along with many other major publishing houses, provide places on their websites which will provide manuscript submission information (like SAGE Path) "suggest a journal" or related publishing outlet based on titles, abstracts, or keywords/descriptors you provide. Some of these services have more advanced features which you must pay for. However, the majority have a simple "journal recommendation" service which is free of charge.

Activity 5.1

For this brief activity, log onto your device and go to: https://us.sagepub.com/en-us/nam/journals. On the SAGE journal tab, there is a section that offers the following services: A My SAGE journals tab where scholars can register for personalized services such as email alerts, managing search alerts, managing account preferences, and creating favorite journal lists. You can peruse this webpage and perhaps, add to the list you generated for your quick write for this chapter.

Using Your Professional and Social Connections

Another way the authors of this text solicit or create lists of journals or other publication outlets pertaining to a topic is to use professional and social network connections. To begin, we often ask our colleagues and cohort members for assistance. You should also ask your academic mentors, colleagues, and/or fellow graduate students (across disciplines) about publication outlets. Many will have suggestions or at least additional considerations for you. Also, many professional organizations have message boards/blogs or list-serves. Typically, if you are member, you can post a question directly to your colleagues about what publication outlets they may recommend or have published with before. They may reply with a single source or may have a curated list to pass along. Please note, if the conversation continues with specific colleagues, pull the dialog off of the list-serve and into a private conversation channel. Your colleagues do not want to be included in a mailbox clogging series of emails which are not targeted to the whole group.

We recommend that scholars (new and seasoned) and graduate students join these list-serves and message boards/blogs as they are also great sources for burgeoning research in the field, avenues for learning more about ongoing scholarly conversations, and, finally, places where new/specialized calls for manuscripts relevant to your field/discipline are frequently posted. Scholars can also join **special interest groups** that exist within professional organizations' umbrellas. As an example, the American Educational Research Association (AERA) has a host of special interest groups (SIGs). Many SIGs sponsor a journal as well as generate calls for special issues of a journal when members of the SIG are named as editors for special issues. A quick perusal of the AERA website during the time of this chapter writing revealed 185 SIGs in AERA alone. The listing is diverse. For example, the Educational Statisticians (SIG #137) lists the following as its purpose, "To increase interaction among educational researchers interested in the theory, applications, and teaching of statistics in social science." They host their own website. Illustrating the depth and breadth of the AERA SIGs, the umbrella organization also hosts SIGs such as Environmental Education (SIG #33) whose purpose is to "advance and critique environmental education research." The SIG lists both a website as well as a Facebook page for its group members.

In some graduate-level and doctoral writing seminars, a course activity may be for class members to each self-select a journal of choice to investigate. Then resources are grouped and labeled in the same fashion as described in this chapter's quick write activity. Writing groups can emulate this process and generate appropriate lists of potential outlets. This kind of activity is still writing activity, it just deviates from composing, revising, and editing.

A final method for generating a list of potential publication outlets involves creative use of social media. Several of the authors of this text also use some of our social media accounts as online professional learning communities. For example, one author uses her Twitter account to academically engage with colleagues around resources, current research, and applications of practice. She follows relevant hashtag conversations and academic voices and invites others to do the same. Another author uses Pinterest and Facebook for the same purposes. These types of online learning communities can also be ripe avenues for exploring or soliciting additional publication outlets.

Curating Your List to Determine Fit

Now that you have your list of potential journals, we want to help you think through a series of specifications you should consider when curating your list to identify the closest fit(s). There are two types of specifications to consider and we will review both below—editor/publisher provided specifications and specifications you may have to investigate and collect as an author. In the graphic organizer which follows, we provide a matrix of specifications you can use to collect information about specific journals and determine your manuscript's fit with the specific journal (Table 5.1).

Provided Specifications

Most reputable publishers provide specifications about the periodical in the "about the journal" sections of the outlet's webpage. You will want to make note of the details of each component that the editors have meticulously included in this series of write ups. For example, in a journal edited by three of this book's authors, the "about this journal" reads as follows:

About Literacy & Social Responsibility eJournal

As we move as an organization to focus on transforming lives through literacy, this peer-reviewed eJournal of the International Literacy Association (ILA) provides an international forum for educators, authors, and researchers from all levels to promote the intersection of literacy and social responsibility for learners of all ages. Some areas of interest include: community engagement, service-learning, informed and

Table 5.1 Matrix of Journal Specifications to Determine Fit Graphic Organizer

Journal Name:

Editor(s) Name(s)

Provided Specifications	Notes from Journal	Fit? (Y/N)
About the Journal		
Access (Paid or Open)		
Frequency of Publication/Deadlines		
Aims/Scope		
Readership		
Types of Manuscripts Considered		
Audience/Reach		
Peer Review Type/Time in Review		
Acceptance Rate		
Submission Guidelines *Make a note of each component below.*		
Collected specifications	**Notes from journal**	**Fit? (Y/N)**
Theoretical Perspectives		
Methodological Perspectives		
Length of Time Since Last Related Topic Published		
Editor and Editorial Review Board Positionality		

participatory citizenship, social justice, activism, the transformative power of literacy, and/or stewardship - among others. Manuscripts highlighting an appreciation for sociocultural and/or linguistic diversity of participants and researchers are encouraged. Manuscripts containing hyperlinked digital supplements/data displays are particularly welcome.

Let's take a minute to break down and unpack all of the information that is provided here. There are several things to note in this "about the journal" write up. The editors first provide information about the ejournal's connection to a larger organization. This should tell the reader that this journal has the capacity to expand readership to a larger body. The reader could, for example, take this information and research the number of members in ILA and their locations to get a better understanding of their global reach. The next line identifies the editors' positionality as leaders of a journal with goals of inclusivity across disciplines or interdisciplinarity—i.e., they expressly invite scholars in the discipline of literacy and those in other areas of education or related fields to submit manuscripts whose work may be aligned to the areas of scholarship they list. Finally, the editors also establish their eagerness to use the affordances of the digital format to foster boundary breaking of traditional, print-based only, scholarly output.

Another area commonly included in the opening "about the journal" section is frequency of publication. This is often articulated by stating the number of times per year a journal is published. Along with frequency information, there is typically an indication of timelines for submission. For example, if a journal is published quarterly, there is often a deadline for submission for consideration for each issue. However, some journals which publish multiple times per year also have **rolling submissions**—meaning they do not stop or start accepting submissions by a certain deadline.

Typically, the next thing to note is the journal's aim or scope. These terms are used somewhat interchangeably to refer to the topic or topics the journal hopes to include. Usually this section is used to frame what is "inclusive" or "exclusive" of the range of topics the editors consider for inclusion. In this section, if not included in the "about the journal section," there can also be information about the specific disciplinary areas that journal considers for inclusion. Again, by way of exemplar, we include the "Aims & Scope" of the journal the authors of this text have edited.

Aims & Scope

Literacy & Social Responsibility eJournal is an international peer-reviewed forum published by the Literacy and Social Responsibility Special Interest Group of the International Literacy Association. This journal provides a venue for educators to promote the intersection of literacy and social responsibility for lifelong learners through policy, research, and/or practice.

In this section, readers should note that the journal editors identify that the manuscripts can be about policy, research, and/or practice. Many journals will identify if they seek one or more of these types of articles. If they do not, this is information you should note when you collect more specifications (as we will outline below).

On the subject of types of articles, typically information about the types of manuscripts considered is also presented. Common formats include full length manuscripts of research, policy or practice, theoretical pieces, responses to published research, and book reviews. Many times, especially in large journals, there may also be particular columns (types of articles) which have their own editor and specifications. For each type of article, the editors/publisher should indicate the word length and other specifications (including rolling deadlines).

The journal publishers or editors should provide information about the journal's target audience. Are they publishing for other professionals/practitioners in the field? Researchers? Policy makers? Is the outlet connected to a professional organization (as in the example above)? Along with the audience, there is typically some indication of the journal's reach. This could be identified by listing how people access the journal's content. Is the journal **open access** and published online? This means that the content can be accessed by anyone around the world for free. Or, is it indexed and/or part of paid subscription services? Audience and reach are important as they can heavily impact how much exposure/circulation an article has in different academic communities and how people are engaging with the content. This exposure and engagement control the associated journal, article, and author metrics, which are discussed in detail in Chapter 8.

Typically, an open access (OA) journal requires peer review and once a manuscript has been accepted, publications are immediately available electronically and are permanently free for anyone to access. Open access publishing typically means the author pays an article processing charge (APC) fee for this open access. These kinds of open access publications are labeled as gold open access journals. Often, institutions have agreements that reduce the fee amount for open access publishing. However, there are other categories associated with open access publishing. The term platinum or diamond open access publishing refers to open access journals that do not charge any APCs. Platinum open access journals are usually underwritten by a university or research entity. Green open access is a term that refers to when an author publishes an article in any category of journal and then self-archives a copy in a freely accessible institutional or online archive, often referred to as a repository which operates as a professional network. An example of such a repository is the archive Research Gate. Yet another open accessing term, bronze open access refers to articles that are free to read, but only on a publisher page. Bronze open access articles are not be available to scholars for later reuse or downloading. Finally, predatory open access journals are of questionable quality and merit. The Directory of Open Access Journal (DOAJ) is a database for open access publishing. According to this directory, the journals listed in DOAJ database have gone through a vetting process specific to the journals' peer review process and the specifications of the journals' editorial board.

You likewise should take note of how the journal editor/publisher discusses the peer review process. **Peer review** is "a process where academicians (or your peers) evaluate the quality of other researchers'/authors' work. The goal of peer review is to ensure published work is "rigorous, coherent, uses past research and adds to what we already know" (Sage, 2020, p. 1). The peer review process provides three things: (1) evaluation, in that only the best pieces are selected for publication; (2) integrity, in that reviewers are ethically removed from the research conducted; and (3) quality, in that the selection and review/revision process improves the overall quality of the published article by providing authors the insight and opinions of experts in their field (Sage, 2020). For these reasons, in higher education, publishing peer-reviewed articles is always preferable to publishing **invited** or **non-peer-reviewed** articles for most employers for these reasons.

As an example, in annual evaluations for most higher education institutions or policy/research groups, you will typically have to provide information about the peer review process along with any article you publish. However, non-peer-reviewed publications also have merit. For example, many non-profits, community organizations, and state entities frequently publish newsletters that reach a rather significant audience in terms of numbers. Occasionally, a scholar may want to contribute to such a publication as a means of informing a wider audience of the general public about issues. Other scholars contribute a letter to the editor or seek to publish opinion pieces in newspapers. It is also common for PhD students to review new texts as a means of generating an initial publication or contributing to guest columns that may be part of a journal's format. We want to stress that typically these kinds of non-peer-reviewed publications are important, but not the kinds of publishing activity or productivity that is generally recognized in the tenure and promotion process for scholars, although some institutions have an "other" category of publication. Generally speaking, doctoral students, newly-minted PhDs, and novice researchers should strive seek out and publish in peer-reviewed journals.

There are six types of peer review and these are described in Table 5.2 below.

Table 5.2 Types of Peer Review

Type	Description
Peer review (Not blinded)	In this case, the editor, author, and the reviewer's identities are all known to each other.
Single blind peer review	In this case, the reviewer's identity is hidden from the author.
Double blind peer review	In this case, the author and reviewer's identities are hidden from one another.
Triple blind peer review	In this case, the editors, author, and reviewer's identities are hidden from one another.
Open peer review	While this is a new type of peer review, an open peer review typically involves publishing an article's review (and reviewer's names) alongside the article.
Post publication peer review	In this uncommon type of peer review, articles are viewed and published following the publications of the article.

In addition to noting the type of peer review process, prospective authors should note the posted "time in review." **Time in review** is how long an article typically moves from the original submission through peer review to a published piece. Understanding the length of time an outlet takes to complete this process is key to aligning your goals of publishing and productivity to a potential selection for "fit." A fuller discussion of the peer review and editor relationship and process is provided in Chapter 6.

The final two areas which should be investigated as part of the classically provided specifications of a journal are the acceptance rate and the manuscript guidelines. We have discussed acceptance rates at the beginning of this chapter, but, as a reminder, acceptance rate is the percentage of manuscripts submitted for publication which were ultimately published. The lower the acceptance rate, generally, the higher the perceived prestige of publishing a journal. However, this number should not be used as an indication of journal or article quality. This concept is discussed in more detail in Chapter 8.

The next sentence we intentionally bolded and capitalized for emphasis. **The manuscript guidelines provided to potential authors by editors and publishers should be the MOST CAREFULLY READ component of the provided specifications.** These specifications offer information about many components of a manuscript including page formatting, citation style, blinding or pseudonym requirements, required permissions/releases for publication of identifiable information or Institutional Review Board (IRB) documentation, allowed/preferred digital inclusions in text and/or supplemental file types, and much, much more. We recommend making note of each guideline separately on the graphic organizer (Table 5.1) provided. Authors who fail to follow and adhere to the manuscript guidelines provided by editors and publishers will frequently achieve an outright rejection by the editors upon submission.

Collected Specifications

In addition to the specifications provided by the publisher and editors, when determining fit of a manuscript for potential publication, there are also specifications that an author will have to find or "collect" on their own. To begin, any of the typically provided specifications outlined above which were not provided by the editor/publishers should be solicited by querying an editor (see the exemplar at the end of chapter for an example). We will describe the process of curating a relationship with an editor in more detail later in this chapter and in Chapter 6. However, there are several specifications which are not directly stated by the editors/publishers but are important components to know and understand as you are identifying whether your manuscript will be a good fit for this publication.

For this set of specifications, we recommend that you begin your inquiry by downloading several issues across several volumes of the journal which have been edited by the current editorial staff. As you review these issues, we want you to note several things about the content. What kinds of theoretical perspectives are represented in the articles within? What kinds of methodologies are represented? Do these perspectives align with your areas of study and the manuscript for which you are trying to find a home? Do the topics of these articles align with the scope, aim, topics, and descriptions of submissions the editors/publishers provided? While overlap across the answers to these questions and your manuscript is optimum, it is not required. However, it does allow you to understand more about how the editorial team and reviewers privilege certain ways of knowing—whether intentionally or unintentionally through the peer review process.

Another consideration in the inquiry of collected specifications is to identify how long it has been since the journal has published topics related to your manuscript. For example, if a very similar piece was published as part of the current volume or a recent volume, this information is something that the author may want to consider. Recent publication of similar topics could mean there is a want/need for more information for their audience or it could mean that a similar article would be less likely to be published at this time. Determining the difference may warrant a query to the editor.

Finally, we encourage you to also review articles written by the editor and members of the listed editorial review board. An editor is chosen for a journal based on their ability and capacity to push the scholarly conversation in a discipline forward. Understanding the perspectives and positionality of the editor and editorial review board will also give you a better understanding of how your manuscript fits with their conceptualizations of the field.

Determining If Your Manuscript Fits a Specific Call for Papers

Specific calls or special issues typically involve a tightly-focused emphasis. Often, special calls are solicited years in advance as a rotating feature of particular journals. In this case, journals invite editor(s) to propose a topic. Other times, specific calls or special issues are proposed by editors or an editorial team in response to a significant event with major impact. As this book is being written and prepared for publication, the COVID-19 pandemic is continuing to explode in waves across the globe. In response, several journals have issued calls for COVID-related topics in terms of educator's, administrator's and researcher's reaction to COVID-related conditions.

The editors will provide information about the specific call's scope, target audience, and possibly, several statements that reflect the range of the special issue. Many specific, special calls will ask for a **precis** or abstract first. This synopsis of what a scholar intends to submit will provide the editor(s) with information on how the special issue may take shape and allow him or her to decide on an array of articles that explore the complexities of the special issue. Take great care to be explicit and meet word counts when such a requirement is established for a specific call. This is also an opportunity for an editor to determine whom to invite to submit (not promise to publish) and to begin to consider the depth and breadth of the responses to their call. It is appropriate to **query an editor** in such instances to determine if what you are envisioning "fits" with his or her vision of the special call. A complete discussion of this practice follows in

Chapter 6. Again, we point readers to the exemplar at the end of this chapter with accompanying sample abstracts.

Preparing a Full Abstract to Send With Inquiry

As with many of the sections in this chapter, it behooves scholars to pay close attention to details provided in a specific call or special issue. When an abstract is requested, word counts matter. Therefore, carefully decide what you will write in response. As discussed and presented in Chapter 4, an abstract outlines the work and research question or purpose, provides a brief description of aspects of the work, generally focusing on the issue, its importance, methods, brief findings, and implications. And, as stated previously, examining the body of research of an editor may provide insight into whether your piece fits with a special issue. Thus far, we have discussed subscription-based journal and book chapter publishing wherein a fee is assessed for members or their institutions, granting access. This is an historical financing model for publications. However, since 2010, **open access** journals have become prevalent.

Considering Initial Practitioner-Oriented or Policy-Oriented Pieces That Align With Research Interests

When publishing, scholars and academics have several goals. Of course, we are all interested in amassing a record of scholarship that will ultimately lead to positive evaluations, promotion, and/or tenure and impact our respective field of study. While we all want to see our research published in top tier research journals in our field, we also should consider how our work will impact day-to-day practice and policy in our field. This requires us to translate our work to be accessible to practitioners and policy makers. We view these as companion pieces to our primary research publications.

Communicating with a practitioner or policy making audience can easily flow from your research, if you are strategic. In most discussion sections, you are asked to write what the implications are of your research—what should be done or done differently, in light of your research findings. This is a good place to start in considering how to frame a practitioner or policy publication. If you conducted an intervention study, detailed information on how to implement your intervention would also be of interest to practitioners, as would the empirical support for your intervention from your literature review. Or, conversely, consider detailed information on how your research impact policy, regulation, or statute making, implementation, and evaluation around your area of study.

Using the same process as described above, complete a separate Table 5.1 to identify practitioner or policy journals or columns that may be viable outlets for your work. Reviewing journals aim and scope, author guidelines and previous issues, as described above (see *Provided Specifications*) will also provide guidance for practitioner or policy submissions. Social networks are also a good avenue to explore for these types of publication outlets. You may get suggestions about editors that are particularly skilled and helpful in providing support for writing for a practitioner or policy making audience. We all want the results of our research efforts to make a difference in our respective field. Having a companion practitioner or policy publication to translate our research into action both informs the field while also serving to build your scholarly productivity.

Activity 5.2 Final Practice Opportunity

Review your list of possible publications one more time. For this last practice opportunity in this chapter, the purpose of this final exercise is to prioritize your list. Have you used the **graphic organizer** presented as a means of determining fit, as well as your own publication needs? For example, if you are on a promotion or **tenure clock**, what journals do you want to publish in but do not have a quick turn-around for review and/or are published annually? Reprioritize your list based on your answers to these and related questions.

Critical Thinking Questions

- As you prepared your list of potential, appropriate journals, is there a hierarchy?
- Who is your research librarian? Have you reached out to meet?
- Have you identified outlets that will yield calls for themed issues or special issues?
- Who in your social network can you ask about research journals and/or other related practitioner or policy focused venues for publication?
- What recommendations presented here were the most useful? Why?

Sample Correspondence With Editor for Specific Call— Special Issue

Dear Dr. XXXX,

We hope this missive finds you well.

Please accept this email as our intent to submit an original manuscript tentatively titled, "Re-Thinking leadership as the emergence of crisis mentoring in pandemic environments: Case study of three school leaders' concerns and use of time", to the *International Journal of Mentoring and Coaching in Education*, for the Mentoring and Coaching in Times of Crises, Pandemics, and Social Distancing Special Issue. We are aware of the November 16 deadline for submission through the *IJMCE* portal.

Attached is our working abstract. We look forward to submitting to the special issue.

Thank you in advance for your consideration.

Sample Abstract #1

Re-Thinking Leadership as the Emergence of Crisis Mentoring: Case Study of Three School Leaders' Concerns and Use of Time in Pandemic Environments

Education in the United States is at a pivotal moment as the COVID-19 global pandemic, coupled with resultant exposure of systemic societal inequities, have converged. While past disasters (2005 Hurricane Katrina; 2016 Baton Rouge floods) have influenced instructional mentorship among South Louisiana principals and assistant principals, those who work with at-risk, vulnerable populations of children from poverty have been especially impacted by the recent pandemic. South Louisiana educational leaders realized the extent of lack of access to connectivity for students from poor, urban communities of Color and recognized limited teacher preparation to teach remotely. Concurrently, teachers were experiencing emotional distress from increased professional and personal pressures. Principals and assistant principals grappled with how to both advance leadership while continuing to provide instructional mentoring in pandemic times. This embedded case study within a multiple case study investigated concerns and use of time of three school leaders for a 25-week period, from March through August 2020, revealing what issues monopolized educational leaders' thoughts and actions regarding instructional mentoring amid continued uncertainty of schools reopening and potentially closing early. Three data sources—reflections, interviews, and documents/artifacts produced by the host districts in response to COVID-19 shuttering of schools—were examined regarding how three school leaders functioned as instructional mentors regarding online teaching and online learning for PK-6 students. Ongoing analysis revealed four important themes: operating in unpredictability and uncertainty, fluidity in responding to shifting directives, addressing teachers' emotional demands, and problematic supervision of instruction. Implications include emerging leadership practice characterized as crisis mentoring.

NAME, PhD-corresponding author
unit—Institution

NAME, PhD (author 2)
unit—Institution

NAME, PhD (author 3)
unit—Institution

NAME, PhD (author 4)
unit—Institution

Sample Abstract #2

A critical focus of elementary teacher education programming is assisting pre-service teachers to use literature and provide access to books as a cornerstone of reading development. Post-Katrina, New Orleans faced alarming yet riveting challenges as it recovered, rebuilt, and underwent a renewal of education. Nowhere is rebirth more apparent than within the public schools. Reports have counted the dead and number of displaced persons, estimated property loss, even tallied months of missed school. One key component missing in post-disaster discussions was lack of access to books. In August 2007, Abramson Science and Technology Charter School opened in New Orleans-East, serving one of the areas most impacted by Hurricane Katrina. Housed in temporary buildings and run on generators until late fall 2007, the school had no library. Due to flooding and wide-spread devastation, the East was devoid of even a neighborhood public library, thus elementary-aged children lacked access literature. While current, national estimates suggest and average of approximately 22 books to one child, in the fall of 2007, in a place called New Orleans East, the number was zero books per child. *Academic-service learning is pedagogy of action.* Thus, this manuscript highlights service, teaching, and research efforts to establish classroom libraries at Abramson in a reciprocal and mutually beneficial service-learning project. The goal was two-fold: establish adequate, culturally sensitive classroom libraries, while involving education majors' opportunities to apply knowledge of quality literature in collecting and selecting books best suited for individual classrooms. Due to wide-spread support and generosity, **8,665** books were delivered to Abramson.

Sample Abstract #3

Chapter Proposal

Numerous studies reveal impediments to arts integration implementation in K-12 settings, however, existing literature fails to organize, analyze, and report studies by the very impediment themes that appear in the literature. This proposed 20–25 page chapter, "Arts Integration Impediments: A Themed Compilation of Current Literature," aims to identify and categorize frequently cited barrier and obstacle themes from the field of arts integration. Themes include: minimal administrative support for arts integration, priority given to testing mandates and pre-scripted curriculum, sparse resources and materials, time constraints, and general education teachers' lack of confidence/self-efficacy with varied art forms. This proposed chapter is an original work which has not been published elsewhere.

The authors' expertise is wide ranging: administration, teacher education, arts integration consulting, K-12 teaching, and working as a practicing theatre artist are several of the perspectives the authors bring to this work. Budget constraints and a decline in arts education classes in schools have positioned general education classroom teachers on the front lines of arts integration (Parsad & Spiegelman, 2012). This chapter, therefore, primarily targets the arts integration practitioner audience. Teacher educators, higher education administration, mentor teachers, preservice teachers, arts integration advocates will also find this chapter relevant to their work. Through the identification of impediments by theme, educational stakeholders can work to change the narrative of arts integration to one that is supported, embraced, and valued.

Parsad, B., & Spiegelman, M. (2012). *Arts education in public elementary and secondary schools: 1999–2000 and 2009–10* (NCES 2012–014). Washington, DC: National Center for Education Statistics, Institute of Education Sciences, U.S. Department of Education.

SUMMARY

As this chapter ends, readers should have a sense of the possibilities for determining "fit" for a publication as well as methods for minimizing outright rejection from editorial teams. This chapter offered intentional issues and tactics for optimizing publishing opportunities. Creating a list of journals to investigate was an important first step in ascertaining if a journal or call for a book chapter "fits" your research. Critically documenting and analyzing both the provided and collected journal specifications was also highlighted. The authors finally provided recommendations reflective of personal experiences and perspectives as editors. We hope our insider knowledge further supports your publishing and productivity goals.

KEY TERMS

Double Blind Peer Review In this case, the author and reviewer's identities are hidden from one another. Thus, you do not know who reviews your work; reviewers do now know whose work they are reviewing.

Generalist Journal A publication outlet broadly focused on a range of topics within a particular field.

Graphic Organizer A visual thinking tool used to organize ideas and express the relationship between ideas.

Interdisciplinary Journal A publication outlet which focuses on bringing together scholarship around a specific issue or method across disciplines and fields of study.

Open Access Online publication that is available at no cost.

Open Peer Review While this is a new type of peer review, an open peer review typically involves publishing an article's review (and reviewer's names) alongside the article.

Peer Review (Not Blinded) In this case, the editor, author, and the reviewer's identities are all known to each other.

Post Publication Peer Review In this uncommon type of peer review, articles are viewed and published following the publications of the article.

Precis A clear, concise summary. Typically, editors request a precis when they want an idea of what your are intending to submit, topic wise. Usually, a word count is specified.

Query an Editor This term refers to the practice of contacting and editor for the purposes of asking a specific question or questions. **(See Chapter 5)**

Rolling Submission Publications that accept submission as they are received, reviewed, and accepted without specific, set dates are using a process called rolling submissions.

Single Blind Peer Review In this case, the reviewer's identity is hidden from the author.

Special Interest Group(s) As part of a professional organization, special interest groups, also abbreviated to the acronym, SIGs, are self-determined groups of individuals who share an interest under the umbrella organization. Some SIGs require dues, other operate as a group that functions loosely around the special interest.

Specialty Journal A publication outlet focused more narrowly on a sub-specialty within a particular field.

Tenure Clock The timeframe provided for your institution for milestones in the tenure process. For example, most universities allow new hires six years to reach tenure with a mid-point evaluation. In some institutions, a third year review occurs, and it may be simply an opportunity to provide the new scholar with feedback, or in some cases it is high stakes and an unsuccessful third year review means a scholar is not allowed to proceed to the six year mark. Institutions also specify what event may stop the clock, such as critical family illness, pregnancy (usually for women), and significant medical issues.

Time in Review Refers to how long an article typically moves from the original submission through peer review to a published piece.

Triple Blind Peer Review In this case, the editors, author, and reviewer's identities are hidden from one another.

REFLECTIVE QUESTIONS

- What research journals that I identified in my field(s) have an open call for manuscripts or a special call for manuscripts that could be an outlet for my work?

- What practitioner journals that I identified in my field(s) have an open call for manuscripts or a special call for manuscripts that could be an outlet for my work?

- Could I create a one year and two-year submission plan?

- Which research journals can I identify as top tier and that I can aspire in which to publish?

- Which practitioner journals can I identify as top tier and that I can aspire in which to publish?

- Which international research and/or practitioner journals can I identify and that I can aspire in which to publish?

- Which Special Interest Group (SIG) research and/or practitioner journals can I identify and that I can aspire in which to publish?

ADDITIONAL REFERENCES AND RESOURCES

Ballenger, R., Kaser, S., Kauffman, G., Schroeder, & Short, K. (2006). Our reflections on writing for publication. *Language Arts*, 83(6), 534–543.

Richards, J. (2014). Academic writing to publication: Some points of departure for success. *Journal of Reading Education*, 39(3), 45–47.

Sage (July, 2020). *What is peer review?* Retrieved from https://us.sagepub.com/en-us/nam/what-is-peer-review

http://jomesonline.com/.

http://www.jeqr.org/.

https://beallslist.net/.

https://doaj.org.

https://explore.researchgate.net/display/support/Getting+started.

https://guides.mclibrary.duke.edu/qualitative/journals.

https://indianacampuscompact.org/pen-to-paper/.

https://journals.sagepub.com/home/eth.

https://journals.sagepub.com/home/mmr.

https://qualpage.com/2017/11/30/publishing-qualitative-research/.

https://tqr.nova.edu/journals/.

https://www.aera.net/https://us.sagepub.com/en-us/nam/title-lists.

https://www.journals.elsevier.com/journal-of-experimental-social-psychology/https://journals.sagepub.com/home/qrj.

https://www.longdom.org/clinical-trials.html.

https://www.researchgate.net/journal/1935-.

WORKS CITED ────────────────

Sage (July, 2020). *What is peer review?* Retrieved from https://us.sagepub.com/en-us/nam/what-is-peer-review

Taba, H. (1967). *Teachers' handbook for elementary social studies.* Palo Alto, CA. Addison-Wesley.

CHAPTER 6

An Editor's Perspective on Submitting Your Manuscript

(Invited Submission, Renée M. Casbergue, PhD & Professor Emeritus)

Our guest author for Chapter 6, Renée M. Casbergue, PhD, professor emeritus from Louisiana State University, advises readers to expect rejection, especially if the fit is not a good alignment for a scholar's work and a journal's needs. The purpose of this chapter is to assist authors as they navigate the editorial process for manuscripts submitted for publication in academic journals. The chapter will address the roles editors may play in the academic publication process as well as review how to identify guidelines for submission, considerations for querying an editor, how to craft a submission letter, and specific considerations for addressing a call for papers for a themed issue. The chapter will also help you understand the possible responses you will receive from editors and what each means for proceeding with your manuscript.

Learning Objectives

There are multiple learning objectives for this chapter. They are:

1. Recognizing the role of editors in publication process

2. Identifying publication guidelines

3. Knowing how and when to query an editor

4. Knowing how to address a call or theme

5. Understanding how to submit your manuscript

6. Learning what to expect in response to your submission

7. Understanding the nuances of guiding the submission process with community partners

8. Navigating co-authoring relationships and the role of a corresponding author

Quick Write # 5

This fifth quick write is designed to help you understand the job of an editor and consider this perspective. What do you think the job of an editor of an academic journal entails? Spend a few minutes writing down all the things you believe an editor is charged with. Consider what their relationship might be to the authors who submit their work and what their roles might be as they work through the editorial process. Take a few minutes to jot down your thoughts and keep them in mind as you read this chapter.

Role of Editors in the Publication Process

As you considered what it is that editors of academic journals do, your first thought was most likely that the editor's job is to decide to accept or reject your manuscript. The editor is the first level of review of your manuscript, and based on the journals' guidelines, the editor can decide to **desk reject** a manuscript if it does not adhere to the guidelines of the journal and not send the manuscript off for review. It is important to know, however, that the editor's job is multi-faceted and one of those facets is coordinating the work of many other individuals who contribute to the final disposition of your manuscript.

Depending on the journal, an **editor** might be the sole decision-maker based on external reviewers' suggestions. In that case, the editor does an initial review of every submission, identifies potential reviewers with appropriate expertise, and sends your manuscript out for review. Once reviews are received, he or she then reads them carefully to ascertain the manuscript's relative strengths and weaknesses and decides about publication. For larger journals, typically those with sizeable readership and a high volume of submissions, there might be a team of associate editors who contribute to the final decision. **Associate editors** are usually appointed based on varying areas of expertise. For a literacy-focused journal, for example, there may be one associate editor with expertise in early/ elementary literacy development, another who has experience with the literacy of adolescents and adults, and perhaps someone else whose expertise is related to literacy standards and policy. The editor's first responsibility, then, is to assign submissions to the most appropriate associate editor. In that case, it is the associate editor who identifies and assigns reviewers and does the initial reading of reviewers' feedback. Depending on the system established for a particular journal, the associate editor may be the person who makes the recommendation to accept or reject a manuscript.

The editor's role then is to review recommendations from all the associate editors and make a final determination about the disposition of a manuscript, keeping in mind the journal's overall publication goals. It is possible that even with positive reviews and a recommendation for acceptance from an associate editor, the editor might still reject a manuscript. That can happen, for example, when the journal has a large backlog of accepted submissions, or when it has already agreed to publish a very similar article from a different author.

One additional editorial role you might see when perusing an organization's publication outlets is the **editor-in-chief**. In some cases, this title designates the sole editor of a single journal, as described above. At other times, though, it refers to the organization's overall head of publications. Many large professional organizations produce multiple publications. The editor-in-chief oversees the publication of professional books, newsletters, and often a variety of journals intended for audiences ranging from practitioners and policy makers to researchers. It is rare that an author of a manuscript would ever correspond with the editor-in-chief of a professional organization, whose role is primarily to ensure that the direction of all the publications adequately reflects the organization's editorial priorities and that the publications collectively meet the needs of the full range of its members.

A final key contributor to the editorial decision-making process is the external **reviewer**. A **refereed journal** is one that sends every manuscript it receives to be reviewed by experts in the field. Most refereed journals use a **blind review process**. This means that the reviewers do not know who has written the manuscript they are reviewing as the editor removes any identifying information, including references to the authors' previously published work before forwarding the manuscript to reviewers. Conversely, the identity of the reviewers will not be revealed to authors. The types of peer review have been more fully explained in Chapter 5. Because reviewers are selected carefully based on expertise that aligns with the content and/or research methodology of the submission, the reviews they produce are pivotal in editors' decision-making process. Figure 6.1 illustrates a typical editorial structure for an academic professional organization.

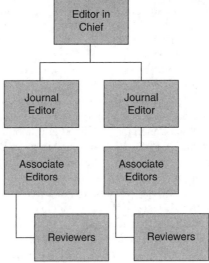

Figure 6.1   Editorial Organizational Chart for an Academic Professional Organization

Source: Renée M. Casbergue

Identifying Publication Guidelines

While some of this information was discussed in Chapter 5 from the perspective of choosing potential outlets, a fuller, editorial explanation for submission is provided here. Given the typical structure described here, imagine the number of people who might be involved in handling your manuscript once you have submitted it. First an editor (often with the help of an assistant who opens and catalogues submissions), then perhaps an associate editor, and typically at least three reviewers will all work with your manuscript. Now consider the amount of time each person might spend with your submission. From the moment you hit submit to upload your documents, countless hours go toward managing and reviewing your work. No one wants all of that effort to be wasted when it is discovered that a submission does not meet the journal's **guidelines**.

Before you consider submitting to an academic journal, it is important to make sure that you understand and follow all guidelines. Mustaine and Tewksbury (2013) surveyed a broad array of journal editors in the social and behavioral sciences to identify common editorial processes and found that most adhere to consistent guidelines. Familiarizing yourself with broad guidelines for professional academic writing as well as journal-specific guidelines will ease you through the process of submitting your work for publication and often garner a more favorable response from reviewers and editors. Guidance typically falls into three categories: methodology guidelines, format guidelines, and publication guidelines.

Methodology Guidelines

Research journals have very specific guidelines about the types of articles they will publish. You will need to search for publication guidance on the journal's webpage to determine if the manuscript you are working on fits its methodological preferences. While it might be tempting to simply examine a series of back issues from the journal you are interested in for this information, that may not give you the full picture of what the editor will consider.

When serving as a co-editor of the *Journal of Research in Childhood Education,* most issues were comprised of data-based research articles, often with a focus on early childhood and children in primary grades. This reflected both the primary focus of submissions we received and the demographics of the parent organization for the journal, the Association for Childhood Education International. Careful examination of the journal's website, however, would have revealed that the journal took a broader perspective than might be presumed based on the contents of most issues. First, the organization at the time considered "childhood" to include birth through adolescence, and thus we would have gladly considered research manuscripts that centered on middle and secondary school populations. And because we received so few submissions with that focus, the chances for acceptance of a well-researched and well-written submission would have been good!

The guidelines also indicated that we would consider reviews of research. Manuscripts of this type required that the review make a significant contribution to the literature and that the author's approach to identifying the research studies included was rigorous and explicitly described. Interestingly, many potential authors I spoke with during "meet the editor" sessions at professional conferences had no idea that such manuscripts might be acceptable.

Finally, as mentioned in Chapter 5, reviewing past issues of the journal might not reflect the most current **editorial stance** of the journal. This is important for several reasons. In particular, journals change somewhat with each new editorial team, and also adapt to changing views of what constitutes high-quality, publishable research. There was a time when qualitative work was perceived as being less rigorous and not worthy of consideration by major research journals. That is rarely an issue currently with widespread acceptance of many qualitative traditions. That does not mean, however, that every journal is open to reviewing studies using all research approaches. Some are very clear that they will only consider quantitative studies, while others are devoted exclusively to disseminating qualitative research. And still others will accept work reflecting a broad range of research traditions. You do not want to put significant time and effort into submitting a manuscript that won't even be considered by a journal because it does not meet the methodological requirements. Checking the guidelines before you begin will save everyone's grief. Again, Chapter 5 touched upon this issue of consulting and adhering to guidelines; here a deeper explanation is provided.

Format Guidelines

Just as all journals will have methodological guidelines, so too will they provide guidance regarding the format of submissions. Before you begin crafting your manuscript, check to see what style guidelines are in place. Broadly, most journals will specify their preferred style, whether those from the American Psychological Association (APA) (https://apastyle.apa.org) or those of the Modern Language Association (MLA) (https://style.mla.org), for example.

While a journal might advise following a specific style, it also may have its own quirks. For example, some journals that require APA style nonetheless vary in whether they want full first names or just first initials for authors cited in the references, regardless of the current APA guidelines. Similarly, journals may also express a preference for heading and subheading format, regardless of the overall style in use. Careful reading of the journal's guidelines is necessary. And in the case of formatting, looking to the most recent issues of the journal *can* provide a good model of the desired format.

The format guidelines will also indicate important considerations like page length and expectations regarding tables and figures. Authors need to recognize that page limitations are usually non-negotiable, especially if a journal includes both digital and print versions. Print journals have a set number of pages allotted for each issue and have budgeted for that amount of page space. Printing expenses often make adding additional pages to an issue cost prohibitive. Typically, **format guidelines** will provide a range for page length, and savvy authors will be sure to conform to those limitations.

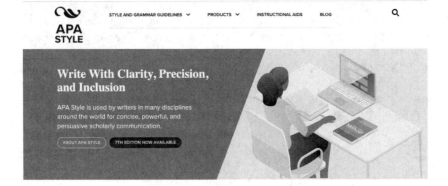

If your manuscript includes tables and figures, you should also look for guidance on how many of each are acceptable. Multiple tables will eat up available page space, so consider adapting tables to combine information. For example, if you are working from a research presentation as suggested in Chapter 3, your presentation may have multiple slides for demographic information about your research sample. Rather than one table for subjects' age and gender and a separate table for SES status and classroom placement, those demographics can easily be combined into one table in a manuscript that readers will be able to examine closely.

You should also consider how many figures are really needed. For example, because much of my published scholarly work focuses on young children's emergent writing, I do need to include figures that illustrate major concepts about how children conceptualize print. Young children's unconventional use of print and invented spelling is often charming and sometimes hilarious. It is always tempting to include multiple examples for sheer entertainment value. It is important to remind myself, though, that entertainment is not the purpose of a scholarly article. Where one writing sample can adequately demonstrate a concept I am describing, I cannot include two more that illustrate the same thing, no matter how much I enjoy those samples as well. It is always important for authors to be economical in their choices of figures. In fact, it is not uncommon that manuscript reviewers are asked to evaluate whether figures are both relevant and necessary; you need to make sure that figures you include are both. While written guidelines may not spell out the number of figures that are acceptable, perusing recent issues of a journal will provide some insight into what is typical.

In addition to guidelines for the number of tables and figures, journals usually have detailed specifications regarding preparation of these materials. The general expectation now is that figures and tables must be ready for publication as submitted. Journals will specify the required file format for pictures (usually TIFF or JPEG), and the required resolution, dimensions, and fonts for any tables, captions, or graphs. It is also important to remember that in most cases, figures will be published in black and white. While using different colors in a bar chart to illustrate the performance of treatment versus control groups at different points in a study makes for an appealing visual presentation, for example, for publication in black and white, authors will need to convert to something like different shading values or symbols to convey the same information in print. Understanding a journal's specific guidelines can save authors time and effort in the latter stages of the submission process.

Publication Guidelines

Beyond the details of methodological and formatting guidelines, many publishers have broader guidelines intended to assure consistency across publications and adherence to professional standards for both the conduct and dissemination of research. These guidelines range from **ethical considerations** to **publishing agreements** between authors and journals once a manuscript is accepted for publication.

There have been numerous attempts to standardize these types of guidelines across professional and academic fields of study (Larson & Cortazal, 2012). These broad publication guidelines are often shared across multiple journals under the umbrella of a publisher like Sage, Taylor and Francis, or Springer for example. Many follow guidelines from the Committee on Publication Ethics (COPE) (https://publicationethics.org), an organization with the aim of ensuring that "ethical practices become a normal part of the publishing culture." Ethical considerations range from questions of who should be included as authors and in what order, to guidance about previous dissemination of work included in a manuscript. They also indicate how to recognize and address issues of integrity like plagiarism and self-plagiarism (something that is sometimes a novel concept for novice authors).

A publishing agreement is a contractual agreement between the journal and the author. It specifies when and how the author can share the work, compensation to which authors are entitled (if any), and who owns the rights to the work.

It is advisable that authors become familiar with these kinds of publication guidelines to avoid common pitfalls and head off disputes that sometimes arise and may stop the publication process in its tracks. Table 6.1 lists some widely recognized resources for these types of broad publication guidelines.

Table 6.1 Sample Resources for Publisher Guidelines
American Psychological Association https://www.apa.org/pubs/journals/resources/preparation-submission
Modern Language Association https://www.mla.org/Publications/MLA-Book-Publications/Resources-for-Contributors
Sage Publishing https://us.sagepub.com/en-us/nam/manuscript-submission-guidelines
Taylor and Francis Publishers https://authorservices.taylorandfrancis.com/publishing-with-taylor-francis/

When and How to Query an Editor

As established in Chapter 5, it is not always easy to discern if the manuscript you are working on will be a good fit for a particular journal. In that case, it is acceptable to query the journal's editor for her or his perspective.

If you find the thought of corresponding directly with an editor at all intimidating, it might be helpful to remind yourself that most editors of scholarly journals are themselves active scholars in the same position as you are when they submit their own work to other journals. They are authors who, like you, will receive both positive and negative reviews of their work. No matter how well known they are in their fields, their manuscripts will still meet with occasional rejection and frequently with requirements for significant revision. As authors themselves, they understand that sometimes further clarification of publication guidelines is needed.

More importantly, most editors would rather answer a succinct e-mail than receive an unsuitable manuscript that, depending on the journal's policies, may nonetheless need to be sent through the entire review process. The key word here is succinct! Be very specific about what you are asking and be as brief as possible. Demonstrate that you have already read the publication guidelines and state exactly why you are unsure if your manuscript would be considered. By way of an exemplar, you might say, for instance:

I see in the publication guidelines that reviews of literature are an acceptable format for this research journal. My dissertation study of kindergarten children's writing in response to reading digital and traditional storybooks includes a review of literature that meshes research related to young children's use of digital devices and research on emergent reading and writing. Much of the review is comprised of studies that include preschool populations. Is a review of this scope something you would consider for this journal that I believe is aimed at researchers interested in literacy development in elementary school settings?

In just four sentences, this query indicates attention to guidelines, a brief statement of the focus of the manuscript, and a specific question of whether the topic is appropriate for the journal.

It is critical to keep in mind that a positive response to a query such as this is simply an indication that the editor will *consider* this work. This response in no way suggests that the manuscript you submit will be accepted for publication. Even a submission with enthusiastic encouragement from an editor will need to be sent out for reviewer feedback and meet standards for high-quality research and writing. Your initial inquiry gives the editor no insight into those qualities of your manuscript. Conversely, authors should not take a negative response to a query such as this as a judgment of the quality of their work. Editors may discourage you from submitting to their journal for a variety of reasons that have nothing to do with how well-researched or well-crafted your manuscript might be. Perhaps the topic of your manuscript doesn't quite fit what the editor understands to be the journal's primary audience. Or the journal may have accepted already as many of your type of manuscript as can be accommodated for the foreseeable future. Even when the response isn't positive, authors are always better off knowing as early as possible in the publication process if they should find an alternate outlet for their work. If an editor indicates it is not a good fit, feel free to follow-up expressing gratitude for their time and perhaps asking if they have a suggestion for a more appropriate publication outlet.

You may wonder, *what is the best means of contacting an editor?* Many journals will have contact information listed for editorial staff. If there is a designated e-mail address listed, use that. Since editors of most academic journals are themselves in academic positions, it is easy enough to locate their university e-mail addresses. However, if they have a designated e-mail address for the journal, you are likely to get a quicker response to an inquiry sent there than to a faculty inbox where it might get buried amid the typical professor's load of e-mails from students, administrators, and various working groups. Telephoning an editor is also rarely a good idea. We all have experienced "phone tag" that can go on for days. Even if you are able to make phone contact relatively quickly, an editor may prefer to give some thought to your query before responding. Written requests allow for more careful consideration.

Appropriate (and Inappropriate) Requests of Editors

Querying an editor to determine if the topic of your work is a good fit for a journal is a good use of your and the editor's time. Editors are also usually happy to help clarify whether the type of manuscript you are preparing meets the journal's guidelines. For example, while the written guidance may indicate that the journal recognizes the value of multiple research traditions, within broad quantitative, qualitative, and mixed methods approaches, there is still lots of latitude regarding what is considered acceptable for a journal. Some more avant garde methods of data collection and reporting of findings will lie outside of what the editor believes will be of interest to the journal's audience. If your manuscript will not follow widely recognized reporting style, it may be a good idea to ask before submitting.

Not every query is appropriate. However friendly and approachable an editor may be, keep in mind that she or he is not your advisor or mentor. As noted above, your questions should be very specific. If an editor responds that your planned approach to reporting data doesn't fit the journal's expectations, it is not appropriate to seek advice about how you might adapt your approach to data collection and reporting. Nor is it an editor's job to help you brainstorm research questions or decide what kinds of practitioner or policy-oriented manuscripts you might produce when feedback from reviewers is that your submission is too technical for the journal's more practitioner or policy-oriented audience. Finally, it is never appropriate to ask an editor to read and respond to an early version of your paper and give you feedback before sending it out for review. Those are requests better shared with your actual advisor, mentor, or writing group.

How to Address a Call or Theme

As you work to find appropriate outlets for your manuscripts, don't overlook the value of calls for papers or themed issues of journals. Themed issues and special calls were presented as a final reflective question in Chapter 5. Here, a deeper explanation is provided. Most journals routinely have a call for papers in the front matter or at the end of a printed journal, and/or on the journal's web page. These calls offer a succinct statement of the types of manuscripts the editorial team seeks. Of even more value are special calls for **themed issues** for which journals solicit submissions. Themed issues of journals usually include a special section with articles that all address a common issue; sometimes an entire issue may be devoted to the theme.

Themed issues are often planned to address a very current issue of concern. For example, in the spring and summer of 2020, calls for papers for themed issues centered on the impact of the COVID-19 virus abounded across multiple fields of study, from medicine and basic science to economics and education. One benefit of submitting to such a themed issue is a significantly shortened timeline for the review process. Because journals want the topic to remain timely, the timeframe from submission to acceptance or rejection of a manuscript may be just a few weeks as opposed to the more typical 6–12 weeks allotted for the review process.

To increase the potential for your manuscript to be accepted for a specific call or themed issue, it is vital that its relevance to the call be evident to reviewers. There are two common ways to ensure that editors and reviewers understand why and how your submission is appropriate for the theme: including the language of the call in the manuscript's abstract and introduction and framing the discussion and implication sections to incorporate the theme. Box Including the language of the call provides a detailed explanation of how an author might respond to an exemplar call for a themed issue.

Including the Language of the Call

Calls for themed issues follow a fairly standard format. They begin with an overview of the issue, contextualizing it and outlining its importance and potential impact on the field of study or profession. Then the call lists specific topics within the broader theme that the editorial team hopes to include.

A call for papers related to the COVID-19 pandemic published by the UNESCO Institute for Lifelong Learning (https://uil.unesco.org) for its *International Review of Education (IRE)* in early April 2020, for example, began with an overview of how the pandemic raised concerns for policy-makers, educators, parents, and children. It then discussed issues of inequality in access to online learning supports, psychosocial consequences of loss of school communities for learning, the stress of economic issues for families, and impact on global aid for education in poorer parts of the world. This was followed by a specific request for topics:

In an effort to generate new knowledge on this new global challenge, and its impact on and implications for lifelong learning, the International Review of Education (IRE) invites papers for a special issue on "Education in the age of COVID-19," covering the following themes:

- *Effects of formal and nonformal education institution closures; and the generalization of online and distance teaching and learning.*
- *Rediscovering family/intergenerational learning in times of confinement.*
- *Psychosocial support in times of crisis.*
- *Inequalities resulting from the crisis (in terms of access to education, quality, learning outcomes, differential impacts in public and private institutions, geographical disparities, etc.).*
- *Lifelong learning and citizenship: Learning to live together again.*
- *Preparing tomorrow: Lessons learned from this crisis and implications for lifelong learning.*
- *International solidarity during and after the crisis: The transformation of education aid patterns and flows* (International Review of Research, 2020).

When submitting to a call like this one, an author can strive to use the same terminology as that included in the call. For example, an author may want to address the potential for widening the gap in achievement between children from upper and lower socioeconomic communities and frame the introduction to a manuscript as the potential for differential learning outcomes. The choice of the word "inequalities" in the call, however, is a clear statement of the editorial slant intended. Introducing the topic in terms of inequalities will help both reviewers and editors recognize that your manuscript views the issues through their preferred lens.

How to Submit Your Manuscript

Once you have identified a publication outlet, and after many rounds of drafting, revising, and editing your work to ensure that it reflects your best thinking and writing, you are ready to submit it to the journal of your choice. In almost all cases now, manuscripts are submitted through an online management system such as *Scholar One* (used by SAGE and many other publishers), Elsevier's *Evise*, or *Editorial Manager* used by Springer, Wiley, and others. Each journal's website will contain a link to the submission system it uses, along with instructions for creating log in credentials if you are submitting to that journal for the first time. Because each of the systems is used by multiple publications, using the link from the journal's web page ensures that you are uploading your work to the correct publication.

Framing Discussion and Implications Sections to Incorporate the Theme

While using the language of the call, particularly in your abstract and introduction, may position your manuscript in a positive light as reviewers begin reading, it is important to follow through later in the manuscript. For example, if you have examined SES-based differences in outcomes for children from the same classroom after schools shut down for the pandemic using a well-designed study that controlled for prior academic achievement among the two groups, under normal reporting guidelines, you could do a very straightforward presentation of results followed by any number of conclusions and implications. Again, though, because the call specifically framed issues related to differential outcomes as inequalities both in the overview and in the fourth bulleted topic, it would be prudent to frame your conclusions and implications in that light. Doing so further implies that your submission would benefit from some treatment of the literature related to inequitable education opportunities and affordances in your manuscript's review of literature. That would allow for you to recursively tie your conclusions to issues raised in your own lit review.

By weaving the language of the call throughout a manuscript, authors consistently signal to the reviewers and editors that the manuscript is indeed aligned with their editorial vision for the themed issue. In my experience as a guest editor of one themed issue of *Childhood Education* related to the legacies of the No Child Left Behind federal initiative, it was surprising how many submissions failed to do that, leaving reviewers as well as my co-editor and I to infer the connection between the call and what was submitted.

Once you are logged in, you will first enter basic information about your manuscript, including the title, authors and their affiliations, keywords, and an abstract. There is usually a tab through which you will upload a cover letter. While often an afterthought when authors have invested considerable time and effort into crafting the manuscript itself, the submission letter may play a part in shaping an editor's decision about your manuscript. At the very least, the letter serves as a polite introduction to your submission. In the case of a manuscript submitted to a themed issue, the cover letter is yet one more opportunity to briefly explain why and how your submission fits the call.

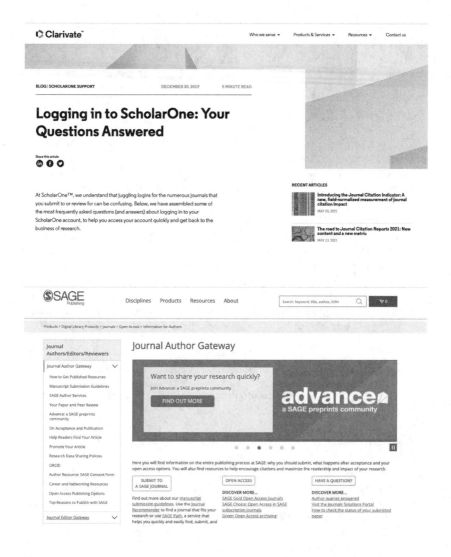

Required Elements of a Submission Letter

Your letter should maintain a professional tone and state succinctly that you are requesting a review of your work (specifying its title) for possible inclusion in the journal (specifying its name). Specify who the author is, and in the case of multiple authors, indicate who will serve as the **corresponding author** to whom all correspondence should be directed. You should also add a statement that all authors have approved of submission of the manuscript to the journal.

Include a very brief description of the type of manuscript you are submitting (e.g., review of literature, quantitative or qualitative research report, commentary, or interpretation of research for practitioners), followed by a statement of the significance of your contribution and why it should be of interest to the journal's readers. Finally, specifically state that the manuscript you are submitting has not been published previously and is not currently under consideration by another journal.

Possible Additional Information

Depending on the circumstances, your letter may also include additional information. As noted, if you are responding to a call for a themed issue, specify the connection between your manuscript and the call. If you have previously queried the editor about the manuscript, also reference that correspondence and the editor's response in your cover letter.

Because editors are increasingly hard pressed to line up appropriate reviewers for the growing volume of journal submissions (Leopold, 2015), suggestions for potential reviewers along with their contact information may be appreciated, particularly if your topic or research methodology entails highly specific or technical expertise. You must follow ethical guidelines when suggesting reviewers, however, and state specifically that you have no relationship to anyone you list, and that they have not provided previous feedback about your manuscript in advance of its submission or about the research project itself.

Uploading Your Paper and Related Documents

The final step in the submission process is actually uploading your materials. The submission system will usually specify acceptable document types, whether Microsoft Word, Rich Text File (RFT), or PDF. The manuscript management system will usually convert Word or RTF submissions to a PDF or HTML file format.

In most systems, you will see separate tabs that enable you to upload any additional required files, including figures and tables. In most cases, each figure or table is uploaded as a separate file. Be sure that you have named the files using the format designated by the journal, for example, "Figure 1.1 (followed by brief figure name)." Typically, there is also a place to designate any captions or summary of these files as well.

Once all materials are uploaded, authors are given the opportunity to review their submission as it appears in the manuscript system. The converted documents will be what reviewers actually see. You will need to make sure that formatting, including the order of the pages, and special characters have not been disrupted by conversion to PDF files. Only once you have done a careful review should you hit the "submit" button.

What to Expect in Response to Your Submission

Once you have submitted your manuscript, it is out of your hands. All you can do is wait for a response from the editor. The time it takes to receive reviews and the editor's decision varies widely across journals, although most strive to arrive at a decision in about eight weeks. The typical length of time is usually spelled out on the journal's home page. Recognize, though, that the length of time specified is often aspirational. Many factors influence the length of time from submission to disposition of your manuscript. Keep in mind that editors must depend on reviewers to agree to perform reviews and to complete their reviews on time. Any difficulty in securing appropriate reviewers and any delay in getting even one review returned on time will stymie an editor's attempt to respond within the timeframe specified by the journal.

Source: iStock

Therefore, you should only inquire about the status of your submission once you have received no response within a reasonable period after the stated time-frame. On rare occasions, a journal's response to a submitted manuscript is unreasonably slow. While some authors may not mind waiting for months on end for the possibility of publishing in a highly valued journal, not everyone can afford to wait. This is especially true for newer scholars in academic settings who face time constraints related to tenure and promotion. It is equally problematic if the content of your manuscript is related to a topic of immediate interest to the field, and timeliness is of the essence. If you are dissatisfied with ongoing delays in securing a response to your submission, you are well within your rights to contact the editor and request that your manuscript be withdrawn from consideration by that journal. Be sure to make this request in writing so that when you submit it to an alternate publication outlet, you can verify that the manuscript is no longer under consideration elsewhere.

Assuming your manuscript does follow the normal review process without significant delays, you will eventually be informed of one of four possible editorial decisions: outright acceptance, provisional acceptance, revise and resubmit, or outright rejection. Explanations for what each editorial response means for a manuscript follow.

Acceptance

Having a manuscript accepted outright with no revisions is the ideal outcome for a journal submission. It is also an extremely rare outcome, even for experienced authors. An outright **acceptance** indicates that no significant edits are required beyond minimal wordsmithing that the editor will do. Even well-known researchers who are tops in their fields of study are more likely to receive provisional acceptance or instructions to revise and resubmit their work.

Provisional Acceptance

A **provisional acceptance** is a very positive response to a manuscript. It generally indicates that only minimal revision is needed. A provisionally accepted manuscript usually meets all the editorial standards of the journal, in terms of methodology (if a research article), and quality of writing. Suggested revisions are often simple requests for clarification, a little more elaboration for an idea that was not entirely clear to a reviewer, or perhaps the addition of a table, figure, or example that will help the flow of the manuscript. If the suggested edits are completed as requested and by the deadline specified, authors can assume that their manuscript will be published.

Revise and Resubmit

A request to **revise and resubmit** an article is a common decision that most experienced authors learn to expect with some regularity. In this case, the required revisions and edits are more extensive. With any luck, reviewers will have provided significant guidance regarding the necessary changes to the original manuscript. For example, authors may be asked to reorganize the paper for better flow, provide much more detail about processes for data collection and analysis, or add more extensive conclusions and implications for practice.

A revise and resubmit response indicates that the reviewers and editor believe that there is sufficient merit to the paper to reconsider it when the suggested revisions are completed. It suggests that the topic is in fact a good fit for the journal; therefore, a suggestion to revise and resubmit should also be viewed as a potentially positive outcome. Unlike a provisional acceptance, though, authors cannot be as confident that their manuscript will ultimately be published by that journal. Once revisions are completed, the manuscript will usually be sent out again for review. While, ideally, the same reviewers who provided feedback about the original version of the manuscript will review it again, in some cases new reviewers will be used. Either the original reviewers or the new ones may not be satisfied with the revisions and might then recommend rejection. Navigating the revise and resubmit process is extensively detailed in Chapter 7.

Rejection

Having a manuscript rejected is never the desired outcome of a submission. A **rejection** is a final response with no option to make edits or revisions and request another review. Authors need to accept that their manuscript needs significant work and is not yet ready for publication. The experience does not have to be entirely negative, however. The review process for a high-quality journal is likely to yield substantive reviews and perhaps a detailed explanation from the editor about why the manuscript was rejected. Savvy authors will use this information to educate themselves about what needs improvement, whether in their research process or in their writing.

What Comes Next?

In the case of provisional acceptance or a revise and resubmit, authors should act expeditiously to respond to the feedback they receive. The editor's correspondence will provide a timeframe during which changes should be made. Authors should be sure to work within that timeframe and provide an updated manuscript by any deadline specified. Authors may be asked to complete simple edits within a couple of weeks. They will usually be given at least four to six weeks to submit more extensive revisions. The exception to this may be if revisions are required for a manuscript to be included in a themed issue with a time-sensitive deadline.

Within the timeframe specified, authors should not rush too quickly to complete extensive revisions. It is usually better to take a couple of days at least to digest the feedback provided and carefully consider the best way to respond. Occasionally, the feedback will be conflicting, with one reviewer suggesting something that is opposed to what a different reviewer wants. The editor's correspondence to the author may provide sufficient guidance to navigate these differences. If not, this is an instance where it is a good idea to query the editor about his or her preferences for resolving any issues. Only when you are satisfied that you have addressed all of the editor's or reviewers' concerns should you then return to the manuscript submission system and follow all instructions for uploading your revised manuscript. In Chapter 7, readers are offered suggestions for using a tool called a reconciliation chart to keep track of requested edits and revisions and document authors' responses to those requests.

The following exemplars allow readers to view sample letters of submission and resubmission from this invited author's perspective. While other similar exemplars appear in related chapters, the value of including several exemplars allows readers to see the continuity of such letters but also how different authors express themselves.

Cover Letter Exemplar

General Submission Cover Letter Exemplar

Date:

[Editor's name and title]
[Journal Title]
[Physical Street Address]
[City, State, Zip code]

Dear [Editor's name]

Please accept our manuscript, *Kindergartners' Writing in Response to Digital and Traditional Books*, for possible publication in [*Journal's Title*]. This is a research report from a study conducted in public schools in two large metropolitan areas. We collected a total of 120 writing samples after children read each digital and traditional picture books. The manuscript details findings related to differences in the content and format of children's writing depending on the type of book read. The manuscript concludes with implications for inclusion of both digital and traditional books in the kindergarten classroom. We believe that our findings and implications will be of interest to early literacy researchers and educators who comprise the primary audience for this journal.

My co-author [co-author's name] and I have both approved this submission. As first author, I will take the lead on all correspondence going forward. Please address any correspondence to me at the address below my signature. This manuscript has not been previously published and is not out for review by any other journal.

We look forward to reviewers' comments about our manuscript. Thank you for your consideration.

Sincerely,

[signature]

[Corresponding author's name]
[Address to which correspondence should be directed]

Resubmission Letter Exemplar

Date:

[Editor's name and title]
[Journal Title]
[Physical Street Address]
[City, State, Zip code]
Dear [Editor's name]

I have uploaded my manuscript, [Title of Manuscript], for further consideration for publication in [Title of Journal]. As we discussed in earlier e-mails, at your suggestion I reorganized the literature review as outlined by Reviewer 2 rather than the structure advised by Reviewer 1.

I do believe that this reorganization has improved the flow of the manuscript.

I have also expanded discussion of practical implications from my research findings as suggested by two of the reviewers. I trust that the manuscript now has more to offer to more practice-oriented readers.

In addition to those major revisions, I have addressed each of the other suggestions raised by the reviewers. Please see the attached reconciliation chart that tracks each of the changes made in this revision.

I hope that the revised manuscript meets your expectations. I look forward to receiving your decision about its disposition. Thank you and the reviewers for your guidance.

Sincerely,

[Signature]

[Corresponding author's name]
[Address to which correspondence should be directed]

SUMMARY

This chapter began by clarifying the roles that editors, associate editors, and reviewers play in the potential publication of a manuscript you have submitted to an academic journal. Following methodology, format, and other broad publication guidelines is critically important to a successful review of your work. Careful consideration should be given to when and how to query an editor if you have questions about the guidelines or whether a manuscript you have in mind might be a good fit for a particular journal. It is especially important to consider fit when responding to a call for papers for a themed issue. When doing so, using the language of the call throughout your manuscript and in your submission/cover letter will help reviewers and editors understand why and how your paper is a good fit. The submission process will vary across journals; instructions in the journal's submission portal should be reviewed carefully before your manuscript and accompanying documents are uploaded. Once you submit your manuscript, you can expect to receive one of four responses: a rare outright acceptance, a provisional acceptance, a suggestion to **revise and resubmit**, or outright rejection. Reviewers' and editors' comments must be considered carefully to improve your manuscript going forward. Attending to all the details entailed in submitting your manuscript to an academic journal will increase your chances of eventual publication in the journal of your choice.

KEY TERMS

Acceptance (or Provisionally Accept) A journal submission decision where no significant edits are required beyond minimal wordsmithing that the editor will do. In academic publishing terms, an accept decision is a category of response that indicates a manuscript submitted for publication is considered both an appropriate fit for a journal and is of significant quality in terms of writing style and scholarship. Outright acceptance decisions are infrequent. In these rare instances, editors typically make any minor revisions, and nothing further is required from authors.

Associate Editor Identifies and assigns reviewers and does the initial reading of reviewers' feedback; the associate editor may be the person who makes the recommendation to accept or reject a manuscript.

Blind Review Process A review process where the reviewers do not know who has written the manuscript they are reviewing.

Co-Authoring Agreements Agreement between collaborators on a project that include not only responsibilities for the project, but details on anonymity and specifics of the project to be disclosed, including determining the publication outlet.

Corresponding Author The team member who takes the lead in all correspondence related to the manuscript submission.

Desk Reject A decision made by a journal editor that your manuscript has been rejected by a journal without being sent out for review.

Editor Responsible for the initial review of every journal submission, identifies potential reviewers with appropriate expertise, and sends your manuscript out for review. Once reviews are received, he or she then reads them carefully to ascertain the manuscript's relative strengths and weaknesses and renders a decision about publication.

Editorial Stance The slight shift that accompanies the change in the editorial team of a journal, and the adaptation to changing views of what constitutes high-quality publishable research.

Editor-in-Chief The sole editor of a single journal or the organization's overall head of publications.

Ethical Considerations Ethical considerations range from questions of who should be included as authors and in what order, to guidance about previous dissemination of work included in a manuscript. They also indicate how to recognize and address issues of integrity like plagiarism and self-plagiarism (something that is sometimes a novel concept for novice authors).

First Author Typically. This is the person who has conceptualized the study, developed research questions, and decided on research design.

Format Guidelines Guidance on the preferred style of a particular journal, such as American Psychological Association (APA) (https://apastyle.apa.org) or Modern Language Association (MLA) (https://style.mla.org), for example.

Guidelines Guidance provided by a journal on methodology, format, and broad publication considerations.

Provisional Acceptance (or Accept With Minor Revisions) A journal submission decision where the manuscript revisions are often simple requests for clarification, a little more elaboration for an idea that was not entirely clear to a reviewer, or perhaps the addition of a table, figure, or example that will help the flow of the manuscript.

Publication Guidelines Broad guidelines intended to assure consistency across publications and adherence to professional standards for both the conduct and dissemination of research; range from ethical considerations to publishing agreements between authors and journals once a manuscript is accepted for publication.

Publishing Agreement A contractual agreement between the journal and the author(s); it specifies when and how the author(s) can share the work, describes any compensation, for publication, and explicitly states who owns the rights to the work.

Refereed Journal A journal that sends every manuscript it receives to be reviewed by experts in the field.

Rejection A journal submission decision that serves as a final response with no option to make edits or revisions and request another review.

Reviewer An expert in a given field of study that aligns with the content and/or research methodology of the submission, the reviews they produce are pivotal in editors' decision-making process.

Revise and Resubmit A journal submission decision where revisions and edits are more extensive; reviewers usually provide significant guidance regarding the necessary changes to the original manuscript.

Themed Issues A journal that devotes a special section with articles that all address a common issue; sometimes an entire issue may be devoted to the theme.

CRITICAL THINKING QUESTIONS————

- What role will a journal editor play as you pursue publication in an academic journal?

- When might you need to correspond with an editor and what will you need to do to project professionalism in my written correspondence?

- How do you feel about writing with co-authors?

- What steps will you ask co-authors to take before you begin writing together?

- How will you deal with any awkwardness that might arise if you suggest a formal co-authoring agreement?

WORKS CITED ————————————————

American Psychological Association (2020a). *Publication manual of the American psychological association*, 7th ed. Washington, DC: APA.

American Psychological Association (2020b). *Tips for determining authorship credit.* Retrieved from https://www.apa.org/science/leadership/students/authorship-paper. Accessed on June 29, 2020

International Review of Research (2020). Retrieved from https://uil.unesco.org/event/call-abstracts-ire-special-issue-education-age-covid-19. Accessed on June 29, 2020

Larson, E., & Cortazal, M. (2012). Publication guidelines need widespread adoption. *Journal of Clinical Epidemiology*, 65(3), 239–246. doi:10.1016/j.jclinepi.2011.07.008

Leopold, S. (2015). Editorial: Increased manuscript submissions prompt journals to make hard choices. *Clinical Orthopedics and Related Research*, 473, 753–755. doi: 10.1007/s11999-014-4129-1

Mustaine, E., & Tewksbury, R. (2013) Exploring the black Box of journal manuscript review: A survey of social science journal editors, *Journal of Criminal Justice Education*, 24 (3), 386–401. doi:10.1080/10511253.2012.759244

Working With and From Manuscript Reviews

Revising and Resubmitting Your Manuscript

Purpose of Chapter

As an editorial team, we have rarely experienced outright *acceptance*. In fact, collectively, we've experienced it just twice; however, all of us have learned and every author learns to accept rejection, as well as learns what can be gleaned as advice from reviewers and revise and then resubmit a rejected manuscript *elsewhere*. We believe that part of the writing and publishing paradigm for scholars is the degree of revision needed between acceptance and rejection.

Learning Objectives

There are several learning objectives for this chapter. They are:

1. Learning to accept reviewers' comments as constructive criticism

2. Trusting editors' decision-making process

3. Developing a mindset that enables acceptance of critique as needed revision

4. Systematically and strategically addressing review comments, edits, and suggestions

5. Acquiring professional diplomacy when disagreeing with a reviewer or editor

6. Writing succinct yet comprehensive resubmission letters

You Received Your Reviews: Now What?

As we stated in Chapter 4, the timeframe for writing a scholarly article or book chapter could be ideally managed within a 12-week timeframe. However, that is an ideal timeframe; depending on what else is occurring in a scholar's professional and personal life, that timeframe could be shorter, but likely a longer timeframe is more realistic. In Chapter 5, the authors of this text discussed the beginning of the publishing process as a scholar or scholarly team selects an appropriate publication outlet and then adheres to all manuscript guidelines once a publication venue has been selected, providing options for determining "fit" and for minimizing outright rejection from editorial teams. Chapter 5 offered strategic and thoughtful approaches for optimal publishing opportunity. And in Chapter 6, an invited author shared definitive, finite aspects of the skills involved in submitting a manuscript from the perspective of a seasoned editor.

A constant the authors have advocated throughout this text thus far is the efficacy of scheduling regular writing intervals that will allow graduate students, new scholars, and novice researchers to achieve success. The degree to which writing a manuscript is attainable and achievable depends on an individual's adherence to sufficiently addressing the requisite sections of a manuscript, and the ability to craft a manuscript that is coherent, deemed appropriate for a journal's audience or a book's overall concept, and is in alignment with the guidelines of the publication. With the 12-week timeframe in mind, also consider that the submission process involves a manuscript undergoing a review process, which likely results in revision, and that manuscripts are published based on editors' decisions and preset publication timelines. The review process is not quick; volunteer reviewers with appropriate content knowledge about a topic need to be secured, contacted, and committed to reviewing with a final review step being the determination of the editors to *accept, accept with minor revisions,* to ask an author to *revise and resubmit,* and the decision to *reject* a manuscript. This process is referred to as the **peer review process.**

Productivity begins with creating a manuscript and publishing ends when a manuscript has been accepted and is scheduled for a publication date, at which point a scholar can list on their curriculum vita (CV) as **in press**. It is important for scholars to recognize that rounds of review and editing components can add several months, at a minimum, to the timeframe. The discipline discussed in Chapters 1 and 2 comes into play here as scholars anticipate the time, effort, and skill needed to take an idea from germination to fruition, from idea to manuscript. Patience is also needed as there is an interplay between when it is too soon to check on the status of a submitted piece and when it is prudent to do so to realistically determine the status of a review. In essence, if a scholar produces a viable manuscript in 12 weeks and can submit it quickly once finished, the first round of review can easily add an additional six to eight weeks minimally, with additional rounds of external peer review possible after each revision submitted by the authors. The more niche your topic, the more likely your manuscript will take more time in review. The entire process from submission to printing can take anywhere from five months to a year without any guarantee of publication. This is independent from the journal's possible backlog of submissions and accepted articles, which can also add time to seeing your article in print. All of us, your authors, have also experienced a change in an editorial team during peer review of a manuscript, which can also add significant time to the process.

Overcoming Initial Emotional Response to Criticism

In the introductory chapter, the authors defined rejection and revise and resubmit, two of the possible four categories of response that a scholar can anticipate when a manuscript has been submitted. To review what was further explained in Chapter 5 about the peer review process, the categories of response from an editor consist of an outright provisional acceptance, wherein the editors(s) accept with minor revisions required by the author(s), revise and resubmit, and reject.

If you are fortunate enough to ever receive either an outright acceptance decision or an accept with minor revisions decision, you should be elated. And then, you should immediately respond to the editor, thank him or her and accept the decision. If a date for resubmitting with minor edits is not given, suggest a date within two weeks. Because of the effort—the deep thinking, writing, editing, and revising time involved just to produce and submit a worthwhile manuscript, not to mention the data collection and analysis on a research article or chapter—when a decision comes back that invites a scholar to revise or resubmit, think of that decision as a gift, not an outright rejection. However, from experience, the authors of this text stress that you may also feel emotionally let down and discouraged when invited to revise and resubmit. This is worth repeating: a revise and resubmit is a *gift*. This category of response indicates a decision by the editor(s) that elements of your manuscript were noteworthy and significant but that other components indicated a need for something additional, and that some aspect is lacking. Perhaps you were provided with significant additional edits, possibly you were given feedback from reviewers and the editor(s) that suggested major revisions such as more depth to sections of the manuscript, or maybe you were asked to clarify a portion of your manuscript before additional reviewing can be provided. Consider a revise and resubmit decision as a request as well as a challenge to do more work for further consideration, which can ultimately improve your work. However, a revise and resubmit is never a promise or an assurance of publication and, frankly, such a decision can feel discouraging.

Quick Write # 6

This sixth quick write is a chance to release emotion and get past the feelings you may experience of discouragement, disappointment, letdown, and failure if you receive a response of a rejection or a revise and resubmit. Open up a new word document or turn to a new piece of paper. Set a timer for three to five minutes. You are going to write about how you are actually feeling about your current manuscript. List the reasons you feel that way. Acknowledge your irritation and vexation, perhaps your frustration and feeling of pride in producing what you have completed. When the timer sounds, stop and reread your thoughts and feelings. Whatever you are experiencing, those emotions are justified. Now put that paper away or close that document because now you are going to take concrete steps to address the edits and revisions suggested by the editor(s). You are now going to engage in the revise and resubmit process if that was the editorial decision handed to you.

Responding to a Revise and Resubmit: Your New Best Friend in Achieving Publishing Success
••

While acknowledging your feelings as important, action is more important. Recall the time you have spent getting a manuscript written and submitted. Time is still of the essence, especially for doctoral students who are balancing the completion of a capstone study with building a publication record that will garner interest for a position in academia. Culling articles from your dissertation study is a way to maximize your efforts. Margaret-Mary, one of the authors of this text, published an issues piece from her dissertation within the first year of her first academic appointment. She received a revise and resubmit that underwent two complete rounds of review before being accepted for publication. Leah Katherine, another author, chose to submit a piece on a smaller study related to but not directly from her dissertation that was first submitted to a leading research association as an award submission. Even though she won the award for her work, the manuscript was not outrightly accepted by the journal to which it was submitted. Rather, she and her co-author also experienced three rounds of revise and resubmit decisions (and over a year in review) before they saw their piece accepted and in print. Another author, Cyndi, quickly submitted her dissertation research for publication, did not initially see the revise and resubmit as a gift, and let the edits sit for a few months before she put her feelings aside and addressed them. And Ty, the fourth author of this text, made the decision to publish a piece from her dissertation but in a practitioner-based journal. She submitted shortly after defending and entering her tenure track role. Despite the type of journal, Ty also experienced a revise and resubmit. At the same time, Ty sent an article from a different small study; the manuscript was outright rejected. We share these experiences as we have experienced numerous decisions of revise and resubmit, collectively in our experience, the most common decision. And while initially deflated with that assessment of a manuscript, learning how to strategically address a revise and resubmit decision, subsequent successfully led to publications. The following process can also be used to maximize your effort and move forward if you have received a rejection.

For newly minted academics, often, the clock for tenure or evaluation starts with your hire date. So, in addition to managing relocation to a new job, presumably to a different locale and home, you will need to publish at an even rate based on the parameters outlined by your institution. New academics in their initial position should consider their dissertation or thesis study as fodder for publication. You will also need to plan to initiate subsequent studies including learning the new processes for study approval at your institution. However, if and when you received a revise and resubmit decision, which new scholars should expect at best, respond as soon as possible to the editor(s). If not sooner, within 24 hours of receiving a decision of revise and resubmit, you should issue a polite, professional response. This is expected.

Before you respond, be sure to carefully read any terms, such as timelines and/or deadlines for resubmission included in the correspondence. The editor(s) should indicate the length of time to resubmit as well as more information about the review process. This second review may require the author to use the track changes feature and or perform an additional upload to a platform as well. Be sure that you understand what you are being asked to do, and if any aspect is unclear, you can seek clarification in your response to the editor(s). Given the amount of time a review process takes, a revise and resubmit process is typically based on the amount of revision or addition the manuscript requires. As indicated in Chapter 6, any missive should maintain a professional tone and correspondence should be stated succinctly.

Your response to the editor(s) should begin with a brief but sincere statement of thanks indicating your appreciation for the review process, the time, attention, and suggestions from reviewers, and editor(s) correspondence. Remember the editors are your colleagues and are likely providing volunteer service in their editorship position. Follow your expression of thanks with a statement that acknowledges any terms, timelines, or deadline. If you need more time, negotiate a reasonable extension up front. At this point in your response, if anything was unclear, this is your opportunity to ask for clarification. End your response with another, final statement of thanks. Be succinct but comprehensive.

Editors Want You to Succeed and Editors Want Quality Journals and Books

Now that you have responded affirmatively that you plan to revise and resubmit your manuscript, you want to put this process in perspective. First and foremost, editors are academics. They were once graduate students, new scholars, and novice researchers, and most recall the struggles of publishing and the stress and pressure of productivity. Most editors want two things, they are editors because they really care about the quality of publications, and they want those who submit manuscripts for consideration to be successful. Both reflect on the editor's reputation and prestige within their field as well as the journal's standing within the field and broadly, within academia. This impetus for quality typically results in editors providing scholars with concrete feedback via well-selected reviewers.

Reviewing, along with being an editor, is typically a voluntary service in which scholars engage. Interested individuals submit their names to journals of their choosing to be considered being named to a publication's review board or are requested to join a board based on their research interests, knowledge of a topic, and/or specific research design and methods. They are also selected based on their own productivity. Reviewers are matched with incoming manuscripts, and reviewers are encouraged to adhere to reviewing guidelines, but also to be encouraging and honest. Commonly, reviewers are asked by editors to provide specific feedback that is designed to strengthen a manuscript. Some reviewers also suggest other publications that, in their opinion, seem to be a better fit for a manuscript.

Especially at the outset of an academic career, we recommend, when possible, working with publishers and editors who have an explicitly stated interest in working with new scholars or scholars whose identities and perspective may not have been well represented in the literature (where appropriate). This information is often communicated in the "About the Journal" section of a publication's website or in a call for manuscripts. For example, calls requesting submission from "researchers at all levels and ranks" or specific "own voices" should be of particular note. The rationale for this is that these editors and publication outlets also see part of their role as editors as mentoring or developing new scholars into the field. As a result, the kinds of feedback requested from reviewers for these publications may be more nuanced—with an eye toward being explicit with new scholars and demystifying the kinds of revisions necessary for viable publication in the outlet you selected (or others).

Oftentimes when journals are geared toward novice scholars, even the editor may weigh in to support the author by providing valuable feedback. We have found as editors that it has been helpful to serve as a reviewer or guest editor for the types of journals that we desire to submit a manuscript for publication. We have found that the role of reviewer provides insight into the styles of writing, organization of the manuscript, and the type of research methods or topics that the editor seeks to include in upcoming volumes.

After all reviews are submitted, an editor or editorial team makes decisions about the viability of a manuscript based on the content of reviews as well as their own decision-making. The authors of this text have experienced editors who were encouraging and realistic, honest, and inspiring. And, to be honest, we have also experienced the opposite. However, knowing that editors seek quality, as well as wanting scholars to experience success, is a helpful mindset.

Gaining Perspective on Mastering the Art of Revising and Resubmitting

The publication process is rarely personal; in most instances, as a double-blind process, reviewers approach the review process objectively. Reviewers follow the review guidelines of a publication and render a review that is typically impartial and professional. Reviewers have a service orientation to provide an unbiased, balanced review. Keeping this perspective in mind is useful as scholars receive reviews. Knowing that reviewers are asked to maintain a neutral and fair stance provides a sense of impartiality. Understanding that reviewers are fair-minded and maintaining this perspective is helpful when receiving reviews and accepting their content as evenhanded and unprejudiced.

Tools for Revision

A single way to approach a review and addressing review comments does not exist. As with goal setting, writing habits, and other writing skills, the art of revision is highly personal. No matter the process a writer choses to use, being thoughtful and systematically addressing all suggested edits is paramount. Addressing a review in a methodical manner assures that all comments will be addressed and communicates your seriousness in the revise and resubmit process. In a revise and resubmit decision, likely the same reviewers that initially read and responded to your manuscript will be tapped to read your resubmission. Hence, it is in a writer's best interest to efficiently respond to suggested edits in an organized manner.

Source: iStock

The Reconciliation Chart: Systematically Addressing Editors' and Reviewers' Concerns

The reconciliation chart emerged through experience and sharing with other scholars. It is a very simple tool that provides a minimal structure that allows an orderly, careful, and systematic way to address reviewers' comments. In the reconciliation chart, there is also space to record editor's comments. The remainder of the reconciliation chart is a simple two-column format where scholars can record reviewers' comments in the first (left) column and provide their response and address comments in the second (right) column in a disciplined, precise, and efficient way, as well as the page number where the revision is located. Reviewers and editors want to know how a writer or writers address edits, so the reconciliation chart can be used to indicate changes in response to a reviewer's or editor's suggestions. Because a scholar is reconciling differences, the terms reconciliation chart is appropriately named. Here is a blank reconciliation chart (Table 7.1). Feel free to add or delete sections if your publication outlet uses a different number of reviewers.

Table 7.1   Blank Reconciliation Chart

Editor's Comments

Reviewer 1's Comments	Author's Response (p. #)

Reviewer 2's Comments	Author's Response (p. #)

(Continued)

Reviewer 3's Comments	Author's Response (p. #)

Begin to build your reconciliation chart by reviewing and capturing what the editor has written. Then, systematically record each of the reviewers' comments *briefly* in the left column. Attempt to use succinct statements, extracted from the more voluminous comments provided by reviewers to capture the essence of the suggestions and critique, as concisely as possible. In the next example provided, a partially completed reconciliation chart is provided (Table 7.2). In this example, all editor and reviewer comments have been recorded. Interestingly, reviewer 1 exhibited a much more voluminous, comprehensive nature of comments while reviewer 2's comments are marked by brevity and a focus on mechanics. However, using the reconciliation chart provided a means of capturing the issues, concerns, and suggestions of each reviewer in an organized and systematic fashion.

Table 7.2 Partial Reconciliation Chart

Editor's Comments

Revise and resubmit; request that you revise and resubmit by 5.15.19

Reviewer 1's Comments	Author's Response (p. #)
...stated research question is, "who has access/opportunity to meaningfully engage with this critical curriculum and method and who is left out?" Inconsistent with the paragraph, "Following case study method	
Provide an explanation of what is meant by quintain or use different word	

(Continued)

Table 7.2 (Continued)

Reviewer 1's Comments	Author's Response (p. #)
p. 3, a quotation that is very clearly a book quoting the declaration of independence but then has a citation after it with no page number; odd structure—recommend reviewing it.	
p. 7, "Passage of the elementary and secondary...civic rights in education." This sentence could be improved with either an explanation of how or with a citation (preferably both).	
p. 7, word choice, "teacher education has encompassed service learning"—do you mean incorporated	
p. 7, "for two decades ... for urban teaching by..." This is the first time specifically urban teaching is referred to—is SL not a pedagogical pathway in other contexts (suburban/rural)?	
p. 8, "specifically, teacher...primacy of reciprocity within the curriculum"—reciprocity between who? Teacher/student? School/community? Student curriculum?	
Methods distracted by "quintain"	
Authors cite Stake, Yin, and Merriam. This is very common in educational research; authors should review "Three approaches to case study methods in education: Yin, Merriam, and Stake" by Yazan published in 2015.	
Not sure it is necessary to redact the names of schools; suggest a bare minimum of substituting with pseudonyms.	
Setting was well framed; lit review was about k-12 education—setting is three college/universities; add discussion in front half, about the relationship between k-12 policy and teacher prep (private universities which, outside of accrediting programs like teacher ed, have some additional buffer between them and state educational policy)	
Empirical materials: This is an unusual word choice; personal preference, and can be ignored by the authors.	
Electronic questionnaire: Who did this go to? What was its purpose? Would you have sent the same survey to teachers and counselors (in LA)? Is this the survey that wasn't used b/c IRB didn't allow it in the Maryland case? And I don't see it in the Wisconsin case either	

Reviewer 1's Comments	Author's Response (p. #)
Missing from the methods; would really prefer to see—positionality(ies) of the researcher and assurances of goodliness/trustworthiness	
Findings/Results Maryland-some tension that I do not feel like the author(s) address.	
First the quoted text of the law should probably be presented in a block quote. COMAR 13A.03.02.06 seems to require service which may or may not be service learning. Following evidence makes SL seem likely; not clear that the projects are service learning.	
This is again reflected on p. 13 in the paragraph about LSSs. I would like authors to acknowledge or address this. Because in the literature review they correctly point out that the curricular structural nature of SL is imperative for desired outcomes.	
p. 15—"post shift in accountability and standards" Is this a shift in state policy? Or a more general shift after NCLB? I can read it both ways. Some clarification would help.	
p. 16—"while these courses align with the social justice mission...they do not, necessarily, align to Maryland's outlined best practices" teachers are not prepared to implement the state's designated best practices (participating in a college class that employs best practices of service learning does not necessarily prepare teachers to use these best practices)- some argument could be made that teaching how to do the best practices without actually doing SL is possible (though there is probably a good justification that learning these practices through experiential education is a stronger pedagogical strategy).	
Drop the paragraph on p. 17 about how you developed an online survey but didn't use it. Why is this in the findings? Nothing was found.	
Settings described are universities. But then there are reviews of specific school districts plans. These certainly seem like settings for the research...	
splitting this into two manuscripts	
p. 19 "In summary...found discrepancies around access"—I believe this practically. But It now seems as if this is a case study	

(Continued)

Table 7.2 (Continued)

Reviewer 1's Comments	Author's Response (p. #)
within a case study (case study of districts within states). I think if the between county differences are so distinct, more time should be spent talking about the counties. Also how much heterogeneity are there within counties. If this is Baltimore city/Baltimore county that is a really unique and pronounced difference. But just something to think about	
How much do you really know about practice by comparing policy?	
p. 19—word choice—"leaving many at a loss...with pragmatics" Is pragmatics the right word?	
Louisiana section needs some clarity and more clear direction. I remind the authors their stated research question is, "who has access/opportunity to meaningfully engage with this critical curriculum and method and who is left out?" -this section not consistent with the three stated purposes on p. 4.	
It is not entirely clear to me the authors are differentiating between service learning and community service Be more specific about the policy language. If you're analyzing policy it's important that the reader understand the data. I the state policy is a community service endorsement, as suggested, and not a service learning endorsement, this has significant implications for the broader argument. If teachers aren't required to perform service learning then a failure to prepare teachers for this does not seem to me a problem of policy implementation (pp. 21–22). For example, the electronic questionnaire found that counselors did not receive training in pedagogy—which is notable, but if they are tracking community service this has nothing to do with policy, and certainly doesn't seem to relate to their actual jobs. p. 20, "Unfortunately, school counselors are also in charge..." Why is this unfortunate? p. 20, "While in policy...service efforts"—This sentence has three clauses, each of which is unclear to me; consider your meaning and rewrite this sentence. p. 21 be more clear about the questionnaire findings. Give specific information. Also, "significantly less than 50%" is confusing. Is this statistically significant? Why not just tell us the number? Why did you pick 50%? Also in this paragraph "preparation to implement policy was lacking"—what is your evidence? p. 21 "Louisiana does not hold its teacher or counselor preparation programs accountable for teaching the tenants..."—Why would they? There is not policy suggesting the teachers/counselors should be? This is not policy implementation in the classroom.	

Reviewer 1's Comments	Author's Response (p. #)
p. 22 "A counselor education graduate..." paragraph. I do not understand it's purpose. Nor do I understand why "promote social justice and advocacy is italicized.	
Wisconsin—consider what it means if there is not policy and how that shapes "policy implementation." Private college's mission can be connected to SL—relate to policy implementation. It is not policy of the state, WDPI, or the college to prepare k-12 teachers for service learning.	
Clarify "bifurcated system regarding teacher preparation and policy." Need a clear connection or explanation of what the bifurcation is	
Some sentences need attention and another round of proofreading needed	
Findings Disagree with the first paragraph; in Maryland there is some contradiction between policy and practice; policy in Louisiana is that there is zero policy for service learning, and therefore it is not a contradiction to have limited to no support for in-service teachers Where is the bifurcation. If districts have autonomy, don't you need to examine the districts themselves to see if practice matches policy	
Service and service learning are confounded again in this section	
"...differences within and across cases lead to unethical impacts for students and teachers" is lacking; where is evidence presented.	
"Perhaps worse...could be penalized or sanctions for policy requirements"—It doesn't really seem like there is evidence presented to support this.	

Reviewer 2's Comments	Author's Response (p. #)
Grammatical issues need attention.	
p. 3 ARISES should be ARISE.	

(Continued)

Table 7.2 (Continued)

Reviewer 2's Comments	Author's Response (p. #)
p. 3 Is EXPECTANCIES the correct word? Or EXPECTATIONS? Also is CONSTRASTIVE the correct adjective or CONTRASTING?	
Authors do intentionally use the word QUINTAIN throughout the paper. I am unfamiliar with this word...	

We took a significant amount of time to catalog and record *each* reviewer's suggestion for reviewers. We read through each comment and recorded it on the reconciliation chart. It took a concentrated effort and substantial time to construct. This was for a revise and resubmit, and we offer this as an example of the amount of effort and time it takes just to begin the revise and resubmit process. The reconciliation chart also illustrates the level of detail needed to sufficiently convey to reviewers and an editor how serious scholars are about addressing all suggestions. See the Exemplar at the end of this chapter for how we addressed each reviewer's comments and included page numbers where that edit occurred. A sample resubmission letter is also included.

Once the chart has been partially completed and all reviewers' comments have been recorded on the left side of the reconciliation chart, the real work of a revise and resubmit begins. Having comments from reviewers recorded in an orderly way allows a writer to address each comment systematically. Overall, be succinct and capture the essence of a reviewer's suggestion. As you consider each comment, remember you are the author and while a reviewer may suggest a revision, you can choose not to make the change. If you decide not to make a particular revision, respectfully, professionally, and clearly, indicate your reasoning on the reconciliation chart.

Also, as you are revisiting and revising your work, you may add new information that was not indicated by the reviewers. Be sure to add these changes to the reconciliation chart as this demonstrates to reviewers that you are committed to the quality of the work. You may consider dividing these tasks among co-authors, who, through discussion, are assigned to tackle different sections. As each comment is addressed, record what you actually did to address the comment in the second (right) column. Be sure to do a final review, as page numbers are likely to shift before the revision is ready to send back for review. Note that in a final reconciliation chart, as presented next, how each comment was addressed as well as the page number where the edit was located is listed.

Using the reconciliation chart as a tool for revision provides a structured way for scholars to address all suggested edits thoroughly and efficiently. From these two examples, it is clear that a great deal of revision was needed to address edits comprehensively and thoroughly. More importantly, the reconciliation chart conveys to editor and reviewer alike how serious a scholar is about attending to each suggestion, and by default, how much a scholar values the reviews themselves.

The Art of Disagreeing With a Reviewer in a Professional, Respectful Manner

Simply put, while reviewers' comments are intended to strengthen and improve a manuscript, and you will address a majority of them while revising, you may not always agree with a reviewer. That's perfectly acceptable. However, disagreeing respectfully is appropriate; frequently it is warranted. While the match between manuscript and reviewer usually works, at times, a mismatch occurs. Sometimes there is a philosophical clash, other times a reviewer lacks knowledge of some aspect of a manuscript. For instance, in the last example, both reviewers did not understand what was meant by the qualitative case study term of "quintain." We simply provided a definition that addressed reviewers' concern in a respectful professional way. In other instances, author and reviewer may just disagree. When that happens, use respectful language, such as *with all due respect, I disagree*, or *respectfully, I disagree*, and state why concisely. If you have evidence that supports why you should not make a particular edit, be sure to provide that evidence (e.g., a link to APA guidelines, a citation supporting your point). For example, "While we appreciate reviewer 1's perspective, we respectfully disagree with the suggested revision. We find the current phrasing corresponds with our sociocultural theoretical frame (Perry, 2012) and stance. The reviewers suggested change comes from a different, cognitive research tradition." Often, the issue really isn't just that you disagree, but at issue is also how you express yourself.

At times, two of the reviewers' suggestions may also directly contradict one another. When this happens, sometimes the editor will offer a suggestion on how to address the conflict. But, when this is not the case, you must follow a similar procedure to the one outlined above with one exception. Again, use respectful language, such as *while I appreciate this suggestion and careful read, I have chosen to use the suggestion offered by Reviewer X to address this issue*. If the editor does not comment on how to address the conflict, it is ok to add a footnote or directly email the editor regarding the contradiction and detail how you, as the author, have chosen to respond. Again, we provide examples of disagreeing professionally in the Exemplar.

Timeliness and Thoroughness

No matter what method is selected to address and attend to suggestions provided by reviewers, being comprehensive is important. In essence, you do not want to skip any suggested edits. Doing so may cause reviewers to doubt the sincerity of the resubmission. Being thorough is expected. In addition, providing the resubmission in a timely manner is equally important. Scholars send a strong message when they thoroughly address all edits suggested and do so in a timely manner. In addition, if the submission portal is electronic, missed deadlines will cause your submission to be identified as a new submission versus a revision, which may initiate a new set of reviewers who may have different views of your work.

Letter of Resubmission

In Chapter 6, invited contributor, Renée Casbergue, PhD, provided sample letters of submission. A resubmission letter is equally important. You want to inform the editor(s) that you have read reviews carefully and made every attempt to address each one. A brief but well-written letter of resubmission can send a strong message that you're a serious scholar. Further, this letter of resubmission will also be where you attach your reconciliation chart.

Every Manuscript Has a Home

Novice scholars require practice and finesse to accurately select a journal for potential publication. It takes significant time and effort to write a manuscript and to prepare a manuscript for submission. Revision and resubmission are also a time-consuming endeavor. Hopefully the contents of this chapter have demystified the process of receiving and responding to a review of a manuscript. However, nothing provides a guarantee of a positive decision. The more one writes, submits, and works through the process of becoming more productive, the higher the likelihood of acceptance. However, sometimes a manuscript is not considered for publication. This can occur at the first review, those conducted by editors who decide not to send a manuscript out for review. Other times, manuscripts are reviewed, but the decision is to not publish. Rejection happens to all writers.

Preparing for Rejection and Turning Around Rejected Manuscripts Quickly: Learning Lessons

If you received a desk rejection, an editor or editorial team decided your piece is not appropriate for the journal, it is natural to feel some sense of disappointment, dismay, and discouragement. On an emotional level, you may want to internalize your efforts and the rejection and subsequently experience a sense of dejection. A rejection is a rejection of a *work product*, not you as a scholar and writer. It is not an indictment of your ability or worth. Indulge in a bit of self-pity and then decide what your next steps will be and remember this is not personal—it's truly not about you, it's about your manuscript. And remember, *every* manuscript has a home. It is your job now to find it. So, take the time to review and catalog what the editor tells you and what the reviewers have provided. Be brutally honest with yourself, and self-reflect: Was your piece's topic a good fit for the journal? Was your review of literature timely and current? Was your piece in need of additional detail? Was your methods section clear, precise, and written in such a way that other researcher could emulate your study? And, did the results of your study significantly add to the field in which you operate as a scholar? Examining your reviews and editor's comment can help you think analytically about your rejection. Once you analyze reviews, you can think about next steps and what you will do with your manuscript.

Every writer has experienced rejection. Rejection can be discouraging, disappointing, and disheartening. Knowing rejection happens to all writers can provide a measure of encouragement and positivity. Mentally, scholars need to prepare for rejection and plan for *when*, not *if* it happens. For many, a rejection serves to make a scholar feel as if the process of publishing is daunting. As we have noted above, rejection is upsetting and unsettling. And while a rejection is not the desired outcome for any writer who submits a manuscript, it is important that scholars address a rejection expediently. This is especially true if you are building a publication record as a doctoral student or novice researcher. You may need to take some time and put some space between a rejection and eventual response. That is typical. However, you can, and should, always salvage a rejection in the shortest timeframe possible.

For example, when you are outright rejected, take some time, no more than a few days, to deal with your emotional reaction. You have put in a lot of work into this manuscript and will now need to redouble your efforts. Remember all authors experience rejection and writing improves through constant work on your craft. However, we encourage you to further reflect on two things after you naturally grieve the end of this submission process with this outlet. First, as you read the reviewers' and editor's comments, reflect on the rationales they give about the article. What suggestions do they give, what questions about the piece do they pose? We encourage you, within a few days, to begin to write reflective notes on the themes of the review that you believe you should address for a subsequent submission and begin to work through them in a systematic manner. Second, you should revisit the process of selecting a new publication outlet using the notes and information you have already culled. If a significant revision is suggested by reviewers, carefully decide if this revision is merited for the piece *in general* or a problem with "fit" *for that particular outlet.*

Leah Katherine, one of the authors of this text, upon outright rejection, strives to edit and "flip" a rejected manuscript to a new, more appropriate venue, within two weeks of the rejection. This means that the piece is getting back into review at a new possible home and more feedback can be solicited without haste. For her, productivity in publishing can mean addressing her emotions by a predetermined end point (two weeks) and moving forward, so that the lengthy process of peer review and publication is not stalled without ending. This strategy also allows Leah Kathrine to once again experience productivity as she takes that rejection, reworks the submission, and resubmits elsewhere. We implore you, do not let all your efforts fail to result in a publication. Follow the same process as outlined for a revise and resubmit, adhere to the new journal's guidelines and the reviewer's suggestions. Then, submit your revised manuscript to a different, perhaps more appropriate journal or publishing venue, in a timely manner. One final reminder, *every manuscript has a home*; finding the right door may require knocking on a couple.

Editing Manuscripts-Editorial Review Boards: Reviewing Increases Writing Skills

If you want to substantially accelerate you acquisition of skills and writing ability, consider reviewing for journals in your field. Reading others' writing and crafting review responses hones writing skills. Reviewing can also boost morale, especially if you compare your writing to others and gauge how you measure up to what you are reviewing. Reviewing allows you a glimpse into what is being submitted which can be a powerful motivator.

Begin this process by familiarizing yourself with the reviewer qualifications and the process for applying to be a reviewer. Craft a letter and update your CV. Apply to two of the journals you targeted. Many times, journal editors will ask the potential reviewer to review an article to determine the skill of the applicant. Only offer to review for manuscripts which solidly fall within your expertise. It is very important for the reviewer to educate herself on the journal aim, scope and audience, and the methodology, format, and publication guidelines for the journal. These vary from journal to journal and in order to be thorough, you must consider the journal when completing your review. While you are reviewing, you should consider the helpfulness of the comments you are providing and how they will contribute to the success of the writer—even if your recommendation is not positive. It is very easy to be critical and reject a manuscript; however, an editor will consider the quality of the review you have provided. The editor will also consider the timeliness of your review.

If you are selected as a reviewer or guest reviewer for a journal, you may be tempted to overextend yourself by agreeing too frequently to review a manuscript in an effort to increase your service or your skills as a writer. You must consider that it is not helpful to either the editor or the researcher who is waiting on your review to be so overextended that you are delinquent in turning in your review or that you are rushed and give a cursory, superficial review. Go for quality and timeliness over quantity.

Exercise 7.1 Creating a Reconciliation Chart

For this exercise, locate a piece of writing that has been reviewed and for which you were provided feedback and critique. It can be a proposal, a dissertation/thesis draft, or a manuscript—either a journal article or book chapter. If you have not yet submitted anything for publication, take a paper you received feedback on in a course. Take a blank reconciliation chart and complete it based on what suggested edits were given to you. Record the feedback in the first (left) column. Work through either a section or several pages, revising. As you revise, record how you addressed the suggested edits and on what page these edits appear. Record this in the second column (right). Practice drafting a letter to the editor explaining your revisions.

Exemplars

Completed Reconciliation Chart

Reviewer 1's Comments	Author's Response (p. #)
… stated research question is, "who has access/opportunity to meaningfully engage with this critical curriculum and method and who is left out?" Inconsistent with the paragraph, "Following case study method	p. 4; clarified connection
An explanation of what is meant by quintain or use different word	pp. 4–5; explained in abstract as well as methods section; added citation of Barela 2007 as further explanation
p. 3, a quotation that is very clearly a book quoting the declaration of independence but then has a citation after it with no page number; odd structure—recommend reviewing it.	p. 3; revised for clarity better placement of citation; italicized Declaration language as indicative of reified knowledge

(Continued)

(Continued)

Reviewer 1's Comments	Author's Response (p. #)
p. 7, "Passage of the elementary and secondary...civic rights in education." This sentence could be improved with either an explanation of how or with a citation (preferably both).	p. 8; reworded, added law citations
p. 7, word choice, "teacher education has encompassed service learning"—do you mean incorporated	p. 7; here, encompass means included, which is our intent in using this term
p. 7, "for two decades ... for urban teaching by..." This is the first time specifically urban teaching is referred to—is SL not a pedagogical pathway in other contexts (suburban/rural)?	p. 8; reworded for clarity regrading urban; we refer to studies that expand cultural horizons and address the context of PK-12 urban public schools in the US. In the Skinner and Chapman (1999) piece, only school size is mentioned; we cannot infer school configuration of the 1832 respondents to Skinner and Chapman (1999).
p. 8, "specifically, teacher...primacy of reciprocity within the curriculum"—reciprocity between who? Teacher/student? School/community? Student curriculum?	p. 9; clarified
Methods distracted by "quintain"	p. 5; qualified in abstract and methods section
Authors cite Stake, Yin, and Merriam. This is very common in educational research; authors should review "Three approaches to case study methods in education: Yin, Merriam, and Stake" by Yazan published in 2015.	pp. 4–5; removed Merriam; cite Stake (2005, 2006, 2010, 2013) and Yin (2009) exclusively in regard to both researchers' work with cross-case analysis; revised to reflect; added Stake, R. (2013). *Multiple case study analysis.* Guilford Press.

Reviewer 1's Comments	Author's Response (p. #)
Not sure it is necessary to redact the names of schools; suggest a bare minimum of substituting with pseudonyms	p. 17; addressed course numbers redacted for further review; we redacted institutions as per IRB requirements and common practice
Setting was well framed; lit review was about k-12 education—setting is three college/universities; add discussion in front half, about the relationship between k-12 policy and teacher prep (private universities which, outside of accrediting programs like teacher ed, have some additional buffer between them and state educational policy).	p. 11; we specifically state "and institutions." However, based on R1, we added a clarifying sentence regarding the relationship between PK-12 policy and teacher prep.
Empirical materials: This is an unusual word choice; personal preference, and can be ignored by the authors.	We elected to use empirical materials as per Denzin & Lincoln, 2011.
Electronic questionnaire: Who did this go to? What was its purpose? Would you have sent the same survey to teachers and counselors (in LA)? Is this the survey that wasn't used b/c IRB didn't allow it in the Maryland case? And I don't see it in the Wisconsin case either.	Removed from the manuscript for clarity and conciseness.
Missing from the methods; would really prefer to see—positionality(ies) of the researcher and assurances of goodliness/trustworthiness.	p. 11; added positionality in phrase "as teacher education, educational administration, and service-learning researchers"; also stated on p. 32. p. 12; clarified that each of the institutions seek, maintain, and are accredited for pre-service teacher preparation by their respective state; clarified Louisiana case.
Findings/Results Maryland-some tension that I do not feel like the author(s) address.	Added further clarification on pp. 14 and 15 on both how the service-learning law is

(Continued)

(Continued)

Reviewer 1's Comments	Author's Response (p. #)
First the quoted text of the law should probably be presented in a block quote. COMAR 13A.03.02.06 seems to require service which may or may not be service learning. Following evidence makes SL seem likely; not clear that the projects are service learning. This is again reflected on p. 13 in the paragraph about LSSs. I would like authors to acknowledge or address this. Because in the literature review they correctly point out that the curricular structural nature of SL is imperative for desired outcomes.	interpreted, and the corresponding accountability structures and requirements outlined by the Maryland State Department of Education (MSDE) which further clarify what "counts" as service-learning in the state. p. 14, reformatted law to block quote. Clarified on p. 15 (where the curricular focus is #2 of the 7 required best practices for service-learning). Also, clarified that MSDE requires LSSs to include submit SL specific plans every four years.
p. 15; "post shift in accountability and standards" Is this a shift in state policy? Or a more general shift after NCLB? I can read it both ways. Some clarification would help.	p. 16; clarified post shift in accountability as NCLB & ESSA.
p. 16—"while these courses align with the social justice mission...they do not, necessarily, align to Maryland's outlined best practices" teachers are not prepared to implement the state's designated best practices (participating in a college class that employs best practices of service learning does not necessarily prepare teachers to use these best practices)— some argument could be made that teaching how to do the best practices without actually doing SL is possible (though there is probably a good justification that learning these practices through experiential education is a stronger pedagogical strategy).	The reviewer is correct regarding the teaching of best practices and/or the importance of experiential education using SL. However, neither the teaching of SL best practices nor experiential education using SL are required for teacher education programs and curricula by the MSDE. Clarified on pp. 17 and 18.

Reviewer 1's Comments	Author's Response (p. #)
Drop the paragraph on p. 17 about how you developed an online survey but didn't use it. Why is this in the findings? Nothing was found.	Deleted per reviewer's recommendation.
Settings described are universities. But then there are reviews of specific school districts plans. These certainly seem like settings for the research...	We clarified to include respective school districts in the settings.
Splitting this into two manuscripts.	Thank you, but with all due respect, we perceive this as one manuscript.
p. 19 "In summary...found discrepancies around access"—I believe this practically. But It now seems as if this is a case study within a case study (case study of districts within states). I think if the between county differences are so distinct, more time should be spent talking about the counties. Also, how much heterogeneity are there within counties. If this is Baltimore city/ Baltimore county that is a really unique and pronounced difference. But just something to think about.	Really appreciate the reviewer's comment as it clarified our thinking. We clarified the selection of the two border districts as both a large percentage of total MD student population and representative of the larger concerns with heterogeneity around SES in the state.
How much do you really know about practice by comparing policy?	When there is no funding or professional support for practices which are dictated by policy (see Table 1), the researchers deduce that SL practice is limited in these settings. Clarified on p. 19.
p. 19—word choice—"leaving many at a loss...with pragmatics" Is pragmatics the right word?	Clarified sentence and deleted pragmatics.
Louisiana section needs some clarity and more clear direction. I remind the authors their stated research question	pp. 21–22; in **Louisiana's policies for service-learning or community engagement in the**

(Continued)

(Continued)

Reviewer 1's Comments	Author's Response (p. #)
is, "who has access/opportunity to meaningfully engage with this critical curriculum and method and who is left out?" -this section not consistent with the three stated purposes on p. 4.	**K-12 setting subheading,** this is somewhat explained; however, we further clarified.
It is not entirely clear to me the authors are differentiating between service learning and community service	pp. 21–22; clarified differentiation
Be more specific about the policy language. If you're analyzing policy it's important that the reader understand the data. I the state policy is a community service endorsement, as suggested, and not a service learning endorsement, this has significant implications for the broader argument.	p. 22; clarified p. 23; clarified through expanded discussion p. 21; clarified why it is unfortunate through expanded discussion; reworded awkward sentence construction
If teachers aren't required to perform service learning then a failure to prepare teachers for this does not seem to me a problem of policy implementation (pp. 21–22).	p. 23; clarified through expanded discussion of statistical significance; added evidence
For example, the electronic questionnaire found that counselors did not receive training in pedagogy—which is notable, but if they are tracking community service this has nothing to do with policy, and certainly doesn't seem to relate to their actual jobs.	p. 24; referred back to Act 295 and discussed the interconnectedness of teaching and counseling as they pertain to student growth and development p. 24; this refers to preceding paragraph about the institution's existing program in school counseling; removed italics
p. 20 "Unfortunately, school counselors are also incharge..." Why is this unfortunate? p. 20 "While in policy...service efforts"—This sentence has three clauses, each of which is unclear to me; consider your meaning and rewrite this sentence.	
p. 21 be more clear about the questionnaire findings. Give specific information. Also, "significantly less than 50%" is confusing. Is this statistically significant? Why not just tell us the number? Why did you pick 50%? Also in this paragraph	

Reviewer 1's Comments	Author's Response (p. #)
"preparation to implement policy was lacking"—what is your evidence? p. 21 "Louisiana does not hold its teacher or counselor preparation programs accountable for teaching the tenants..."—Why would they? There is not policy suggesting the teachers/counselors should be? This is not policy implementation in the classroom. p. 22 "A counselor education graduate..." paragraph. I do not understand it's purpose. Nor do I understand why "promote social justice and advocacy is italicized.	
Wisconsin—consider what it means if there is not policy and how that shapes "policy implementation." Private college's mission can be connected to SL—relate to policy implementation. It is not policy of the state, WDPI, or the college to prepare k-12 teachers for service learning.	p. 30; the lack of policy is addressed, the need for preparation is also discussed.
Clarify "bifurcated system regarding teacher preparation and policy." need a clear connection or explanation of what the bifurcation is.	p. 31; addressed as neither due to lack of policy
Some sentences that need attention and another round of proofreading needed.	pp. 29–31 proofed for clarity and flow.
Findings Disagree with the first paragraph; in Maryland there is some contradiction between policy and practice; policy in Louisiana is that there is zero policy for service learning, and therefore it is not a contradiction to have limited to no support for in-service teachers Where is the bifurcation. If districts have autonomy, don't you need to	p. 31; with all due respect, we disagree; absent a full expansion of what constitutes Community Service Diploma Endorsement, authorized by Louisiana Act 295, he finding was that such a policy existed yet was misunderstood... the focus was counselors p. 31; added clarity to the role

(Continued)

(Continued)

Reviewer 1's Comments	Author's Response (p. #)
examine the districts themselves to see if practice matches policy	of teacher prep and lack of bifurcation
Service and service learning are confounded again in this section	p. 31; we respectfully draw attention to: "For all three cases/states, pre-service training for implementing service-learning or civic engagement in the K-12 setting was not included as a required condition for certification or program accreditation for teacher/counselor/school personnel preparation.
"...differences within and across cases lead to unethical impacts for students and teachers" is lacking; where is evidence presented.	p. 31; added clarity and further explanation
"Perhaps worse...could be penalized or sanctions for policy requirements"—It doesn't really seem like there is evidence presented to support this.	p. 32; added clarity for our discussion as well as an addition citation: Schneider (2016)
Reviewer 2's Comments	Author's Response (p. #)
Grammatical issues need attention.	Addressed throughout; addressed issues and each author read for grammar, usage, and reviewed references as well
p. 3 ARISES should be ARISE.	p. 3, Addressed, used arise
p. 3 Is EXPECTANCIES the correct word? Or EXPECTATIONS? Also is CONSTRASTIVE the correct adjective or CONTRASTING?	p. 3, Addressed, used contrasting
Authors do intentionally use the word QUINTAIN throughout the paper. I am unfamiliar with this word...	pp. 4–5, Stake developed the notion of quintain, which we clarified; added Stake (2013) and Barela (2017) as means of clarification

Sample Revision Letter to Editor

Re: "Preschool Teachers' Perceptions of Rough and Tumble Play vs. Aggression in Preschool-Aged Boys" **#(manuscript number)**

Dear Dr. XXXXX,

We are submitting a revised copy of the above-numbered manuscript for consideration in *Child and Youth Care Forum*. In this substantial revision, we have addressed issues raised in your review letter and by reviewers (see attached reconciliation chart) by clarifying the behavior definition (p. 7), rewording the research question/hypothesis (p. 4), clarifying the dependent variable (p. 8), adding additional information on the ICCs, and reporting bivariate correlations.

We greatly appreciate the thoroughness in the review process and feel we have a much improved report of research as a result.

Sincerely,

Author 1, Ph.D.
Associate Professor
State University

cc: Author 2
      Author 3
      Author 4

SUMMARY

This chapter included detailed information of how to address acceptance and rejection when submitting manuscripts for publication. A structured, systematic method for addressing requested revisions was presented. Reviewing was also discussed as a method for improving writing and gaining a better understanding of the submission process. In the next chapter, the science of publication metrics is delineated.

KEY TERMS

Double-Blind Process A double-blind process is one in which neither the writer who submits a manuscript nor the reviewer who assess the manuscript know of one another's identity. The double-blind process is utilized to prevent bias in reviewing.

In Press In press, publications are defined as manuscripts that have been submitted for review, accepted through the review process, and scheduled for publication. Most institutions encourage scholars to add such publications to their CVs as indications of productivity.

Peer Review Process In the peer review process, evaluation of a submitted manuscript is conducted by individuals with similar interests and content or topic proficiencies as the authors of the work (peers). In some instances, methods are a reason for a peer to review a submitted manuscript.

CRITICAL THINKING QUESTIONS

1. What methods might work best for you as a means of revising and resubmitting a manuscript?

2. What might be your first steps when revising a manuscript for revision and resubmission?

3. What potential journals might be good choices?

ADDITIONAL REFERENCES AND RESOURCES

https://authorservices.taylorandfrancis.com/journal-suggester/.

https://writingcenter.gmu.edu/guides/reverse-outlining.

Goldberg, N. (2010). *Writing down the bones*. Boston, MA: Shambhala.

Goodson, P. (2016). *Becoming an academic writer: 50 exercises for paced, productive, and powerful writing*. Thousand Oaks, CA: SAGE.

Hacker, D., & Sommers, N. (2011) *Rules for writers*. Boston, MA: Bedford/St. Martin's.

Noll, E., & Fox, D. (2003). Supporting beginning writers of research: Mentoring graduate students' entry into academic discourse communities. In C. Fairbanks, J. Worthy, B. Maloch, J. V. Hoffman, & D. L. Schallert (Eds.), *Fifty-second yearbook of the national reading conference* (pp. 332–344). Oak Creek, WI: National Reading Conference.

Richards, J. (2014). Academic writing to publication: Some points of departure for success. *Journal of Reading Education*, 39(3), 45–47.

Sunstein, B., & Chiseri-Strater, E. (2006). *FieldWorking: Reading and writing research*. Boston, MA: Bedford/St. Martin's.

Turner, J., & Edwards, P. (2006). When it's more than you, Jesus, and the pencil: Reflections on an academic writing mentorship. *Journal of Adult & Adolescent Literacy*, 50(3), 172–178.

Beyond Impact Factor

Understanding Scholarly Metrics and Increasing Exposure (Invited Submission, Andrea Hebert & David Dunaway)

In the last decade, citation metrics as a measurement of research impact have emerged as a major consideration when deciding where to publish. This chapter explores how research impact is measured, and how research impact and research exposure are intertwined. Therefore, this chapter will introduce some of the most common metrics used to measure academic output and discuss ways to increase the visibility of one's research.

Learning Objectives

There are several learning objectives for this chapter. They are:

1. Understand how citation metrics are used to measure research impact

2. Identify the most common citation metrics used to measure research impact

3. Explain the limitations of the most common citation metrics

4. Calculate simple author-level metrics

5. Identify some of the alternative measures of research impact and quality and describe when these alternative measures are used

6. Formulate a plan to increase the visibility of research

Understanding Scholarly Citation Metrics

You may be wondering why a chapter about citation metrics has been included in a book about academic writing, productivity, and publishing. Publishing is not just an expectation but a requirement for most faculty at research institutions, regional institutions, and liberal arts institutions. However, simply publishing is not enough to guarantee positive evaluations or promotion and tenure. The trend of rating and ranking universities has trickled down to rating university departments and individuals. Many universities use various quantitative measurements, called **metrics**, to gauge university, department, and faculty research productivity, and departments often use metrics to evaluate faculty for tenure and promotion.

Academics need to know why they are measured, the different ways they may be measured, what those measurements are, how they are calculated, and what they mean. They need to understand the limitations of the measurements and the potentially problematic ways metrics can be used. Faculty, especially junior faculty, may have little voice in how they are evaluated, but understanding the metrics used for these measurements can help faculty navigate the system strategically. For better or worse, metrics may also influence what academics write about and where they choose to submit their work, especially before earning tenure or promotion. Understanding the basics of how scholarship is measured empowers new graduate students, novice researchers, and new scholars to make informed decisions about publication venues and methods of distribution.

Institutions and departments have different standards and requirements for evaluation inclusive or exclusive of attaining promotion and tenure, and researchers must work within the confines of their department's bylaws and faculty handbooks. However, if the metrics used by an institution or department for promotion and tenure evaluations do not accurately reflect a researcher's impact, the researcher should be able to voice the reasons why the required metrics are not capturing their impact and should be able to offer alternative measurements and argue for their validity (Chapter 10 presents information regarding tenure in depth).

Some departments rely heavily on bibliometric measures. **Bibliometrics** is a field of study devoted to quantitative measurement of scholarly output and impact. It is not necessary to understand all bibliometric measurements [there are at least 108 author-level indicators alone (Wildgaard, Schneider, & Larsen, 2014)], but academics do need a basic understanding of how the most common metrics are calculated, what they mean, and how they are used. While most academics complete graduate school with a basic concept of **Journal Impact Factor** (JIF), they may be unfamiliar with some of the more granular metrics. We will focus on the three levels of metrics that are most used to evaluate faculty work: article, journal, and author-level metrics (see Table 8.1).

All these metrics have weaknesses, but despite shortcomings, they are used because they are impartial and save evaluators from reading and evaluating every piece of writing produced by a faculty member. Although the measurements are impartial, an evaluator with an imperfect understanding of metrics can misinterpret what the metrics indicate. There are different citation rates across disciplines, which can lead to unfair comparisons for article, journal, and author metrics. Some measurements try to normalize these differences, but these measurements are usually lesser known and are used infrequently. Citation metrics cannot measure the quality of scholarship and imperfectly measure the impact of scholarship. For example, without looking at a citation in context, it is impossible to judge whether the article is being cited in an argument contradicting its content or in an article of poor quality. In addition, citation counts do not measure the influence of an article on those who read the article but do not produce research themselves. In other words, a **citation count** cannot reflect an article's impact on practice.

Table 8.1 Key Metrics

Article-Level Metrics

citation count—number of citations an article receives

Journal-Level Metrics

JIF—number of citations to a journal for a given year divided by the number of citable items published in that journal for the prior two years

$h5$-index—the largest number h such that at least h articles in the last five years of that publication were cited at least h times each

SJR—the average number of weighted citations received in the selected year by the documents published in the selected journal in the three previous years

SNIP—the number of citations given in the present year to publications in the past three years divided by the total number of publications in the past three years

Author-Level Metrics

h-index—the number of papers (h) that have accumulated at least h number of citations

$i10$-index—the number of articles an author has published with at least 10 citations

Citation count—total number of citations an author receives for all articles published

Source: Andrea Hebert and David Dunaway

Despite these shortcomings, metrics will continue to be used as a measurement of scholarly productivity and impact. Each institution and department will have different evaluation guidelines, and many of these guidelines will specify the metrics which will be used in summative (retention, promotion, or tenure) decisions. Therefore, scholars need to know how to retrieve and interpret the relevant citation metrics to navigate the system effectively.

Article-Level Metrics

Article-level metrics attempt to document the impact of a single article. The most basic metric is a citation count, usually from Web of Science, Scopus, or Google Scholar. This is a simple metric, but a foundational component for journal-, author-, and even institutional-level metrics. Citation counts will vary across databases. Web of Science includes citations from journals, books, and conference proceedings, whereas Scopus includes these as well as patents. Google Scholar citation counts tend to be higher because Google Scholar often has multiple versions of the same article and includes some sources not included in Web of Science and Scopus, such as theses and dissertations.

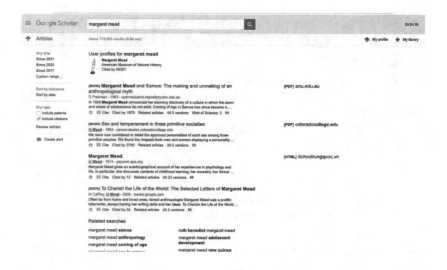

There is usually a lag time between the publication of an article and the peak of its popularity; as a result, most new articles have very few citations. This lag time can affect the author-level metrics of early career researchers. Unless an article quickly becomes a seminal work in a field, the frequency of new citations usually tapers off after a few years, although there are rare "sleeping beauty" articles. These sleeping beauties are articles which receive little recognition at the time of publication but after an extended period begin to receive more attention and a higher citation rate.

Journal-Level Metrics

Journal-level metrics are used to gauge the quality of a journal in which faculty are publishing. The JIF is the most commonly known journal-level metric, but there are other measurements of journal impact, with each measurement generating its own journal rankings.

Garfield and Sher created the JIF to guide the selection of journals to include in the Science Citation Index (SCI) (Garfield, 1999). Garfield (1972) also perceived the JIF as a tool for libraries to use to make collection development decisions and to help authors decide where to submit articles. The JIF is the number of citations to a journal for a given year divided by the number of citable items published in that journal for the prior two years:

$$JIF = \frac{\text{Number of citations to a journal in 2021 for articles published in 2019 and 2020}}{\text{Number of citable items published in 2019 and 2020}}$$

Although Garfield (1972) created the JIF, he acknowledged the measurement's potential shortcomings even before the use of the JIF to create Journal Citation Reports in 1975, including the potential underrepresentation of non-English language journals, the "inordinate influence" a very highly cited article can have on a journal's ranking, and an inaccurate representation of the impact of a journal which publishes few articles even though those articles are highly cited (p. 473). He continued to point out what he considered to be inappropriate uses for years, including using a journal's JIF to compare authors and to measure article impact instead of using an actual citation count for the article (Garfield, 1999).

While JIF is one of the most popular journal metrics, Scopus and Google Scholar both have journal rankings that are widely used. Google Scholar uses the *h*5-index that measures a journal's impact based on the most recent five complete years of articles. "It is the largest number *h* such that at least *h* articles in that publication were cited at least *h* times each" (Google Scholar, n.d.). For example, if a publication has an *h*5-index of 38, 38 of the articles published in the last five years have been cited at least 38 times.

Scimago uses data from Scopus, an abstract and citation database by Elsevier, to rank journals by their Scimago Journal Rank (SJR) indicators and bases its score on three years' worth of data as opposed to JIF which uses two. SJR "is the average number of weighted citations received in the selected year by the documents published in the selected journal in the three previous years" (Scimago, n.d.). Weight is determined by journal prestige. For a full explanation of how Scimago calculates the SJR, including how it determines prestige and factors prestige into its calculation, see the Scimago Research Group's "Description of Scimago Journal Rank Indicator" in the *Additional Readings and References* section.

The Centre for Science and Technology Studies calculates a **SNIP** (source normalized impact per paper) measurement which makes it easier to compare citation impact between different fields of study by normalizing citations to correct for different fields of study's citation practices. Like SJR, SNIP is calculated using three years of citations from Scopus. It is "the number of citations given in the present year to publications in the past three years divided by the total number of publications in the past three years" (Centre for Science and Technology Studies, 2019). You can learn more about how the citations are normalized in the SNIP calculation by reading the Waltman, van Eck, van Leeuwen, and Visser (2013) article in the *Additional Readings and References* section.

Some institutions require faculty to publish in journals with high impact factors for evaluation (including tenure and promotion), and some must indicate the impact factor of the journal in which their article has been published for evaluation purposes. This is seen as one of the most common misuses of the impact factor because the journal impact factor does not measure the impact of an individual article and does not judge the quality of an individual article (Alstete, Beutell, & Meyer, 2018, p. xiii; Gingras, 2016). The first recommendation of the influential *Declaration on Research Assessment* called for the end of using journal-based metrics to measure a researcher's contributions or "in hiring, promotion, or funding decisions" (American Society for Cell Biology, 2012).

Author-Level Metrics

Author-level metrics attempt to measure the productivity and influence of an author. The most common author measurement is the Hirsch index (*h*-index). The *h*-index was developed by J. E. Hirsch, a physicist at the University of

California, San Diego. The *h*-index is defined as the number of papers (*h*) that have accumulated at least *h* number of citations. It can best be understood by seeing a calculation (see Example 8.1).

Example 8.1 *h*-index

List publications in descending order of citation count (i.e., the most frequently cited to the least frequently cited). The point at which the number of citations falls below the article number is the *h*-index. In this example, article 7 received more than 7 citations, whereas article 8 received fewer than 8 citations; therefore, the *h*-index is 7.

Publication	Times Cited
Publication 1	75
Publication 2	52
Publication 3	29
Publication 4	17
Publication 5	11
Publication 6	9
Publication 7	9
Publication 8	4
Publication 9	3
Publication 10	1

Activity 8.1

List your (or your major professor's) publications from most to least cited. Using the example above, calculate the *h*-index. Use a different database to

identify the citation rate for each publication and recalculate, noting how the
h-index changes.

Web of Science, Scopus, and Google Scholar will generate an author's h-index
based on the articles contained in their respective databases; as a result, an author
may have a different h-index from each database. An author's h-index can never be
higher than the number of papers published by the author. This can put early-
career researchers at a disadvantage. If two authors have each published an equal
number of papers, but the overall citation count for one is significantly higher, it is
possible for both authors to have the same h-index; in fact, the author with a lower
citation count could possibly have a higher h-index (see Example 8.2).

Example 8.2

In this example, Author A's h-index would be 6, whereas Author B's h-index
would be 7. Even though Author A accumulated 336 citations and Author B
accumulated only 80, the h-index would indicate that Author B's research
impact is higher than Author A's. Viewing an author's h-index out of context can
be deceptive.

Publications	Author A	Author B
Publication 1	80	19
Publication 2	72	13
Publication 3	60	12
Publication 4	51	11
Publication 5	44	8
Publication 6	**20**	7
Publication 7	5	**7**
Publication 8	2	1
Publication 9	1	1
Publication 10	1	0

Chronicle the publication history of two of your favorite researchers. List each researcher's publications from most to least cited work. Calculate each researcher's h-index and compare to their overall citation rate. Do you feel this index accurately captures these researchers' impact on your field?

In addition to calculating an author's h-index, Google Scholar uses the i10-index, which is the number of articles with at least ten citations. For example, if an author has seven articles with at least ten citations each, the author's i10-index would be 7. Once again, this puts authors with articles that have accumulated high numbers of citations at a disadvantage. Author A could have seven articles that each have ten citations, meaning that Author A's i10-index is 7, but if Author B has seven articles and all of them have more than 20 citations, Author B also has an i10-index of 7 despite having more than twice as many citations as Author A.

Egghe (2006) created a lesser known (and not as widely used) metric that tries to correct for this—the g-index. In short, the g-index gives more weight to more highly cited articles. After placing an author's publications in decreasing order of citations, the g-index "is the (unique) largest number such that the top g articles received (together) at least g^2 citations" (Egghe, 2006, p. 131). As in the case of the h-index, the g-index is best understood by seeing a calculation (see Example 8.3).

Example 8.3

Let's take a second look at Author A (with a total of 336 citations and an h-index of 6) and Author B (with a total of 80 citations and an h-index of 7). Author A would have a g-index of 10, and Author B would have a g-index of 8. How is this calculated? Once again, this is easiest to understand when viewed as a table. Start by listing the publications by the number of citations, from highest to lowest. When the articles are ranked in decreasing order of citations, the g-index is the largest number such that the top g articles received a total of at least g^2 citations.

Calculations for Author A			
Publication Number (g)	Number of Citations	Square of g (g^2)	Total Number of Citations
Publication 1	80	1	80
Publication 2	72	4	80 + 72 = 152
Publication 3	60	9	152 + 60 = 212
Publication 4	51	16	212 + 51 = 263
Publication 5	44	25	263 + 44 = 307
Publication 6	20	36	307 + 20 = 327
Publication 7	5	49	327 + 5 = 332
Publication 8	2	64	332 + 2 = 334
Publication 9	1	81	334 + 1 = 335
Publication 10	1	100	335 + 1 = 336

The total number of citations earned by Author A's top 10 publications is greater than 10^2, therefore Author A's g-index is 10.

Calculations for Author B			
	Citation Count	Square of g (g^2)	Total Citation Count
Publication 1	19	1	19
Publication 2	13	4	19 + 13 = 32
Publication 3	12	9	32 + 12 = 44
Publication 4	11	16	44 + 11 = 55
Publication 5	8	25	55 + 8 = 63
Publication 6	7	36	63 + 7 = 70
Publication 7	7	49	70 + 7 = 77

(Continued)

(Continued)

Calculations for Author B			
	Citation Count	Square of g (g^2)	Total Citation Count
Publication 8	1	64	$77 + 1 = 78$
Publication 9	1	81	$78 + 1 = 79$
Publication 10	0	100	79

The total number of citations earned by Author B's top eight publications is greater than 8^2, therefore Author B's g-index is 8. Author B's index cannot be higher because publication 9 only received 79 citations, which is less than 9^2.

Activity 8.3

Using the same two researchers from Example 2, calculate the g-index. This provides additional insight.

Key Points

As a graduate student or novice researcher, the onus to determine what is considered acceptable at your institution or desired institution is a writer's responsibility. As stated, how metrics are considered fluctuates across institutions, even if they are within a similar category, and the metrics used vary from institution to institution. Knowing how metrics are applied is important information as writers make decisions about where to publish. The following three key points should guide your publishing decisions:

- There are multiple measures of research productivity and impact at the article, journal, and author level.

- Citation rates vary across fields and disciplines.

- Check with your unit, college, and institution's specifications.

Other Measurements of Scholarly Impact

There are alternative ways to measure the impact of scholarship outside the confines of traditional citation metrics. These alternatives try to address the limitations of citation metrics, including **noncitation impact**, meaning research that may be read and which may influence practice but which may not produce citations from other researchers, and the impact of scholarship in fields of study that rely heavily on monograph publishing. These measurements, sometimes referred to as "fuzzy" metrics (Roemer & Borchardt, 2015), do not rely on citation metrics and can include acceptance rates, library holdings, and subscription data.

Acceptance Rates

Some departments, units, and colleges rely on the acceptance rate of journals as a measure of journal quality. Journal acceptance rates can be difficult to find and are sometimes unavailable; however, even when acceptance rates are available, they are often self-reported without an explanation of the methodology used for calculating the acceptance rate. Concerns exist over how some journals calculate their acceptance rates as well as concerns that the rate may not accurately reflect the quality of the journal, and at least one publishing company representative advised against using acceptance rates for research evaluation (Alstete et al., 2018). The acceptance rate of a journal can vary from year to year depending on the number of submissions received. And, some journals consider subsequent revisions as part of their total count, either as a rejection or acceptance.

If you need to find the acceptance rate of a journal, you can look for this information in several places. Some journals report acceptance rates on their websites. Acceptance rates for some journals can be found in Cabell's Directories. (Cabell's Directories is a proprietary database; contact your institution's library to find out if it has a subscription.) Journals published by the American Psychological Association (APA) report annual acceptance rates along with the methodology for determining acceptance rates. As a last resort, authors can contact the journal editor directly, but the accuracy of the acceptance rate will depend on the accuracy of the editor's records.

Library Holdings

Library holdings for monographs can be gathered through WorldCat (https://www.worldcat.org/). WorldCat allows you to search the catalog holdings of thousands of libraries from around the world. WorldCat will give a fairly complete listing of the number of libraries that own a monograph as well as identifying the libraries that own it. Library holdings do not reflect book usage, but Roemer and Borchardt (2015) make the case that library holdings can "provide an important backdrop of discovering qualitative measures, such as *which* libraries own your publication" (p. 43). In other words, if high-profile research libraries have added a monograph to their collections, that information can indicate the potential impact of the monograph's scholarship.

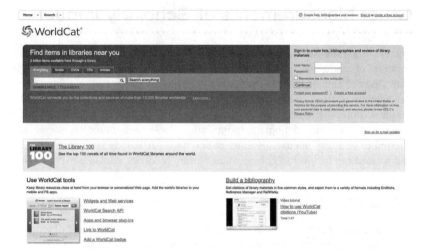

Subscription Data

If a journal lacks a JIF, SJR/SNIP, and acceptance rate, a researcher may want to consider subscription data about the journal. In theory, these data can indicate the size of a journal's audience by including both the number of libraries with journal subscriptions as well as the number of individual subscribers (Roemer & Borchardt, 2015). This is one of the more unreliable/unconvincing of the fuzzy metrics. Shrinking library budgets often mean that even prominent journals are dropped in lean budget years, and many libraries rely on interlibrary loan and document delivery to make up for gaps in their collection.

Altmetrics

Altmetrics attempt to measure the immediate, nonscholarly impact of research. Altmetrics acknowledge the changing landscape of how academic information is shared and used by capturing information about the number of article and chapter downloads and views, tweets, news mentions, likes, shares, mentions in blogs, etc. Altmetrics can give a snapshot of the reception of newer articles that have not had time to generate citations in other scholarly articles and may be able to predict the future scholarly impact. Early career researchers can use altmetrics to address the lag time it takes for articles to generate citations. Some databases now include tools that display altmetrics, such as Altmetric (https://www.altmetric.com) and PlumX Metrics (https://plumanalytics.com). Even if an institution does not include these tools in their databases, it is possible to download an Altmetric plugin to see the Altmetric data for any article with a **Digital Object Identifier** (DOI).

As a newly minted PhD or novice researcher, determine what is acceptable in your unit, department, college, or institution; this information assists writers in making decisions about where to publish. The following two key points can guide your publishing decisions.

Key Points
• •

- Some departments use alternatives to citation metrics to measure research impact and quality.

- Altmetrics attempt to measure the immediate, nonscholarly impact of research.

Increasing Exposure
• •

Many publishers offer suggestions on increasing the visibility of their publications; following a publisher's suggestions is an effective way to increase the visibility of your work. Remember, the metrics used to measure the influence of a journal are based on the number of citations its articles receive. So, journal publishers are invested in the success of the articles they publish. The following sections incorporate some of these suggestions and go into additional details. You should begin incorporating ways to maximize the exposure that your article will receive during the writing and submission stage and follow through with additional attention after publication. Keep in mind that increased exposure and impact are not always reflected by citation metrics, but without visibility, scholarship has little chance to make any impact.

Selecting a Publication Venue

When selecting a journal in which to publish, make sure the journal is indexed in a database that researchers in your field use. Journals often include information about indexing on their sites. If this information is not present on the journal's site, EBSCO's Serials Directory and UlrichsWeb Global Serials Directory list this information for most journals. These are proprietary databases; you may need to contact your institution's library to find out if you have access to them.

Consider publishing in an open access journal. Open access articles are more freely available than those behind paywalls, and some studies suggest that articles published in open access journals are more highly cited than articles published in traditional journals. Funding for publication in open access journals can be written into grants, and some institutions offer financial support to authors who chose to publish in open access venues.

Some scholars have reservations about publishing in open access journals because of the proliferation of low-quality journals which use a pay-for-publication model, but there are many quality open access journals, including journals that are listed in Web of Science's SCI (Science Citation Index) and

SSCI (Social Science Citation Index). Both JCR and Scimago allow users to narrow results to open access journals. In addition, the Directory of Open Access Journals (doaj.org) maintains a list of reputable open access journals (look for the DOAJ seal) and provides open access education.

Keywords and Search Engine Optimization

If asked to provide keywords as part of your submission, select them strategically and very carefully. Consider using variants of terms used in your title and abstract to maximize the likelihood that keyword searches in databases will retrieve the record.

In addition to the keywords you supply with the article, as you write your article, you can increase the chances of your article coming up in Google and Google Scholar searches by deliberately including relevant keywords when appropriate in your title, abstract, section headings, and figure, table, and graph captions.

Links

Journals often give authors access to free digital copies of their articles for distribution through a link for download, usually for a set period or for a certain number of downloads. This link can increase your readership by making your article immediately available to researchers and can remove the barrier which paywalls present to researchers without a journal subscription.

Institutional Repositories

If you are not publishing in an open access journal, there are legal ways to increase the availability of your publication to those without access to personal or institutional journal subscriptions. Many author agreements allow authors to post **preprint** copies in an **institutional repository** (IR). A preprint is usually a copy of an article before it has gone through the peer-review process. Check your publication contract to determine what rights you have retained. An institutional repository is a digital archive that facilitates preserving and distributing the scholarly output of the institution's researchers. Content varies between IRs, but many include presentation slide decks, whitepapers, and datasets in addition to article preprints. If your institution does not have an IR, there are alternative outlets for depositing your preprints, such as SSRN (https://www.ssrn.com).

Attribution and Scholarly Profiles

Correct attribution is fundamental to ensuring that scholars receive recognition for their work; there are many authors with the same or similar names working in different (and sometimes the same) fields, and it is not uncommon for articles to be credited to the wrong person because of similar names. Multiple author identifiers exist to facilitate work attribution, including ORCiD, ResearcherID, and Scopus Author ID. These author identifiers are unique and persistent; in other words, they are like a DOI for a scholar's name. ResearcherID is linked to Web of Science and is now also associated with Publons, a Clarivate Analytics product, which aims to give academics credit for peer-review contributions while maintaining the anonymity of the peer-review process. Authors with publications indexed in Scopus are automatically assigned a Scopus Author ID. ORCiD (https://orcid.org) identifiers are nonproprietary and are used by multiple publishers and are sometimes used by funding organizations in grant applications. Your ResearcherID and Scopus Author ID can be linked to your ORCiD account. Many journals now ask authors to submit their ORCiD identifier along with their article submissions.

Google Scholar allows users to set up profiles. Users can configure their Google Scholar profiles so new publications are automatically added to their list of existing works. Users can edit their lists of works to ensure articles are being correctly attributed to their profiles. Google Scholar will also calculate the h-index and i10-index of authors with profiles based on the items indexed in Google Scholar. When creating a profile, users can list tags for areas of interest. Users have the option to designate profiles as public or private. A public profile is an easy way to make your bibliography available to a wide audience of researchers. The tags used for areas of research interest are linked to public profiles of other Google Scholar users with the same research interests; this makes it easier for people with similar research interests to discover your work. You can also see when and by whom your articles are being cited.

Web Presence

Self-promotion on the web can be an effective way to increase the visibility of your research and can increase altmetric measurements for new publications. Because many academics maintain a Twitter presence, it can be an effective platform for promoting your work, especially if your followers retweet your posts. When you tweet about your articles, include a link to the article (this is a good place to use the link some publishers provide for free copies of your article). If your publisher does not provide a link to free copies, but you have deposited a preprint version of the paper in an IR, you can include a link to the preprint. If you maintain a professional blog, including references and links to your articles can increase awareness and readership.

Academia.edu and ResearchGate (www.researchgate.net) describe themselves as academic social networks. Although they both have social networking aspects, they are most often used as repositories for articles. If your institution does not have an institutional repository, these may be places to deposit your articles. Make sure to check your author agreement to see if there are restrictions on what you may post; you may only be able to post a preprint version. Failure to abide by the author agreement is a violation of copyright.

Activity 8.4

1. Select a field of study. Find the journal rankings for the field of study in Journal Citation Reports, Scimago, and Google Scholar. Compare the top ten journal titles from each source.

2. Select a second field of study and locate its top ten journals as listed in Journal Citation Reports, Scimago, and Google Scholar. How do the JIF (JCR), the SJR (Scimago), and the $h5$-index from Google Scholar of the top journals compare to those you located in exercise # 1?

3. Select an author with a Google Scholar profile. Compare the h-index generated by Google Scholar for that author with the h-index generated by Web of Science.

4. Using the publication information for the following author, compute the author's h- and g-index.

Publication 1	245
Publication 2	223
Publication 3	182
Publication 4	65
Publication 5	58
Publication 6	49
Publication 7	40
Publication 8	33
Publication 9	20
Publication 10	18
Publication 11	18
Publication 12	17
Publication 13	15

Publication 14	14
Publication 15	13
Publication 16	12
Publication 17	11
Publication 18	10
Publication 19	7
Publication 20	6

5. Using the "Only Open Access Journals" filter in Scimago's journal rankings, locate reputable Open Access Journals in your subject area.

Key Points

- Authors can take steps to increase the exposure of their research.

- Publishing in open access journals or depositing preprint versions of paywalled articles in an IR allows researchers with limited access to institutional databases and journal subscriptions to access research.

- A carefully curated scholarly profile makes it easier for people to discover your research.

- Self-promotion on the Web can be an effective way to increase the visibility of new research and can increase altmetric measurements for new publications.

- Increased exposure does not ensure an increase in impact, but research without exposure cannot generate impact.

SUMMARY

In this chapter, we covered the basics of article-, journal-, and author-level metrics as well as alternative measurements of research productivity and impact. Understanding what these metrics mean and their limitations empowers authors to navigate the world of scholarly publication deliberately and can help them create a more nuanced description of their research portfolio. While recognizing metrics do not necessarily measure the quality of research, we acknowledge the role these metrics can play in promotion and tenure decisions and discuss ways to increase the visibility of research to increase the likelihood of citation.

KEY TERMS

Altmetrics Altmetrics are scholarly impact measures based on activity in online tools and environments, such as social media, online reference managers, blogs, and scholarly social media networks such as ResearchGate or Academia.edu (Priem, Groth, & Taraborelli, 2012).

Bibliometrics According to Pritchard (1969, p. 349), bibliometrics is "the application of mathematics and statistical methods to books and other media of communication."

Citation Count Citation count refers to the number of times a scholarly work is cited by other works.

Digital Object Identifier A digital object identifier or DOI, is an identifier used to uniquely identify certain items. Systematized by the International Organization for Standardization, DOIs are used primarily to recognize academic, professional, and government information, particularly journal articles, research reports, and other types of official publications. They are also used to identify data sets and other kinds of information resources, including certain commercial videos.

g-index The g-index is the number of papers (g) whose sum of citations are at least g^2.

h-index The h-index is the number of papers (h) that have accumulated at least h citations.

h5-index The h5-index is the h-index based on articles published in the last five complete years.

i10-index The i10-index is the number of articles published by an author that have received at least ten citations.

Institutional Repository An institutional repository is a digital collection of information output by an organization such as a university or a company.

Journal Impact Factor Journal Impact Factor (JIF) is an indicator created by Eugene Garfield to rate a journal's impact by calculating the total number of times the articles in a journal were cited in the two years prior to the year that the JIF is calculated divided by the total number of articles published during that time. It is a dynamic measure that changes with time.

Metrics Metrics are quantitative assessments used to assess and compare performance or production.

Noncitation Impact Noncitation impact refers to the impact made by research that may be read and which may influence practice, but which may not produce citations in academic works.

Preprint A preprint is the version of an article before it has undergone peer review.

SJR (Scimago Journal Rank) SJR is calculated using data from Scopus. It is "the average number of weighted citations received in the selected year by the documents published in the selected journal in the three previous years" (Scimago, n.d.).

SNIP (Source Normalized Impact Per Publication) SNIP is "the number of citations given in the present year to publications in the past three years divided by the total number of publications in the past three years" (Centre for Science and Technology Studies, 2019). As its name suggests, SNIP weights citations to correct for different citation rates across fields of study.

CRITICAL THINKING QUESTIONS

1. Which measurements would describe your research impact in the most favorable light?

2. Is there one measure that can represent all aspects of your research quality, productivity, and impact? If not, why?

3. Consider your academic identity. What can you do to raise your profile?

   a. Do you have an ORCiD?

   b. If you do, is it linked to your Researcher ID and Scopus Author ID?

   c. Do you have a Google Scholar profile? If so, is it configured to automatically update your list of articles?

      • Do you check your Google Scholar profile periodically to make sure all articles appearing in your list are correct?

ADDITIONAL REFERENCES AND RESOURCES

https://beallslist.net/Maintains a list of potential predatory journals and publishers.

Rele, S., Kennedy, M., & Blas, N. (2017). LMU librarian publications & presentations. *Journal Evaluation Tool*, 40. Retrieved from https://digitalcommons.lmu.edu/librarian_pubs/40

Rousseau, R., Egghe, L., & Guns, R. (2018). *Becoming metric-wise: A bibliometric guide for researchers.* Oxford: Chandos Publishing.

Scimago Research Group (2007). Description of Scimago journal rank indicator. Retrieved April 7, 2020, from https://www.scimagojr.com/SCImagoJournalRank.pdf

Waltman, L., van Eck, N. J., van Leeuwen, T. N., & Visser, M. S. (2013). Some modifications to the SNIP journal impact indicator. *Journal of Informetrics*, 7(2), 272–285. doi:10.1016/j.joi.2012.11.011

WORKS CITED ——————————————————————

Alstete, J. W., Beutell, N. J., & Meyer, J. P. (2018). *Evaluating scholarship and research impact: History, practices, and policy development.* Bingley: Emerald Group.

American Society for Cell Biology. (2012). San Francisco declaration on research assessment. In Paper presented at the Annual Meeting of the American Society for Cell Biology. Retrieved from https://sfdora.org/read/

Centre for Science and Technology Studies (2019). Methodology. *CWTS Journal Indicators.* Retrieved from https://www.journalindicators.com/methodology

Egghe, L. (2006). Theory and practise of the g-index. *Scientometrics*, 69(1), 131–152. doi:10.1007/s11192-006-0144-7

Garfield, E. (1972). Citation analysis as a tool in journal evaluation. *Science*, 178(4060), 471–479.

Garfield, E. (1999). Journal impact factor: A brief review. *Canadian Medical Association Journal*, 161(8), 979–980.

Gingras, Y. (2016). *Bibliometrics and research evaluation: Uses and abuses.* Cambridge, MA: MIT Press.

Google Scholar (n.d.). Google Scholar metrics. Retrieved April 5, 2020, from https://scholar.google.com/intl/en/scholar/metrics.html#metrics.

Priem, J., Groth, P., & Taraborelli, D. (2012). The altmetrics collection. *PloS One*, 7(11), e48753. doi:10.1371/journal.pone.0048753

Pritchard, A. (1969). Statistical bibliography or bibliometrics? *Journal of Documentation*, 25, 348–349.

Roemer, R. C., & Borchardt, R. (2015). *Meaningful metrics: A 21st century librarian's guide to bibliometrics, altmetrics, and research impact.* Chicago, IL: Association of College and Research Libraries.

Scimago (n.d.). Help. *SJR—SCImago Journal & Country Rank* [Portal]. Retrieved April 4, 2020, from https://www.scimagojr.com/help.php

Wildgaard, L., Schneider, J. W., & Larsen, B. (2014). A review of the characteristics of 108 author-level bibliometric indicators. *Scientometrics*, 101(1), 125–158. doi:10.1007/s11192-014-1423-3

Considerations for Productive Collaborative Relationships for Writing

This chapter specifically addresses the logistic and stylistic choices, rewards, and potential concerns when collaborating with other researchers while designing and authoring research with a goal of publication. Given that many institutions and units value collaborations across campus and across institutions, and that rich collaborative relationships and/or partnerships can foster productivity, collaborative research and corresponding writing can yield positive publication outcomes including books, book chapters, and journal articles. Working with collaborative partners can be an efficient strategy for maximizing your publication output. For example, it is only through collaborations that interdisciplinary work is generated—allowing for germination of unique perspectives that make significant contributions to multiple fields of research. The saying, "many hands make light work" highlights one of the primary benefits of collaborative partners which is to accelerate your research and publication trajectory. As authors, we have found that collaborative research and writing relationships have also been very insightful, having greatly informed our thinking and expanded our frames of reference through the collaborative process.

Learning Objectives

There are several learning objectives that relate to successful authoring collaborations with colleagues. Those objectives are:

1. Learning how to create networks of writing support through writing circles and accountability partners

2. Learning to cultivate relationships with potential collaborative partners for research

3. Learning effective strategies for working within collaborative relationships

4. Learning to navigate challenging situations in collaborative relationships

Identifying a problem and proposing a solution or line of inquiry to investigate through the research process is simple when these topics are your ideas and/or passion. In this way, the research process and subsequent writing can typically be clearer and more easily managed. As a result, many scholars prefer to be the sole explorer (or author) on their research journey. However, many other scholars find they enjoy the synergy and creativity that comes from working with collaborative partners.

Regardless of your stance on going solo or working within and across the confines of a group, all new scholars and novice academics should have the tools to, at minimum, collaborate where necessary. For some academics, especially those with additional administrative loads, collaborative research and coauthoring is necessary or encouraged by an institution's policies. Further, when engaged in institutional or researcher-driven grant funded projects, partnerships, within or across institutions, are typically required. In these cases, coauthoring is both expected and prudent as each investigator can bring a unique perspective to the research. Even more concretely, the guidelines of a grant may also require coauthorship which utilizes the expertise of practitioner-scholars as well as academics.

Therefore, for many of the readers of this text, establishing and maintaining collaborative partnerships/relationships are vital activities. Yet, to be successful, collaborative relationships must be carefully cultivated over time and have the capacity to impact one's research—whether by improving your skill as an academic writer or by collaborating around research questions and corresponding designs and reporting. For the purposes of this chapter, we will discuss the two main types of collaborative relationships utilized for increasing productivity in research and publishing. These are: (1) uniquely supportive collaborations around writing feedback like writing groups and accountability partners, and (2) collaborations with partners which result in collaborative research. We will also discuss the affordances and challenges inherent in collaborative relationships and provide a few concrete strategies for how to maximize benefit and minimize challenges. To get you started thinking about how/where you can cultivate collaborative relationships, attempt the quick write below.

Quick Write # 7

For this quick write, you will be asked to create a list of potential collaborative partners from whom you may solicit feedback *on your writing*. Open a new document or grab a favorite writing pad and quickly generate a list in five minutes or less. Record the following headings: colleagues in my field of study at my institution, colleagues in my field of study at other institutions, and researchers or professionals outside of your field.

- List three colleagues in your institution who might be viable collaborative writing partners. These colleagues can be either in your discipline or outside of your discipline. They can include both faculty and undergraduate or graduate students.

- List three colleagues in your field of study at other institutions. These colleagues might be from professional organizations you are involved with or that you have met at professional conferences.

- List three researchers or professionals in a related field of study inside or outside of your institution. These colleagues should be in related fields of study which you have read and cited in your scholarship.

Save your work and continue to add potential writing feedback partners. Refer to this list often to maximize the impact of your collaborations.

Supportive Collaborations for Thinking and Writing Feedback

The first category of collaborative relationships which can be utilized for increasing productivity in research and publishing are those which are uniquely supportive collaborations around thinking and writing feedback like writing groups and accountability partners. We want to draw a specific distinction between these supportive collaborations around writing feedback and those which are around collaborative research and coauthoring because they can and do serve very different purposes and, therefore, have different qualities, affordances, and challenges.

Writing Groups AKA Writing Circles

Writing groups, also known as **writing circles**, can serve a key role in achieving writing goals. Vopat (2009) based his notion of writing circles on the earlier work Daniels (2002) literature circles where in a social context, collaboration and shared authentic literacy experiences contributed to writing growth. Vopat (2009) defined writing circles as, "small groups...meeting regularly to share drafts, choose common writing topics, practice positive response, and in general, help each other become better writers" (p. 6). Central to writing circles is voice and choice. Roberts, Blanch, and Gurjar (2017) further defined writing circles as a collaborative structure used to encourage written products.

According to Plakhotnik and Rocco (2012), in a study of Latina students, writing support circles assisted graduate students who lacked skill in writing, who were writing in a second language, and with students who lacked confidence in writing. By creating a sense of community, reluctant adult writers can excel within the writing support circles structure. The notion of employing writing circles has been implemented in many different contexts such as with adult learners in the accounting field (Huber, Leach-López, Lee, & Mafi, 2020). Fleming et al. (2017) found that the use of the monthly meetings to work on and discuss projects and garner feedback through writing circles increased the scholarly productivity of junior faculty. In essence, writing circles are a conduit to improve writing stamina, quality, and support a novice scholar's trajectory in becoming a more proficient writer. The key functions of the writing circle are structure and accountability. Writing circles are typically very structured where writers meet at the same time, in the same location, and write for a specified amount of time. A writing circle may be what you need to ensure you sit and write. A common writing circle agenda is outlined in Table 9.1.

Leah Katherine, one of the authors of this text, has participated in writing circles at her university. She has also participated in a variation of a writing circle which takes place over the course of an entire day. In this example, which her university calls a "writing retreat," the day's writing is divided up into one or two half days. This allows for time to write larger pieces and also receive more intensive feedback. Often additional "ground rules" are set for the writing circles. For example, in Leah Katherine's university sponsored writing circles and retreats, no self-depreciation of thinking or writing is allowed, and all writing accomplished must be shared and celebrated. She has found that this culture of asset perspectives, positive thinking, and self-affirmation leads to greater productivity within the writing circle and beyond it. Additionally, through these experiences, Leah Katherine has not only received valuable thinking and writing feedback from colleagues outside of her field, but also, over time, developed meaningful interdisciplinary research collaborations and relationships across her campus. We will discuss these types of collaborations in greater detail later in the chapter.

Having supportive others assist you in your writing will propel you forward in your publishing and productivity goals because these individuals can and should serve as critical friends. Your collaborative relationships in writing circles can offer you critical feedback on both your arguments and writing style and celebrate when you reach key milestones. Earlier in this text, we discussed setting goals that are strategic, time bound, and specific. In your writing circle, we encourage you to maximize this collaborative relationship beyond sharing your goals. These individuals are also ones that may inform you that the goal is too large or may help you break a large task into smaller chunks. They can also help you think through your timeline, and, depending on the interdisciplinary or disciplinary nature of your partnership, provide insight into the best outlets for your work.

Table 9.1   Agenda for Writing Circle (1.5 Hours)
Five minutes or less—At the beginning of the session, each member comes with a targeted specific and measurable goal on a current writing project for the writing session.
Minutes 6–60—Each member writes independently to accomplish their short-term goal for the writing session.
Minutes 61–85—Members switch work with one other member and offer suggestions in a predetermined format (writing or oral).
Minutes 86–90—Each member shares and celebrates their writing successes for the day, no matter how small, and proposes new short-term writing goals to be completed prior to the next writing circle for feedback.

Just because a writing circle has the word writing in it doesn't mean all writing circles have members compose during meeting time. Some writing circles are not a time for crafting but a time for sharing predrafted writing and checking-in. As authors, we see this type of writing circle as more of an **accountability group**. When coauthor of this text, Tynisha, was a novice scholar, she joined a writing circle, only to learn that it was more of an accountability group. This group of novice scholars, who were from a variety of disciplines, met once a month. During this time, writers physically met in the same space. They used the time to set goals and to share accomplishments toward to previously set goal. The gem was that this small group of 3–5 novice scholars could also serve as readers and initial audience for each author's work. They would send portions of writing to the writing group, either as a whole or in pairs, in between meeting times and provide feedback to the author on the designated day and time for the writing group. What was most rewarding for Tynisha was that the writing circle agreed that authors would not send whole manuscripts but a portion of a manuscript that would take readers no more than 30 minutes to both read and respond to, with suggestions in writing and orally. The goal of this type of writing account-ability is to build self-efficacy as writers, facilitate the writing process among novice scholars, and to combat against competition through building an intentional community of collaboration across independent writing projects. See Table 9.2 for a potential structure for a writing accountability group.

Today, writing circles and accountability groups can and do take on many forms. Some are web-based where writers meet at the same time, but aren't in the same physical location. Writing circles may be highly structured where individuals are invited to participate and others casual in nature where one can drop in at will. Also, the culture of the writing circle may vary on the participants or the facilitator. For example, participants in the writing circle may be within the same academic discipline or may be interdisciplinary. As in our examples, writing

Table 9.2   Structure for Writing Accountability Group
Each member comes with a report on their prior goals for a current writing project.
Each member provides feedback on a previously read draft of a colleague's work and offers suggestions.
Each member proposes new short-term writing goals to be completed prior to the next writing group for feedback.
Members provide feedback on one another's short-term writing goals.
Group concludes.
Members send new writing to predetermined colleague or group by predetermined date and time.

circles may consist of time for free writing or participants may be required to bring a piece to workshop. Because writing circles can look and feel very different, you must decide what type of writing circle is best for you and you may even choose more than one writing circle to be a participant.

Source: iStock

What Is an Accountability Partner?

We discussed, above, active engagement in a writing circle is one way to have accountability toward academic productivity. Traditional accountability partners are also valuable. **Accountability partners** can be counted on to provide critical feedback and keep a writer honest. If you know someone is going to ask you about your productivity, such as your latest project or when a manuscript will be submitted, or an impeding deadline, you count on providing it.

Identifying accountability partners is important because this collaboration is truly about relationship. With most accountability partners, the relationships are reciprocal, and you are also in the position of holding your colleague/partner accountable to their goals as well. As you think about choosing an accountability partner, think about what you need first. This short list details some criteria that can help in selecting someone that will support your efforts. As you consider these criteria, reflect on responses for both your potential partner and for yourself. Compatibility across multiple of these categories is key for productive partnership.

- Knowledge of academic research and publication

- Current scholarly productivity

- Availability
- Ability to be critical and honest while being also maintaining professionalism
- Intersectionality of scholarly pursuits
- Institutional affiliation

In reviewing this list, you may have identified more than one individual who can serve as an accountability partner. The individuals may be at your current institution, in your doctoral program, or not in higher education at all. This choice is yours based on what you need from your accountability partner. The four authors of this text are at three different institutions and all are in different units, but we serve as accountability partners for each other. Because of the relationship we have with each other, how we communicate varies among us. This is a result of our long-standing relationships, our knowledge of one another's fields, our cultivated respect for one another, and the various projects we have worked on together. We all also have additional accountability partners outside of our authorship group that keeps us on track and ensures we are making progress toward our goals.

In fact, it is possible that as a scholarly writer, you could have more than one accountability partner. For example, you may have one partner within your institution who helps you maintain reasonable goals for your local expectation. Simultaneously, you may have another accountability partner in your field at another institution who helps you keep an eye on your own trajectory as a scholar in your discipline. As stated throughout the chapter, you will have to decide what works for you as a scholar. Before proceeding to the next section on our second category of collaborative relationships, we encourage you to again brainstorm potential new partnerships through the quick write below.

Quick Write # 8

For this quick write you will be asked to create a list of potential collaborative partners for research—possible coauthors for projects and publications. While it may seem very similar to Quick Write # 7, this exercise stresses not just collaborative writing, but this exercise is expansive in asking you to consider potential collaborators beyond writing and to consider collaborators for research, grants collaborations and partnerships, various possible editing collaborations, and to identify proximity and intentional collaborators. Open a new document or grab a favorite writing pad and quickly generate a list. Record the following headings: colleagues in my field of study at my university, colleagues in my field of study at other universities, professionals in the field outside of the university.

- List three colleagues in your university who might be viable collaborative partners. These colleagues can be both in your discipline or outside of your discipline. They can include both faculty and undergraduate or graduate students.

- List three colleagues in your field of study outside at other universities. These colleagues might be from professional organizations you are involved with or that you have met at professional conferences.

- List three professionals in your field of study that are outside of the university. These professionals can be partners you have engaged with in the community through service-learning or recipients of this service.

Save your work and continue to add potential partners. Refer to this list often to maximize the impact of your collaborations.

Collaborative Relationships for Collaborative Research AKA Coauthoring

Collaborative research has various connotations. For some scholars, collaborative research is the high impact practice of engaging in research with either undergraduate or graduate students or community partners. In this chapter, we use the phrase collaborative research as a means of defining a research relationship between scholars either at the same institution, different institutions, different disciplinary areas, or similar disciplinary areas. While we understand that many faculty have expectations of cultivating research through the high impact practice of faculty-student engaged research, in this chapter we will explore other avenues for collaboration.

Collaborating for research and writing, or **coauthoring** has many benefits, and it can have drawbacks. Interwoven throughout this section will be elements that highlight the many dimensions of coauthorship. Coauthoring or collaborative research relationships are valued differently at different types of institutions and, therefore, may be valued differently by readers of this text. For example, liberal arts or mission-driven institutions may more strongly encourage collaborative and coauthored works. The benefit of a strong, collaborative research relationship can be of great value when scholars anticipate and consider the expectations of annual evaluation, promotion, and tenure. These colleagues are able to speak to your role in scholarly pursuits by using concrete examples. As a result, the authors of this text would encourage novice scholars to, at minimum, find collaborative researchers outside of your scholarly home or institutional home for this purpose. In the following subsections, we outline specific considerations around collaborations for coauthor including: choosing coresearchers with whom to coauthor, writing responsibilities, decisions about publication processes, generating cohesive collaborative writing, and revising collaborative writing. We also subtly shift from using just collaborator(s) and collaborations to partners and partnerships.

Considerations for Choosing Collaborative Research Partners for Coauthoring

Given the intimate nature of coauthoring relationships, careful consideration of any collaborative research partnerships for coauthoring is required. Sometimes coauthoring relationships are predetermined by your institutional contract. For example, perhaps some part of your job is collaborating with institutional research or administration to conduct research on programs, initiatives, or partnerships facilitated by the institution. But, the considerations below should be considered when relinquishing control over some component of your scholarly career to another person by choice. These collaborative research relationships should only be entered into because, after careful consideration, you believe the collective product will be much better quality or have greater impact than you could achieve solo. In short, a choice of coauthorship is always a cost-benefit analysis. So, what kinds of considerations should be considered when choosing to enter into **intentional partnerships** for research and writing versus **proximity partnership or partnership of convenience**? Every doctoral student should schedule a discussion of these options with their major professor, and newly minted PhD and novice researchers should schedule a similar discussion of these options with their appointed mentor to explore these options and differences. We have identified several considerations below for readers' reflection. By no means is this an exhaustive list, but, instead, the main considerations we have found helpful in our decision-making.

- Similar/different research questions, disciplines

- Similar/different methods/skills

- Similar/different theoretical perspectives commonly utilized

- Similar/different career trajectory/career goals

- Similar/different perspectives on positionality of the researcher

- Similar/different institutions

- Similar/different writing acumen

- Similar/different time/effort/resources available for additional projects

- Similar/different ethical stances toward research and writing

If you don't know the answers to these queries, we suggest you have open and honest conversations about these upfront with potential collaborators and future partners *prior* to entering into a collaborative research agreement. Ultimately, the choice about how much agreement or disagreement you can manage across any of these considerations is yours. However, we would encourage you to align your choices with your overall goals for your career and the particular research projects you have in mind.

Gaining Clarity on Research and Writing Responsibilities

In collaborative research and writing, identifying how you will collaborate, and the clarity of roles and responsibilities is key. Often, in these relationships in our experience, the type and kind of research collaboration dictates how the project may be divided up. For example, in Leah Katherine's experience with several cross institutional collaborations, one author may serve as a content expert and be in charge of the framing of the question, choosing a theoretical frame, drafting the related literature review, applying for study approval, and writing the corresponding discussion of results for the manuscript. A second author may serve in the role of methodologist and frame/write the methods and findings sections. Other coauthors, with less research expertise but more recent practical experience, may be in charge of the writing up of the implications for policy and practice. Across these decisions, while expertise and role should guide choices across the collaboration, clear communication is key.

While this may seem redundant, and it has been emphasized in this chapter and others, negotiation and open communication is paramount when collaborating on seeking out publication venues. For example, locating a venue is a shared responsibility and should be an ongoing activity with research and writing partners. Typically, collaborators share fields of study or are aware how individual's research interests intersect. Sharing responsibility for locating publication venues typically results in multiple publication opportunities. Sometimes partners take turns so to speak, and each one takes the lead in locating a publishing outlet for ongoing research. Other partners take time at regular intervals to come together and discuss publishing possibilities. This could happen monthly or quarterly, but each partner comes to a sharing session with several possibilities. Other times, a research finding results in reaching out to someone with more experience, bringing an additional member into an existing collaborative partnership.

Cultivating these kinds of a relationship takes time and commitment. Partners have to be committed to productivity and each has to take an active stance on locating "good fits." Once a publication has been mutually agreed-upon, then the same process suggested in Chapter 3 comes into play. Below, those considerations are slightly modified but basically repeated.

- Who is responsible for sections? What are these decisions based on?

- Based on these decisions, your fields' traditions, and your style guides, how will you determine the order of authorship?

- How will you collaborate? Which tools will you utilize?

- Who sets a timeline for when will each section will be completed?

- Where will drafts be stored, and how will the drafts be labeled and saved?

- To whom is the drafted section sent (order for exchanging drafts)?

- Who will revise and edit sections?

- Who will be the corresponding author?

Again, the collaborative research and writing process is a continual negotiation. One key area of negotiating is the identification of order of authorship. In different fields, it means different things and holds different weight. It is important to know what it means for your context what the role of first authorship entails. For others, the order of authors does not have any significance. Another primary collaborative writing consideration is the role of corresponding author. Oftentimes the first author is typically the corresponding author, but that is not always the case. The corresponding author has a responsibility of being the author in communication with the editor or publisher as well as the team. While the person who handles the front and back matter should have a strong attention to detail, the corresponding author must be attentive to all email communication and stay connected.

Open communication can mitigate compromising relationships, we repeat this because it is so significant. In collaborative writing relationships, care should be taken to preserve those relationships. All the authors must commit to being open to ongoing discussions about the division of responsibilities, acknowledge each author's strong points and still developing areas, and thus be cognizant in order to advance the work to be completed. Finally, continued negotiation is key to collaborative writing. If your life circumstances change in the middle of a project, be upfront with your collaborators about how this may change or alter your time commitment to the project and ability to meet predetermined deliverables on time. This type of clear communication and designation of roles across a collaborative research and writing relationship is described in a recent study which follows.

Source: iStock

A recent scholarly project by Margaret-Mary, Leah Katherine, and Tynisha, three of this book's authors, showcases how the research question and method itself can drive division of research and writing responsibilities. Through the use of a cross comparative case study design, each author used their respective state as the case boundaries and separately researched and wrote up the results for their state (Maryland, Wisconsin, Louisiana) case. From there, each of the authors collaborated as the cases were brought together and a cross case analysis was conducted. Leah Katherine took the lead role, setting deadlines and accepting responsibility as the point person, responsible for submitting the initial conference presentation proposal and informing the copresenters of acceptance, logistics, and presentation details. However, what made this collaboration fruitful was both the individual and the collaborative process.

Using the presentation method described above, each author, while responsible for her case, created the slides needed for a presentation which took place in Galway, Ireland, in the fall of 2017. The authors came together to write the presentation introduction, which was not difficult because the research questions were shared as well as the theoretical framework. Each of the conclusions was then complied and through on-line discussion, the authors identified the implications when sharing the findings for the presentation. However, what made this a collaborative success was not that it was a cross-comparative case study, but that each author had a clearly articulated role, and there was accountability within the group. Working toward a conference presentation proposal deadline also helped.

Then, the actual presentation became a springboard to two separate articles: one article detailed the cross-case study, the second focused on just the findings of the Louisiana case. In the article about the Louisiana case, we elected to take on a fourth collaborator and partner because our findings led us to the field of school counseling because the three of us lacked background and knowledge of this field. As collaborators, we again negotiated roles, who would take the lead, who would edit and how editing would occur, and, again, who would be responsible for being the corresponding author. Clear, open communication was paramount. We had to trust and rely on one another, but this process was also a way to address accountability to the writing process.

As an aside, both manuscripts were published in late 2018, illustrating the time-consuming process of publication productivity, but also, that, as a team, we immediately began to write each article after presenting and using presentation feedback to clarify our study. Collaborative writing can help novice scholars navigate and overcome the blank page, and if working with a more seasoned author, provide wonderful examples of mentoring. However, there are pitfalls if there isn't a sense of clarity on the roles and responsibilities among the collaborators. Collaborative writing requires a level of trust and subsequent responsibility that requires authors to collectively determine who will do what and by when. A great deal of honest negotiation is required. In collaborative writing experiences, authors are relying on each one to fulfill agreed-upon obligations by predetermined deadlines.

Creating Cohesive Collaborative Writing

When approaching collaborative writing, one significant difference from solo authoring is to be mindful of consistency of tone, voice, and style to ensure that your collaborative writing is cohesive. For example, whomever constructed the literature review for the research and presentation should also take the lead on writing this section. In tandem, whomever constructed the methods section of the research and presentation should subsequently lead the efforts to write this section and so on. The purpose behind the consistency is that the individual who conceived this section most likely already has a mental outline and all the resources to write a solid draft.

In addition, to the drafting activities, timelines are key because all authors should have their eyes on the parts of the manuscripts at some point to ensure consistency of tone and voice, as well as manage transitions, and sharing accountability toward completion. Writing routines are discussed in detail in Chapter 2. Transitions and powerful words were described earlier in the chapter as well. The transitions in collaborative writing is even more important from one section to another because there may be slight yet discernable variations in tone and style as a result of differing writing styles. Paying close attention to how the transitions are crafted ensures that the slight variations in unique, collaborative writing styles don't impede the overall flow and cohesion of the manuscript. One author should be designated to read for cohesion, style, and tone in addition to adherence to manuscript guidelines from the selected potential publication outlet. There are significant benefits to collaborative writing. As a collaborative text, we understand first-hand what it means to negotiate, set clear divisions of labor, timelines, make concessions for voice and word choice, and, most of all, agree on the publication outlet.

Revising Collaborative Writing

Revising with coauthors also requires organization and clear delineation of responsibilities. If a piece is a revise and resubmit, oftentimes the corresponding author will be the one who receives the editorial and reviewer feedback. In addition, it is oftentimes the corresponding author that generates the reconcili-ation chart and identifies everyone's responsibility with timelines in a third col-umn on the reconciliation chart or by color-coding responsibility. Margaret-Mary, Leah Katherine, and Tynisha have undergone several resubmission processes together and with other coauthors. Whomever is the corresponding author typically identifies which coauthor is most logical to respond to appropriate reviewer comments by first color-coding the comments and then assigning that person in column 3. Because each person is working on a different set of com-ments, a timeline should be constructed to ensure that flow and voice is main-tained throughout the manuscript. Table 9.3 illustrates how we approached reviewers' comments and how we assigned responsibility. Note that as first author, Leah Katherine assumed more responsibility; however, these decisions were negotiated.

Table 9.3 Illustration of How to Assign Responsibility in a Reconciliation Chart

RECONCILIATION CHART		
Editor comments		
Request that you revise and resubmit by 5.15.19		
Reviewer 1 Suggestions	**Edits/Pg#**	**Responsibility**
...stated research question is, "who has access/opportunity to meaningfully engage with this critical curriculum and method and who is left out?" Inconsistent with the paragraph, "Following case study method..."	p. 4; Clarified connection	Leah Katherine
An explanation of what is meant by quintain or use different word	pp. 4–5; Explained in abstract as well as methods section; added citation of Barela 2007 as further explanation	Leah Katherine
p. 3, a quotation that is very clearly a book quoting the declaration of independence but then has a citation after it with no page number; odd structure—recommend reviewing it.	p. 3, Revised for clarity better placement of citation; italicized Declaration language as indicative of reified knowledge	M-M
p. 7, "Passage of the elementary and secondary...civic rights in education." This sentence could be improved with either an explanation of how or with a citation (preferably both).	p. 8; reworded, added law citations	M-M

Comment	Response	Reviewer
p. 7, word choice, "teacher education has encompassed service learning"—do you mean incorporated	P. 7; with all due respect, encompass means included, which is our intent in using this term	M-M
p. 7, "for two decades...for urban teaching by..." This is the first time specifically urban teaching is referred to—is SL not a pedagogical pathway in other contexts (suburban/rural)?	p. 8; reworded for clarity regrading urban; we refer to studies that expand cultural horizons and address the context of PK-12 urban public schools in United States. In the Skinner and Chapman (1999) piece, only school size is mentioned; we cannot infer school configuration of the 1832 respondents to Skinner and Chapman (1999).	Tynisha
P. 8 "specifically, teacher...primacy of reciprocity within the curriculum"—reciprocity between who? Teacher/student? School/community? Student curriculum?	p. 9; clarified	Leah Katherine
Methods-distracted by "quintain"	P. 5; Qualified in abstract and methods section	Leah Katherine
Authors cite Stake, Yin, and Merriam. This is very common in educational research; authors should review "Three approaches to case study methods in education: Yin, Merriam, and Stake" by Yazan published in 2015.	pp. 4–5, Removed Merriam; cite Stake (2005, 2006, 2010, 2013) and Yin (2009) exclusively in regard to both researchers' work with cross-case analysis; revised to reflect; added Stake, R. (2013). *Multiple case study analysis*. Guilford Press.	M-M
Not sure it is necessary to redact the names of schools; suggest a bare minimum of substituting with pseudonyms	p. 17; Addressed course numbers redacted for further review; we redacted institutions as per IRB reqs and common practice	Tynisha

(Continued)

Table 9.3 (Continued)

Setting was well framed; lit review was about k-12 education—setting is three college/universities; add discussion in front half, about the relationship between k-12 policy and teacher prep (private universities which, outside of accrediting programs like teacher ed, have some additional buffer between them and state educational policy)	p. 11; we specifically state "and institutions." However, based on R1, we added clarifying sentences regarding the relationship between PK-12 policy and teacher prep.	Leah Katherine
Empirical materials—This is an unusual word choice; personal preference, and can be ignored by the authors.	We elected to use empirical materials as per Denzin and Lincoln, 2011.	M-M
Electronic questionnaire: Who did this go to? What was its purpose? Would you have sent the same survey to teachers and counselors (in LA)? Is this the survey that wasn't used b/c IRB didn't allow it in the Maryland case? And I don't see it in the Wisconsin case either		Leah Katherine address
Missing from the methods; would really prefer to see—positionality(ies) of the researcher and assurances of goodliness/trustworthiness	p. 11; added positionality in phrase "as teacher education, educational administration, and service-learning researchers;" also stated on p. 32. p. 12; clarified that each of the institutions seek, maintain, and are accredited for preservice teacher preparation by their respective state; clarified Louisiana case	Tynisha
Findings/Results Maryland—some tension that I do not feel like the author(s) address.		Leah Katherine address
First the quoted text of the law should probably be presented in a block quote. COMAR 13A.03.02.06 seems to require service which may or may	See my comment on p. 14	Leah Katherine address

not be service learning. Following evidence makes SL seem likely; not clear that the projects are service learning. This is again reflected on p. 13 in the paragraph about LSSs. I would like authors to acknowledge or address this. Because in the literature review they correctly point out that the curricular structural nature of SL is imperative for desired outcomes.		Leah Katherine address all these findings edits
p. 15—"post shift in accountability and standards" Is this a shift in state policy? Or a more general shift after NCLB? I can read it both ways. Some clarification would help.	p. 16; clarified post shift in accountability as NCLB & ESSA	M-M
p. 16—"while these courses align with the social justice mission... they do not, necessarily, align to Maryland's outlined best practices" teachers are not prepared to implement the state's designated best practices (participating in a college class that employs best practices of service learning does not necessarily prepare teachers to use these best practices)—some argument could be made that teaching how to do the best practices without actually doing SL is possible (though there is probably a good justification that learning these practices through experiential education is a stronger pedagogical strategy).	Leah address Here, I suggest we go back to Dewian philosophy of learning by doing...	Leah Katherine address
Drop the paragraph on p. 17 about how you developed an online survey but didn't use it. Why is this in the findings? Nothing was found.	In an effort to be transparent, creating an instrument but not being allowed to use it is noteworthy; moved to methods section	Leah Katherine
Settings described are universities. But then there are reviews of specific school districts plans. These certainly seem like settings for the research...	We need to politely disagree...	Leah Katherine address

Table 9.3 (Continued)

Splitting this into two manuscripts	Thank you, but with all due respect, we perceive this as one manuscript	Leah Katherine address
p. 19 "In summary…found discrepancies around access"—I believe this practically. But It now seems as if this is a case study within a case study (case study of districts within states). I think if the between county differences are so distinct, more time should be spent talking about the counties. Also how much heterogeneity are there within counties. If this is Baltimore city/Baltimore county that is a really unique and pronounced difference. But just something to think about.		Leah Katherine address
How much do you really know about practice by comparing policy?		
p. 19—word choice—"leaving many at a loss…with pragmatics" Is pragmatics the right word?		Leah Katherine address
Louisiana section needs some clarity and more clear direction. I remind the authors their stated research question is, "who has access/opportunity to meaningfully engage with this critical curriculum and method and who is left out?"—this section not consistent with the three stated purposes on p. 4.	pp. 21–22; in **Louisiana's policies for service-learning or community engagement in the K-12 setting subheading,** this is somewhat explained; however, we further clarified.	M-M address ALL LA suggestions

It is not entirely clear to me the authors are differentiating between service learning and community service.	pp. 21–22; clarified differentiation
Be more specific about the policy language. If you're analyzing policy it's important that the reader understand the data. The state policy is a community service endorsement, as suggested, and not a service learning endorsement, this has significant implications for the broader argument. If teachers aren't required to perform service learning then a failure to prepare teachers for this does not seem to me a problem of policy implementation (pp. 21–22).	p. 22; clarified
For example, the electronic questionnaire found that counselors did not receive training in pedagogy—which is notable, but if they are tracking community service this has nothing to do with policy, and certainly doesn't seem to relate to their actual jobs.	p. 23; clarified through expanded discussion
p. 20 "Unfortunately, school counselors are also incharge…" Why is this unfortunate? p. 20 "While in policy…service efforts"—This sentence has three clauses, each of which is unclear to me; consider your meaning and rewrite this sentence.	p. 21; clarified why it is unfortunate through expanded discussion; reworded awkward sentence construction
p. 21 be more clear about the questionnaire findings. Give specific information. Also, "significantly less than 50%" is confusing. Is this statistically significant? Why not just tell us the number? Why did you pick 50%? Also in this paragraph "preparation to implement policy was lacking"—what is your evidence? p. 21	p. 23; clarified through expanded discussion of statistical significance; added evidence

Table 9.3 (Continued)

"Louisiana does not hold its teacher or counselor preparation programs accountable for teaching the tenants…"—Why would they? There is not policy suggesting the teachers/counselors should be? This is not policy implementation in the classroom.	p. 24; referred back to Act 295 and discussed the interconnectedness of teaching and counseling as they pertain to student growth and development	
p. 22 "A counselor education graduate…" paragraph. I do not understand it's purpose. Nor do I understand why "promote social justice and advocacy" is italicized.	p. 24; this refers to preceding paragraph about the institution's existing program in school counseling; removed italics	Tynisha will address
Wisconsin—consider what it means if there is not policy and how that shapes "policy implementation." private college's mission can be connected to SL—relate to policy implementation. It is not policy of the state, WDPI, or the college to prepare k-12 teachers for service learning.		
Clarify "bifurcated system regarding teacher preparation and policy." need a clear connection or explanation of what the bifurcation is.		Leah Katherine
Some sentences that need attention and another round of proofreading needed.		M-M will take lead
Findings Disagree with the first paragraph; in Maryland there is some contradiction between policy and practice; policy in Louisiana is that there is zero policy for service learning, and therefore it is not a contradiction to have limited to no support for in-service teachers where is the bifurcation. If districts have autonomy, don't you need to examine the districts themselves to see if practice matches policy	p. 31; with all due respect, we disagree; absent a full expansion of what constitutes Community Service Diploma Endorsement, authorized by Louisiana Act 295, the finding was that such a policy existed yet was misunderstood.… the focus was counselors	M-M Tynisha

Reviewer 2 Suggestions	Edits/Pg#	Responsibility
Service and service learning are confounded again in this section	p. 31; we respectfully draw attention to: "For all three cases/states, preservice training for implementing service-learning or civic engagement in the K-12 setting was not included as a required condition for certification or program accreditation for teacher/counselor/school personnel preparation.	
"...differences within and across cases lead to unethical impacts for students and teachers" is lacking; where is evidence presented?	p. 31; added clarity and further explanation	
"Perhaps worse...could be penalized or sanctions for policy requirements"—It doesn't really seem like there is evidence presented to support this.	p. 32; added clarity for our discussion as well as an addition citation: Schneider, 2016	
Reviewer 2 Suggestions	Edits/Pg#	Responsibility
Grammatical issues need attention.	Addressed throughout; addressed issues and each author read for grammar, usage, and reviewed references as well	Tynisha
p. 3 ARISES should be ARISE.	p. 3, Addressed, used arise	Tynisha
p. 3 Is EXPECTANCIES the correct word? Or EXPECTATIONS? Also is CONSTRASTIVE the correct adjective or CONTRASTING?	p. 3, Addressed, used contrasting	Tynisha
Authors do intentionally use the word QUINTAIN throughout the chapter. I am unfamiliar with this word...	pp. 4–5, Stake developed the notion of quintain, which we clarified; added Stake (2013) and Barela (2017) as means of clarification	Leah Katherine

As coauthors engage in the revision process, we have found that the use of "track changes" to be very helpful to ensure that the revisions are accurately captured and included in the reconciliation chart. As coauthors there must be agreement on the platform to use to track revisions and in saving the various drafts of the document. Some like using Drop Box, Google Drive/Google Docs, One Drive, or even email exchange of drafts. What is most important is that there is agreement on the platform being used at the revision stage. As coauthors, when it is your turn to revise the document, you want to see the markups and what was done. If the platforms vary, you may not be able to see the revisions and repeat work. Or, for many of us, worst of all, having the time-consuming task of transition the manuscript across platforms and then reformat the manuscript.

As stated earlier in the chapter, timeliness is important. It is easy to miss a deadline in a coauthoring relationship. It is imperative that the corresponding author sets deadlines by working backwards from when the resubmission is due. As authors, we have highlighted the realities of life. At the stage of revise and resubmit, life can (and in our experience often does) get in the way. As a result, it is quite possible that someone may have to pick up more responsibility at one time or another during revision. As coauthors frequent, ongoing communication between one another will minimize difficulty and lead to success.

Regardless of which format you choose to utilize to make changes across authors, prior to the deadline for resubmission, the corresponding author is ultimately responsible for reviewing the entire document, inclusive of all of the documented edits, ensuring a coherent voice, and writing the letter of response to the editor. Prior to submitting the reconciliation chart within the letter of response, remember to remove the third column which identifies revision responsibility.

Navigating Complexity and Challenging Situations Arising From Collaborative Relationships for Writing
• •

As noted, collaborative endeavors are potentially fraught with opportunities for misunderstanding and potential disappointment whether they are supportive collaborations for thinking and writing feedback or collaborative research relationships for coauthoring. We suggest mitigating as many of these potential pitfalls by starting from an asset frame.

Identifying Strengths
• •

In any collaboration, the sharing of responsibilities is paramount. These divisions can be best determined by knowing your collaborative partner well and understanding the strengths of each partner. For example, if your writing circle partner has a very tight time schedule due to family or other personal commitments, can you shift when they receive your draft to accommodate for more time for feedback? If your writing circle or accountability partner is a seasoned scholar or a person with some control over your contract or career, how do you disagree with their suggestions politely in a way that showcases your respect for their disagreement with how to proceed. For an example from coauthoring relationships, front and back matter can be tedious, so which author has strong organizational and attention to detail? This is very important for the back matter especially because this author will be the one who will ensure formatting, that every citation in the manuscript is in the works cited and will make sure all stylistic protocols are addressed.

In the writing of this text, two of the authors are very detail oriented. They immediately notice when the font has shifted, or that the font size has changed, they note when headings are amiss, and they keep the team consistent with style. Because of their skill sets, these authors also took the lead to ensure that all the citations are correct in text as well as in the works cited section. This was a continual negotiated process, but two of us led on details. Negotiating the responsibilities in consideration of coauthor strengths helps make the writing process run more smoothly. As lead author on this text, Margaret-Mary assumed responsibility for establishing a revision strategy, for following up, and for final edits. In tandem, Cyndi checked reference sections for each chapter for APA style issues.

To mitigate conflict, collaborate to think strategically and honestly about what each member of each partnership brings as their strengths. Have that member be in charge of that area. If the group doesn't know each other's strengths yet, have an open conversation about people's personal insights into their own strengths up front prior to engaging in the research and writing processes. These strengths could be everything from their areas of expertise in research or the manuscript production process to the person who is best with using digital tools and resources. Consider all possibilities.

Dealing With Conflict

Despite our best efforts to be proactive, sometimes conflict is unavoidable. These conflicts could arise during the research process or the writing process. When partners continuously do not "hold up" their side of the collaboration, whether this is in reviewing your work or collaborating as a coauthor, you should address concerns both professionally and with expedience. It is important to remember that, while these conflicts impact you, we have found that the source or point of conflict is RARELY about you at all. However, you can and should professionally express your concerns by setting up an in-person/digital meeting, or, as a last resort outlining these concerns in email. Sometimes, no oftentimes, in these circumstances, your collaborative writing partner's life circumstances have changed and their ability to contribute the relationship has also changed. Yet, they have not had the time, nor energy, to consider how their actions may be impacting you or your career. Where possible, offer strategies and solutions which may assist them (and you) to move forward with the manuscript based on the challenges they articulate. For example, perhaps their role should shift from writing the methods section to the implications? Again, it is important to clarify any change in authorship which may accompany revisions to your original authoring responsibilities.

These kinds of explicit conversations around concerns can sometimes offer your collaborator a chance to reflect on their role relationship and make the requisite changes to recommit to the partnership. Consequently, this explicit conversation could force you to reevaluate your role or perceptions of your role in the partnership. For example, in supportive collaborative relationships for writing, if your partner is unable to provide constructive criticism without "becoming personal," this may be an opportunity for you to evaluate your perspective on "what is personal," or, alternatively, to consider whether you want to propose the establishment of new "ground rules" for the writing circle or accountability partnership.

For coauthoring relationships, when partners find it difficult to resolve differences of opinion within the research process itself, this should be a "red flag" for a novice scholar. For example, for many researchers, there are some conflicts of opinion, particularly around ethics, which may not be able to be resolved. If you are on a tight timeline regarding productivity and publication, you may have to weigh the benefits of continued collaboration against a prolonged and possibly contentious collaborative process. If conflicts are particularly contentious at this stage, we would caution you to reconsider the partnership before investing more time into the endeavor. In fact, for any prolonged conflict that has been addressed clearly and professionally, we would caution you to reconsider the partnership.

As was stated previously in this chapter, coauthorship is always a cost-benefit analysis. If you no longer believe the time and effort invested, or will be invested, it is important to notify your writing collaborators as soon as possible. We would advise you that this is, what many people in academia would call "burning a bridge," so we advise only choosing this option when your bridge is already clearly on fire.

If you choose to end any partnership (supportive or coauthoring), we also encourage you to reflect, in writing, on the prompts below to attempt to avoid similar conflicts in the future.

- What was the original concern?

- How did you communicate the original concern?

- How was it received?

- What role did you play in attempting to resolve the conflict?

- How might you address a similar concern with a collaborative relationship for writing differently in the future?

Navigating Between Goals

As the relationship with your writing partners grows and develops you may notice that the goals you have for your scholarship may shift. This change is normal and expected. Communicating your goals to your writing partners is not only freeing but also can ensure that your writing partners serve as accountability partners and supporters for you. For example, if you are eligible for third year review, promotion or a sabbatical, communicate this to your writing partners. Inform them of what is expected of you and the responsibilities you need to assume to be best prepared for achieving the goal. Or, if your role at your institution (or your institution itself) is changing, be sure to let your writing partners know.

As writing partners, we all have different professional goals and milestones. This is true when your writing partners are at different institutions. For example, Tynisha spent many years at a liberal arts, teaching-focused institution. Although, she had a deep passion for research and advancing her scholarly agenda, she knew that on some collaborative proposals and publications, she was not going to be the first author or serve as the corresponding author and when to allow another writing partner and collaborator to assume the responsibility and learn. In a collaborative, writing relationship as described in various iterations in earlier chapters, this is when everyone has a role in contributing to the success of a publication. One person does not take on the responsibility and add additional names. That is not collaborative writing nor do we as authors endorse **writing mill** strategies. Rather, we have learned to negotiate among partners as to who has the initial idea, who has the time to commit, and who wants to contribute, but with lesser responsibility. Again, this calls for high levels of communication.

At times the goals of one collaborator may not be compatible with others and the collaborator must step away from the writing relationship for that particular publication. It is okay to indicate your limitations. These may be because of your scholarly focus, personal, or professional expectations.

For example, Margaret-Mary's subfield of educational research is access to opportunity, including arts-based pedagogy and arts integration. For her first sabbatical at her institution, she wanted to specifically pursue arts-integration and the A+ model. She was awarded a sabbatical which resulted in a publication and an edited volume of an international journal. And while Tynisha, Leah Katherine, and Margaret-Mary have been publishing together for almost a decade, Tynisha and Leah Katherine have not published with Margaret-Mary in the area of arts education. For Tynisha and Leah Katherine, this is not an area of scholarly expertise. While Tynisha and Leah Katherine may engage in thoughtful conversation and support Margaret-Mary in this subfield, they do not actively publish with Margaret-Mary in this area. Because this was a point of communication and understanding among the three coauthors, it never emerged as an issue.

In a similar way, Cyndi and Margaret-Mary are in the same unit and college at their university, but not in the same program fields. They are also very different researchers, operating in different paradigms. However, they found common ground around an opportunity to collaborate on a state mentoring grant for mentor teachers. They worked together on the grant, the resultant professional development, three presentations, and two articles. They did not involve Leah Katherine or Tynisha. While they shared their work as a point of interest, they were also up front and open about pursuing this line of inquiry as a team of two.

Coauthorship at its core is about *relationship*. Relationships take work and require over communication. As scholars, this is true as we are trained to know our individual fields of study and defend an argument. As detailed throughout the chapter, while framed very positively, our goal is that you avoid the pitfalls of a coauthoring relationship because the cost can be grave. While a negative experience may not have a direct impact on your professional productivity in the immediate future, it may make it difficult to trust and work with others. Collaboration and interdisciplinary scholarship have proliferated and is accepted across all types of institutions. In addition, your reputation can hinge on a coauthoring relationship that has gone sour. The goal is to be as open and honest throughout the coauthoring partnership in order to have productive collaborative publications.

SUMMARY

In this chapter, we addressed strategies for creating networks of writing support through writing circles and accountability partners. We also offered suggestions for cultivating relationships with potential collaborative partners for research, effective strategies for working within collaborative relationships, and navigating challenging situations in collaborative relationships. The building of these skills over time can maximize productivity for newly minted PhD or novice researchers and assist them in their journey to becoming successful within the academy while maintaining strong collegial relationships.

KEY TERMS

Accountability Group Small groups that meet regularly to provide support and feedback to group members on writing goals.

Accountability Partners Colleagues who meet regularly to provide critical feedback to each other on writing goals.

Coauthoring Collaborating with other scholars for research and writing. There is an expectation of negotiating authorship according to style guide specifications across any scholarly product resulting from this type of collaboration relationship.

Intentional Partnerships Hamel, Ryken, Kokich, Lay, and King (2006) define intentional partnership as a systematic inclusion of multiple voices (preservice, mentor, university professor, principal, supervisor) to build shared and mutual understandings across institutions.

Proximity Partnership or Partnership of Convenience This kind of a partnership is typically created because of proximity of one entity to another. A common example is a university that partners with a local school system.

Writing Circles Small groups that meet regularly to work on their writing often with different structures and formats.

Writing Mill Strategy A writing mill is a group of scholars who agree to add one another to all subsequent publications, despite significance of contributions. Such an entity is typically not considered ethical and many professional organizations' code of ethics, style guides, and institutions of higher learning have specific polices against ghost authorship.

CRITICAL THINKING QUESTIONS

1. Who do you already have in your professional circle that you may consider inviting to join a formal writing circle?

2. What working relationships do you have with others that you might consider transforming into a collaborative relationship?

3. What strategies do you currently use in your collaborative writing relationships?

4. What new strategies have you learned that you might consider incorporating?

5. Consider a negative collaborative relationship you have experienced. How might you use some of the strategies from this chapter to reorient future relationships?

ADDITIONAL REFERENCES AND RESOURCES

Clausen, C., Lavoie-Tremblay, M., Purden, M., Lamothe, L., Ezer, H., & McVey, L. (2017). Intentional partnering: A grounded theory study on developing effective partnerships among nurse and physician managers as they co-lead in an evolving healthcare system. *Journal of Advanced Nursing*, 73(9), 2156–2166.

Katsarou, E., Picower, B., & Stovall, D. (2013). Creating intentional partnerships in Urban spaces. In *Moving teacher education into urban schools and communities: Prioritizing community strengths*. Oxsfordshire, UK: Routledge, p. 120. Retrieved from https://www-taylorfrancis-com.proxy-ln.researchport.umd.edu/chapters/edit/10.4324/9780203118658-17/creating-intentional-partnerships-urban-spaces-schools-communities-teacher-preparation-programs

King, G., Servais, M., Forchuk, C., Chalmers, H., Currie, M., Law, M., ... Kertoy, M. (2010). Features and impacts of five multidisciplinary community–university research partnerships. *Health & Social Care in the Community*, 18(1), 59–69.

Lindquist-Grantz, R., & Vaughn, L. M. (2016). The journey and destination need to be intentional: Perceptions of success in community-academic research partnerships. *Gateways: International Journal of Community Research and Engagement*, 9(1), 1–21.

Meidl, T., & Sulentic Dowel, M.-M. (2018). *Handbook of service-learning initiatives in teacher education programs*. Hershey, PA: IGI Global.

Risko, V. J., & Walker-Dalhouse, D. (2009). Parents and teachers: Talking with or past one another—or not talking at all? *The Reading Teacher*, 62(5), 442–444.

Sulentic Dowell, M.-M., & Meidl, T. (October, 2016) *Expanding elementary teacher education teacher education through service-learning: A handbook on extending literacy field experiences for 21st century teacher preparation*. Landham, MD: Rowman and Littlefield.

Thompson, J. D., Lucena, J. C., Lima, M., & Jesiek, B. (2015). Special session: Building intentional community partnerships. Retrieved from https://docs-lib-purdue-edu.proxy-ln.researchport.umd.edu/cgi/viewcontent.cgi?article=1039&context=enegs

Villicaña, M. O. (2018). *Developing intentional partnerships between community colleges and four-year institutions*. NASPA. Retrieved from https://dev.naspa.org/blog/developing-intentional-partnerships-between-community-colleges-and-four-year-institutions

Wallerstein, N., Muhammad, M., Sanchez-Youngman, S., Rodriguez Espinosa, P., Avila, M., Baker, E. A., ... Duran, B. (2019). Power dynamics in community-based participatory research: A multiple–case study analysis of partnering contexts, histories, and practices. *Health Education & Behavior*, 46(1_suppl), 19S–32S.

Yeh, T. L., & Wetzstein, L. (2020). A continuum of transfer partnerships: Toward intentional collaborations to improve transfer outcomes. *New Directions for Community Colleges*, 2020(192), 21–35.

WORKS CITED

Daniels, H. (2002). *Literature circles: Voice and choice in book clubs and reading groups.* Portland, ME: Stenhouse.

Fleming, L. W., Malinowski, S. S., Fleming, J. W., Brown, M. A., Davis, C. S., & Hogan, S. (2017). The impact of participation in a research/writing group on scholarly pursuits by non-tenure track clinical faculty. *Currents in Pharmacy Teaching and Learning*, 9(3), 486–490.

Hamel, F. L., Ryken, A. E., Kokich, M., Lay, O., & King, J. (2006). Intentional partnerships: Generating learning within and across institutional contexts. *Association of Independent Liberal Arts Colleges for Teacher Education (AILACTE) Journal*, 3(1), 41–59.

Huber, M. M., Leach-López, M. A., Lee, E., & Mafi, S. L. (2020). Improving accounting student writing skills using writing circles. *Journal of Accounting Education*, 53, 100694.

Plakhotnik, M. S., & Rocco, T. S. (2012). Implementing writing support circles with adult learners in a nonformal education setting: Priority, practice, and process. *Adult Learning*, 23(2), 76–81.

Roberts, S. K., Blanch, N., & Gurjar, N. (2017). Exploring writing circles as innovative, collaborative writing structures with teacher candidates. *Reading Horizons: A Journal of Literacy and Language Arts*, 56(2), 2.

Vopat, J. (2009). *Writing circles: Kids revolutionize workshop.* Portsmouth, NH: Heinemann.

Leveraging Your Scholarship

Lagniappe Scholarly Considerations

Purpose of Chapter

• •

The distinctly Louisiana term, *lagniappe*, means "a little something extra." As a scholar, it is important to illustrate the flow of scholarship that supports your research agenda. This means two things: (1) you will constantly have scholarship in varying degrees of readiness and completeness, and (2) you should always seek ways to leverage your existing scholarship across several formats and to/for differing audiences. "A little extra" in this case is thinking both *comprehensively* about your research and thinking *strategically* in terms of leveraging efforts and opportunities.

Likely, as a scholar building a career as an academic, you will have works that are published, you will have pieces that are in revision mode, and you will have manuscripts that are simply submitted and in review with a journal. You will also have working draft manuscripts that are just being considered. Keeping an active agenda means paying attention to the state of your productivity, with an eventual eye to publication. This means you must actively track your productivity. In addition, you will also have other projects in various stages of completion (conceptualizing questions to data collection) at any given point in time.

Additional "lagniappe" academic activity illustrates how your agenda has been productive and that you have a current focus in supplemental—a little extra—areas that will produce scholarship and increase productivity in all areas of your research agenda as well. This chapter is designed to assist doctoral students and new scholars in leveraging their scholarly success through entrée into diverse categories of academic proposals such as grant proposals, fellowships, book proposals, and more public facing scholarship like **op-eds**, **white papers**, and **policy briefs**.

Learning Objectives

There are four learning objectives for this chapter:

1. Understand how a scholar can track, leverage, and maximize research impact

2. Identify additional venues as potential outlets to leverage and maximize research impact, including the following: top tier conferences, book chapters, grants/funding, and public scholarship

3. Identify alternative outlets such as opinion pieces, letters to editors, policy briefs, and/or white papers to leverage and maximize research impact

4. Formulate a concrete plan to utilize various media outlets to increase the visibility of your research

Quick Write # 9

For this quick write, you will be asked to create a **jot list** of possibilities—possible venues for research beyond manuscripts, or for different kinds of manuscripts such as opinion pieces, letters to editors, policy briefs, and/or white papers. Open to a new document or grab your favorite writing pad and quickly generate a list. Record the following headings: top tier conferences, book chapters, grants/ funding, and public scholarship.

- List three top tier conferences that you would like to submit a proposal for and attend.

- List three foundations that provide grants for your area of research and the grant amount.

- List three funding agencies. (For this list you may want to contact your office of institutional effectiveness or research, or office of grant development to get a sense of what grants have been successful and well received from foundations at your institution.)

- List three edited books with multiple authorship that appeal to your interests and research.

- List two to three mainstream media outlets. Consider more widely read venues to give your work greater visibility in the general public. Look for publication outlets with a wide readership across print and digital formats.

Save your work and refer to this list often to maximize the impact of your research.

Unifying Features and Distinctive Characteristics of Proposals

Manuscripts and proposals have several elements in common. Both demand a strong purpose and should be crafted to a specific audience, two constructs that are a constant in all solid academic writing. Like manuscripts, proposals are organized, focused, and adhere to format specifications. Proposals have requisite elements, and depending on the source, they may be standard, such as introduction, objectives, and sources cited, or they may be unique, for example, including a theoretical frame and scholarly significance.

Conference Proposals

Professional organizations want to create conference programs that are a mix of originality, fresh, cutting-edge research, practical offerings, and entertainment. Conference registrations are steep, averaging anywhere between $200.00 and $600.00, depending on the field. Above all else, professional organizations want their members to feel satisfied with their overall conferences experience. However, professionals attend conferences to continue their learning and share their expertise. The backbone of any conference is the presentations. For the author(s), adhering to three essentials can lead to success when submitting conference proposals: (1) following the required framework for a proposal, (2) adhering to word counts, and (3) including the conference theme into your proposal. These are essentials and obeying a call for proposals honors the time volunteer reviewers spend on you considering your submission. Typically, reviewers are given a rubric that includes the requisite sections and classically, how authors have adhered to the conference theme. Submitting to a platform requires patience and budgeting time for any mistakes. A common mistake is to ignore one of the required areas of the proposal. Another common mistake is to exceed the established word count for specific sections, including titles and abstracts. These are the technical issues with submitting a conference proposal. One effective way to help conserve time and prevent error is to craft the proposal in a document and copy and paste into the platform.

The benefits of an accepted proposal are significant. Presenting at a professional conference allows scholars the opportunity to get valuable feedback from peers in their field of study and potentially in related fields. Reviewer feedback on your proposal is a prime mechanism for considering strengths and weaknesses and can be incorporated into the actual presentation. Questions, critiques, and comments offered while presenting are also excellent ways to gather response and advice and make your work stronger. As a rule, every presentation should become a manuscript. Feedback garnered *during* a presentation can additionally help strengthen a manuscript! Presenting at professional conferences also provides scholars with a venue to establish themselves and their research within a field, seek out potential collaborators, and locate additional professional activity such as connecting with specialized interest groups of organizations for smaller research areas as discussed in Chapter 5.

Chapter Proposals

Writing a chapter for a book, particularly an edited book, can serve as a great springboard to new research or a synthesis of existing research without the formulaic writing for a journal. Depending on your area of research, you may see

various types of calls for chapter proposals. At conferences, book author/editor(s) may have solicited a call for chapters or call for chapters may come through your national or regional professional organizations' social media outlets or list-serves.

Responding to a chapter call can vary based on the publisher and the book author/editor(s). Regardless of the call to submit a chapter, it is imperative to follow the guidelines for the proposal. If you are unsure if your work is a fit for the book, query the author/editor(s). As you prepare your query, you should be able to succinctly describe the purpose of the proposed chapter, and how it fits within the scope of the book.

The preparation of the proposal should be mapped out and inclusive of the goal of submission to meet the proposal deadline. Most book author/editor(s) will request an outline of the chapter. Similar to crafting a presentation proposal, the more detailed the outline, the easier it is to write the chapter. Also, most proposals for chapters will require a references page as well as an early identification of figures and tables. While the noting of figures and tables may seem insignificant, as the author of the chapter, you may be responsible for paying for the inclusion of these, particularly if requested in color. Also, the book author/editor(s) may need this information for their publisher. Finally, we always recommend having a strong conclusion to the chapter proposal linking to the overall purpose of the book and other chapters. This will demonstrate the value of your work as a significant contribution to the overall text.

Writing Grants/Funding Proposals

Grants or other funding proposals are an excellent way to leverage your scholarly success to expand your productivity and publishing. The first step in getting your research or program funded is having a good question or program which you have piloted and have reported on in journal articles, op-eds, white papers, and/or policy briefs. With this initially published work, you can leverage opportunities to support an expansion of the research question or program with initial or additional funding streams. We recommend that you begin with a **concept template**, similar to the one in Table 8.1 below. Consider these points when requesting grant writing assistance, engaging with program officers, and developing partnerships or working with collaborators (Table 10.1).

Identifying Funding Sources

After you have identified a fundable question or pilot project to expand, you need to spend time locating funding sources. This process is both time consuming and requires careful planning. Therefore, we first recommend that you identify your departmental contact in your institution's **Office of Research and Sponsored Programs (ORSP)** (the name may differ from institution to institution) at the beginning of your career/tenure at each institution to both introduce yourself and your research interests and agenda. In this way, you can identify what resources your institution has for assisting you in identifying, applying for, and managing funding for faculty research. You can also learn what regulations and or policies are in place for different types of funding or sponsored projects at your institution. For example, some grants require institutional matches or other financial commitments. Knowing how or if your institution allows for some of these obligations can be a key factor in determining whether you can or should apply for a specific funding call or source. Another policy you will want to ask about is how your institution calculates **percentage of effort**, or the amount of time you spend on funded work.

On a positive note, this time spent building your network of resources at your institution is invaluable as your ORSP may subscribe to databases for private or nongovernmental grant calls or may be aware of organizations with a past history of funding specific types or categories of projects. Memberships in grant-identifying databases (e.g., SPIN, NOZA—see *Additional References and Resources* section of this chapter for a starter list of sources) can yield potential funding opportunities directly to your email inbox, as can subscribing to grant newsletters (e.g., GrantNews). Further, to apply for funding as a member of an academic institution, most proposals must be **routed**, or approved, through these offices and, in some cases, university administration or governance structures. Learning the procedures for your institutional routing is not just helpful at the beginning of your process for seeking funding, but it is paramount so that you know how much time you need to allot for the approval process. A good rule of thumb is to share your intent with your direct supervisor and possibly dean.

To identify further funding opportunities, we recommend starting with the people and organizations with which you are already associated. For example, all of the authors of this text belong to the American Educational Research Association (AERA) and several other discipline-specific professional research organizations. Many professional associations offer some funding opportunities, and

Table 10.1   Sponsored Project Concept Template

Grant Opportunity:
Funding Source:
Due Date:

Project Title: Name of the project to be submitted for funding (not just the name of the grant opportunity).

Principal Investigator:

Co-Investigator(s): If any

Method: Briefly describe the process of developing, implementing, and evaluating this project. Explain the key milestones and deliverables of this project.

Estimated Timeline: Please provide an estimated completion of deliverables. What parts of the project will you complete each year? Lay out how you will meet the deliverables of the source and the sequence of those events.

Roles and Responsibilities: Describe your partners and what part of the overall project they will be responsible for.

Budget: The budget can be provided as an approximate range. If you are unsure where to begin with budgeting, please provide a list of items and TIME you will need to successfully complete your project (e.g., summer stipend, course release, graduate assistants, participant support costs, supplies). Note any supportive resources available to you in your college for assistance and lead time required.

Additional Resources or Follow-up Needed: Please note (if applicable) any key areas such as budget, ongoing research or collaborations that need to be created, addressed, or completed before submission.

some are specifically set aside for advanced graduate students in support of their dissertation or early career academics. Being aware of rolling deadlines for these **Requests for Proposals** (RFPs), or grant announcements, is key to being prepared to submit a substantive and competitive proposal. If there are other nonprofit or for-profit organizations which you know offer funding in your area, you may want to comprise a list of organizations and sponsors which offer rolling funding applications. In addition to the RFP, there is typically a **notice of intent (NOI)** to actually participate. You also may want to follow these organizations on social media, so you get up-to-date information on funding as it is posted.

Next, use the web to research funders with whom you are not yet familiar. You may wish to start by visiting the United States (US) government's Grants.gov website, download their app, and follow them on social media. Their community blog, YouTube videos, and Twitter feed all offer timely videos and advice on how to use their sites for searching and applying for funding from the over 900 programs and 26 federal grant-making agencies. Also, check state and local/municipal government web sites to see what grants or funding they offer. Often, state and local governments administer many federal and private grants and will list these as well. For scholars who are outside the United States, typically ministries of education, government agencies, and specific arms of government also conduct periodic RFPs.

Once you have identified a possible funding source, read the call for proposals very thoroughly. Note every grant requirement and every grant priority. Grant *Requirements* are the minimums your program, research, or project must meet to apply. Grant Priorities are typically the things the funder would prefer to sponsor if given a choice among programs which meet the requirements, and often priorities are tied to additional points for a proposal. They are worth your time to consider and address. The tighter your proposed research, program, or project is to the identified priorities, the higher the likelihood that your proposal will be favorably reviewed and considered. Similarly, try to learn as much as you can about the organization who solicited proposals and its sponsored programs. This information is typically available on the funder's website or social media and should be carefully analyzed prior to beginning the writing process.

We encourage you to think of a grant opportunity as a partnership with another organization. Therefore, after you have gathered all of the information you can and before you begin to collaborate with partners or write anything, ask yourself:

- What is the mission of the granting organization? Does it align to your research, project, or program?

- Would you want to work closely with this grant organization?

- Does this grant organization frequently fund research or projects like yours?

- Does your research or project qualify for this particular grant program?

- Does your research or project meet all of the grant requirements?

If your tentative answer to these questions is yes, we recommend that you schedule a time to meet the **Program Officer** by phone or video conference. The RFP typically lists the name of a contact person, the Program Officer, who manages the grant process for the organization. Therefore, Program Officers are usually experts in the application process. When you speak with the Program Officer, you should:

- Communicate about your organization, its achievements, and your proposed research, program, or project.

- Confirm that proposed research, program, or project is eligible for the advertised funding.

- Ask any specific questions you have about the grant announcement and clarify any components which are unclear to you.

Questions at this stage are expected, and one of the biggest problems most novice grant writers make is not including a requirement in the application as a result of a misconception (e.g., not realizing there was a financial match required, rather than an in-kind match). Make sure to have all of your specific questions written down to take full advantage of your meeting and ask any follow-up questions which arise immediately. You want to be respectful of the time of the Program Officer and showcase your expertise and organization. If you are ultimately awarded the grant, the Program Officer will typically be your main contact with the organization. Therefore, you want to start the partnership off with respect and professionalism.

Writing Proposals for Funding

As a **Principal Investigator (PI)**, or the person who is in charge of the preparation, implementation, and administration of a grant, you have the ultimate responsibility for the writing process. Writing a grant or funding proposal is both a science and an art. The science of writing proposals for funding includes having complete clarity on the requirements of the call for proposals and articulating the particulars of your research, project, or program, including its importance, the methodological approach, and the procedures and timeline for its **deliverables**, or the products produced by the funding, and the evaluation plan. Grant writers must familiarize themselves with the grant guidelines, both those found in the specific funding announcement and the universal guidelines for all proposals submitted to an agency or foundation.

The art of writing a proposal for funding denotes to the need to tell the story of the research, program, or project in a way that is persuasive to the audience, the reviewers who are contracted to read and rate proposals. This style of writing has to be both factual and convincing. Convey the framework of your project and how it fits with the organization's mission. Explain how your research, program, or project fits in the larger landscape of the discipline and community. Being able to describe these contextual components in a persuasive way can aid your proposal's success. For government funding, you are asking the agency to commit taxpayer money to your enterprise. Why does your research, program, or project merit funding over others?

To aid your argument, make your proposal as organized and easy to read as possible. Use the requirements of the grant as headings to aid in clarity and assist your reviewers in being able to find information easily. Most grant calls or solicitations for funding are peer reviewed. Similar to the peer review process for a manuscript, reviewers are asked to evaluate the quality of the potential contribution of the work you propose. Remember, peer reviewers are generally busy academics who review several grant proposals in a limited timeframe for the agency or organization. As has been mentioned above, pay close attention to the requirements and articulate detailed responses to these. Making it easy for the reviewers to find the information they are looking for under each category gives your proposal the best chance of being considered for funding.

The two areas of writing where you will need to pay very close attention to the desired structure from the funding organization are the budget and the evaluation. These areas are not the place to take artistic license. Keep your writing as close to the actual vocabulary identified in the funding RFP as possible. Typically, you will work with your contact in your institution's ORSP to develop your budget and the corresponding budget narrative. But, be fastidious in aligning your budget categories to the desired categories of the potential funder. A second area to be very clear and adhere to closely is the requirements in the evaluation section of a grant. Frequently, funders identify certain evaluation structures or methods required. In your proposal, be very clear how you will meet these requirements including what metrics (or data) you will collect or solicit and use within these identified structures/methods. For example, if both quantitative and qualitative methods are required, address both. These are two areas where peer reviewers habitually lose confidence in an otherwise fundable proposal. Allowing yourself ample time to address these important sections will ease the stress that can come from working on a tight timeline.

Finally, seek any required letters of partnership, MOU's, or supervisor's signatures and approval *well in advance* of a due date for uploading. It is wise to note while you are reviewing the RFP what external documents are needed and begin contacting others so that this is in process while you are writing the grant narrative. While collaborators and partners were discussed in depth in Chapter 9, it bears repeating that communication is essential when contacting potential grant partners. Knowing your institution's internal procedures and requirements are extremely important. Understanding how platforms work and understanding that it may take time to upload a proposal is also important. It is always a good idea to have your proposal ready for upload at least a day prior to uploading. In that way, if the system kicks a section back (perhaps it is too large and needs to be compressed), or you have forgotten an element, you have time to rectify any mistakes. For example, in a recent proposal, Leah Katherine identified that she needed an investigator biography while uploading a final proposal. Because she was uploading the day before the deadline, she was able to compose and edit an adequate biography. The extra day meant that she was still able to post her best work and wasn't rushed to "post something" so she wouldn't miss the deadline—crises averted.

Timeline for Writers Seeking Funding

The myriad of requirements and considerations, including the time required to get a proposal routed through the institutional systems, points to the need to start the proposal development process early. Ideally, most ORSP offices ask for proposal development to begin six months in advance of submission. This time not only allows your idea to develop, but it also allows you to complete several drafts and revisions. In addition, if your institution offers services such as formatting tables and creating graphics, you want to be able to review what is provided to you, and you may need to ask for edits and revisions. This is typically critical to the development of a strong, competitive proposal. It is advisable to ask ORSP office what level of support you can expect prior to beginning your grant writing process. The more support you have for ancillary tasks gives you more time to focus on developing your proposal.

Recommendations for Writers Seeking Funding

The authors of this text recommend a few additional tips for those seeking to leverage their publishing and productivity for funding. First, we recommend signing up or applying to become a peer reviewer for funding agencies. Understanding how grants are judged and the how the various evaluation systems work is invaluable. Most funding agencies will also pay you a small stipend for your time. But, be aware that the process can be time consuming. Therefore, you should identify how many proposals you could be assigned and the turn-around time for evaluation, in consideration of your other responsibilities, prior to signing up.

By way of example, for one grant funding agency, Leah Katherine was flown to Florida, United States from her home for two days to participate in a peer review process. For her, the experience was invaluable. She learned the priorities of the funder as well as the internal evaluation system for judging the quality of submissions. As a result, she much better understood how certain programs "won out" over others who may be, on their face, similarly qualified. However, prior to the experience, she didn't appreciate how much time went into serving as a reviewer. Prior to the trip, she was asked to preliminarily review ten applications—all over 100 pages. Once on site, the peer-reviewers compared preliminary evaluations, discussed (often called paneling), and worked diligently for over eight hours per day to come to consensus on scores for each proposal as a team. While she was paid a stipend for her time and her meals and travel were covered, she decided not to proceed the next year with serving as a reviewer due to the time commitment. During the next summer, she started a new faculty appointment and didn't feel a second experience with the same funder was going to contribute to her further professional development or grant writing expertise. This was particularly true for her when she compared the lack of novelty in a second experience with the time needed for her new responsibilities and moving.

Second, similar to the process of review for a manuscript, many proposals for funding are not accepted on their first submission. You should not be discouraged, however. You should automatically receive the peer review feedback on your grant proposal with the decision not to fund from the agency. If you do not receive this information, you should request this from the Program Officer. Depending on the cycle of funding (or rolling deadlines), you can utilize the feedback to make revisions or additions to the proposal and apply again. Much like a revise and resubmit opportunity discussed in-depth in Chapter 7, grants get better and improve when refined and revised as per reviewers' comments. Persistence in seeking funding matters. One of the authors of this text applied for funding in three successive cycles from an agency before successfully securing funding. Consider rejections of grants submitted but not funded with detailed reviews as the equivalent of a "revise and resubmit" for an article.

Fellowship Proposals

A fellowship proposal can be a graduate or postdoctoral funding opportunity designed to assist those entering a particular field of study with opportunities to grow their research agenda and develop skills to launch into their career. A common mistake made in writing a fellowship proposal is to only focus on your current research; winning proposals focus on the development of skills that will move the fellow into the next phase of their career. As with everything we have discussed, the best advice for developing a fellowship proposal is to start early and adhere to any guidelines provided. The use of the specific guidelines or categories is the heading for outlining and writing a strong fellowship proposal. Carefully including these headings will ensure all areas of the proposal are addressed. Finally, be careful to proofread your document. The relatively small fee of hiring an editor, around $50.00, may be helpful as you will have spent many hours with the document. With high stakes documents such as this, a more objective set of eyes may be worth the small investment.

In order to craft a coherent fellowship proposal, you must be clear of your ultimate career path. Consider the following:

- Are you interested in teaching, the scholarship of teaching and learning, advising and student mentoring through undergraduate research or working at a research-intensive university?

- What research experiences have you had that you would like to build upon through the fellowship?

- What methodologies would you like to explore or extend? How could the fellowship assist with this?

- What experiences would this fellowship offer which could assist with your career development? How?

Focus on highlighting the experiences you have had that showcase your potential, noting publications, awards, and research, or technical skills. Rather than leaving this open ended for the reviewer, delineate a training plan around the goals you have for yourself professionally and state how these experiences will prepare you for success. Lastly, consider the mission of the funding organization. How does your proposal align to this mission? How will your fellowship project contribute to the funding organization?

There are also requests for proposals for junior, mid-career, and senior career scholars to extend or explore new research areas. Many state-level, regional, and national organizations offer such requests for proposals, usually with a partial or full sabbatical to complete the project and its deliverables. Foundations also offer such proposals. These kinds of proposals are highly sought after and thus, very competitive. They are also extremely worthwhile. As with fellowship proposals, there must be a fit between what you intend to do and the organization's stated mission. Again, be sure to address all areas of the proposal and take care to edit and proofread your document thoroughly. For newly minted PhDs and novice researchers, these may be future goals that can be considered early but acted upon later in your career.

Editing a Special Issue of a Journal

As an example of a future goal, as a scholar, you may rely upon and particularly engage with a certain journal in your field. Typically, this is one that is prestigious, respected, and/or an esteemed publication in a field. While a novice scholar would certainly not expend time vying for a guest-edited journal issue, that is certainly an aspiration that can greatly benefit a mid-career scholar. Reviewing for such a journal would be an important first step, and a secondary step may be to track calls for guest-edited issues for two to three years to gauge what gets accepted and what is not being represented, and how your expertise may fill a gap.

Guest editing a special issue of a journal positions a scholar more firmly within a field and is a worthy future goal. In a similar way, editing a scholarly volume may also be an appropriate future goal to stretch oneself as a scholar and situate oneself as a key contributor in their field. We strongly suggest that graduate students consider reviewing for publications early in their career, especially volunteering to review a special issue; the experience is invaluable and positions a young scholar to understand a journals' goals, aims, an what is being accepted for publication.

Book Proposals

Writing a book proposal may seem like a daunting task, and it is a significant undertaking in terms of both time and effort. A book proposal is a much larger endeavor than journal articles or even book chapters. This means the time and effort involved is magnified compared to a journal article or book chapter. Books can be a great way to share your expertise on a given subject, and many PhD and new scholars opt to convert their dissertation to a book proposal. As with any other type of submission, it is important to carefully review the publisher's submission guidelines for book proposals before you begin writing. While publishers' guidelines may vary, most publishers require a summary of the proposed text (including any key features and pedagogy), a detailed table of contents, and a sample chapter. Unlike other types of submissions that conduct blind reviews of the submitted work, publishers want author biographies to ensure that the authors of the book are well qualified to address the proposed content.

Book proposals ask authors to identify the market for their book (primary and secondary audiences) as well as similar books on the identified topic (competition). It is important to understand the market for your book. Publishers are profit-driven, and while many entertain proposals on topics and issues similar to current publications, they seek proposals that will garner sales and add to the current list of books they publish. As with other publications, you need to carefully consider how your book will fit into the market.

Sabbatical Proposals

Institutional sabbaticals are awarded differently and may involve rank or time at an institution. Most sabbaticals can be awarded for a semester at full pay or a year at half salary. Approaching the task of writing a sabbatical proposal should include the same level of rigor and detail involved in other types of proposals. Essentially, you are requesting that your university continue to pay you while you are away from your teaching and service responsibilities. You need to submit a plan that demonstrates how your institution's investment in your sabbatical is in their best interest in terms of your productivity during the sabbatical year and beyond. Make it clear what the benefit will be to your department, college, and university. Often, a plan to substitute your classes or recommendations for covering your classes is also required. We recommend that you collaborate with your department chair or supervisor to work through some of these details and logistics as well as secure their support for your application early in the process. Often, your supervisor and academic Dean are some of the first people to approve or "forward" your application through an institutional process. Understanding where any supervisors' concerns lie and creating a plan to address them early will help you to put your application in the best position possible to be approved.

While sabbatical proposals may look different, depending on the institution, they share common features. Your proposal should include your goals and objectives for your sabbatical to include a project plan with timelines. Highlight experiences you have had that put you in a great position to complete the goals outlined in your sabbatical. Demonstrate how you have completed activities that have prepared you for the project you are proposing. For example:

- Have you recently collected a lot of data that you can analyze and publish during this time?

- Are conditions right for you to travel and collect data while you are released from your teaching responsibilities, potentially with collaborators from other universities?

- Have you prepared a statement of how courses you typically teach can be "covered' while on sabbatical?

In our experience, sabbaticals are usually rank-ordered so these elements included in a sabbatical proposal may give you an edge over other applicants. A note of caution: be sure not to *overpromise* what will be accomplished during your sabbatical in an effort to make your proposal stronger; seasoned professionals will see this as a shortcoming. Always make sure you can deliver what you have committed. When considering your sabbatical activities, plan to submit a thorough, well thought-out proposal. It is much better to complete all of your proposed activities than to overpromise and come up short; in essence, as coauthors, we all live by the phrase, "it is better to a thorough job of less than a superficial job of more."

A sabbatical application may be the opportunity for you to extend a current research project, start a new research project, write a book, or engage in a different scholarly activity. Carefully and thoroughly read the guidelines for the sabbatical and talk to other colleagues at your institution who have had successful sabbatical applications. Some institutions provide or require specific sabbatical funding. If you need funding for application, this needs to be ascertained *years* before you apply for a sabbatical in order for you to identify and apply for appropriate funding streams.

Also, in your application, don't be modest. As authors of this text, we will reiterate—DON'T BE MODEST. Ask for what you need to meet your scholarly goals while on sabbatical. If required, create a budget to support your research needs such as memberships, conference travel, site travel to gather data, or technology funding to support your research needs.

As an example of leveraging the affordances of both grant and sabbatical proposals, Leah Katherine applied for a year-long sabbatical following her successful application for tenure and promotion. However, as her institution does not provide full funding for a year-long sabbatical, she had separately applied for and received two different sources of grant funding, which paid the remainder of her salary for the academic year. She was able to tie her grants and their associated deliverables and scholarly products to her sabbatical application. Not only did this make her sabbatical application more competitive, since it was tied to additional funding offsetting some of the associated cost of her sabbatical, but she was also able to showcase to the university, her personal (and fiscal) commitment to her sabbatical project and the institution's needs. This kind of successful productivity required long-range planning over several years including a keen observation of what funding was available and likely to become available in her area of interest and field. In a similar vein, Margaret-Mary recently was granted a second sabbatical, She was able to articulate that she completed all proposed activities (and attach artifacts as evidence) on her last sabbatical, and she submitted a detailed list of "deliverables" from her second sabbatical.

Public Scholarship

Another way to leverage your influence and increase your visibility as a scholar is through public scholarship. While many definitions of public scholarship exist across the media sphere, we prefer to use a working definition born out of an interdisciplinary and inter-institutional working group of scholars concerned with the evaluation and promotion of members of academia. According to Ellison and Eatman (2008),

> *Publicly engaged academic work is scholarly or creative activity integral to a faculty member's academic area. It encompasses different forms of making knowledge "about, for, and with" diverse publics and communities. Through a coherent, purposeful sequence of activities, it contributes to the public good and yields artifacts of public and intellectual value. (p. 1)*

This working definition of public scholarship acknowledges the many ways that knowledge and cultural products created by academic institutions should benefit society. While this is a fairly new concept utilized in evaluation structures in higher education, scholarship or scholarly products for the public good have been an evaluation focus for many institutions outside of higher education. For example, many agencies who provide funding for sponsored projects, programs, and research, like the National Science Foundation, have required Principal Investigators to employ alternative methods of sharing information and knowledge created through funded projects for public use. Getting the knowledge out of the academy and onto the streets is a key goal of public scholarship. However, public scholarship does not assume that knowledge only comes from the hierarchical structures of the academy. Public scholarship also "recognizes that new knowledge is created in its application in the field and therefore benefits the teaching and research mission of the university" (Yapa, 2006, p. 73).

Types and Style of Public Scholarship Products

Public scholars attempt to bring rigorous research and critical products to the public sphere to illuminate and/or address some of the most vexing social problems of the present. Traditional scholarship is written for a scholarly audience with the goal of contributing to the larger knowledge base of a discipline. Yet, public scholarship entails a specific commitment to producing public artifacts or texts in order to probe how scholarship can play a role in stimulating broader discussion of challenging social concerns. Some public scholarship takes the form of traditional writing like publishing op-eds or other articles in newspapers or magazines in traditional print-based outlets or online platforms like websites and blogs or white papers and research reports. Increasingly, public scholarship is being produced in the form of arts and multimedia. These can include graphic displays and info-graphics, apps and entire websites, exhibitions, public lectures (in person or on video streaming services), art exhibitions or performances, and many others.

As the audience for public scholarship is not the academy, but the public, the writing or other scholarly products produced are typically created using plain, clear language or forms, largely free from discipline-specific jargon, or vocabulary. This approach allows the largest audience to engage in the dialogue. With an understanding that the issues that matter most are those which affect the largest number of people, public scholars seek to translate or demystify research or creative products for the public good.

Writing Policy Briefs

Policy briefs are one type of public scholarship which merit an individual consideration for scholars. Unlike public scholarship whose audience is the general public, policy briefs are written to translate research for government policymakers and other people interested in influencing or formulating policy, sometimes referred to as think-tanks. Typically, researchers or academics are asked to write a policy brief to provide a concise but clear outline of a particular topic or problem, provide several policy-based options on how the topic or problem may be addressed, and finally make specific recommendations. Policy briefs can take different formats, and there are many templates available online. Before writing your policy brief, which is a piece of persuasive writing at its core, it is important to research the audience of your brief. You should, at minimum, research answers to the questions below:

- What has been this person or organization's stance, or voting record where applicable, on this topic?

- How does this person or organization view similar or related issues?

- How does the person or organization's ontology (worldview) or mission/values align to your topic?

- How has funding, or other tangible benefits, been allocated around this issue recently and in the more distant past?

- Whose perspectives or positions have been valued on this topic in the past?

- Whose perspectives or positions have been ignored or silenced on this topic in the past?

Knowing the answers to these and related questions can help writers to begin to frame their policy brief in ways that will be more persuasive to the target audience or stakeholders. The authors of this text have found that a **one-pager**, or a one-page document which provides key details and recommendations, is the preferred format for many national and state government agencies and policy makers (see Table 10.2). Specifically, a maximum word limit of 1,500 words or less is considered ideal. As policy makers are very busy and your topic is one of

Table 10.2 One-Pager Template

Title of Brief
This title should quickly and clearly communicate the contents of your brief in a memorable way.

Executive Summary
This section is usually 1–2 paragraphs long and the location where the overview of the topic is grounded in research and the policy solution is introduced.

Scope of the Problem
This section is usually about a paragraph and meant to persuade the audience of the problem's importance and need to intervene using policy.

Policy Alternatives
This section should fairly articulate the current policy approach to the problem and convincingly explain several proposed options or alternatives. Bullet or key points work best here.

Policy Implications or Recommendation
This section should clearly outline the concrete steps which need to be taken to address the policy issue. In this section, numbered steps make clear the sequence and actions you advocate.

Further References or Recommended Resources
This section should include the sources (with links) you used to frame your policy brief. This doesn't need to follow any particular citation style, although a concise annotated bibliography is easiest for a nonacademic audience to follow.
You can also include a link to a personal website which can include longer form documents like journal articles, research reports, or white papers on a topic.

Contact Information
Provide your contact information including all of your social media addresses and handles. You want the policy maker to consult you if they have further questions.

many complex issues being addressed at any given time, using your time and space wisely is paramount. Beyond the overview, or one-pager, having a second more comprehensive research report or white paper to supply (as a link) to a policy maker and their staff can be helpful.

Evaluating Public Scholarship in the Academy

Although many people initially pursue careers in research because they are interested in having a positive impact on society in their sphere of influence or discipline, many constrictions encumber this aim. The pressure to be productive in publication is the most impactful impediment to public scholarship for many faculty. The evaluation, tenure, and/or promotion requirements which frequently accompany academic appointments typically identify a limited scope for what "counts" as a scholarly product. Frequently, only scholarship that has been in juried (blind-peer reviewed) outlets with a certain reach or impact and scholarly presentations to a national or international audience "count" for the purposes of meeting scholarly academic, evaluation, tenure, and promotion requirements. For more information, scholarly metrics and indexes have been discussed in detail in Chapter 7.

To understand the impact and value of public scholarship, many institutions in the academy will need to expand their focus of evaluation to include a broader range of creative and critical work, value local and regional work (especially ones created through engaged scholarship), treat curriculum and program design as a scholarly achievement, and appreciate public presentation of knowledge as a respected accomplishment (Ellison & Eatman, 2008).

However, some institutions have expanded their framework of what "counts" for the purposes of academic evaluation, tenure, and/or promotion. Typically, higher education institutions with a mission-based or regional focus place greater value in and a stronger impetus on public scholarship.

Most institutions also have an "other" category of publication. That being the case, we have a word of caution. Before you decide to engage in public scholarship with the goal of receiving "credit" on your evaluation, tenure, and/or promotion materials, we highly recommend carefully examining your university's policies and procedures documents to identify how or if the various types of public scholarship products will count at your institutions. At the very least, confer with those who are more senior than you to determine if the effort and output will be recognized as viable scholarship at your institution.

SUMMARY

Publishing and productivity in scholarly areas beyond peer-reviewed articles and book chapters are important to consider. What is equally important is to know and understand how your institution values such productivity, including how your institution views and rewards grants, fellowships, and sabbaticals. As we have stressed in previous chapters, getting mileage out of your research, ideas, and scholarly pursuits is working smarter. Pursuing grant proposals, fellowships, possible book proposals, and sabbaticals, as well as more public facing scholarship like op-eds, white papers, and policy briefs involves understanding how each type of scholarly product will be perceived and valued at your institution. One commonality across almost all of these lagniappe scholarly considerations is that they involve a high degree of institutional support and expertise to leverage your scholarship and increase your influence.

KEY TERMS

Concept Template An organizational document that outlines a project. Typically, they include all key sections and elements of a proposal, piece of writing, or other submissions.

Deliverables These are goods or services created as an outcome of a project. Examples of deliverables include written reports or documents, in-person services, public presentations, or even curricula.

Jot List A tool used to organize thoughts for an essay.

Notice of Intent (NOI) As the name implies, a notice of intent is an official notice, supplied by the author(s), indicating intent to participate. NOIs are nonbinding; however, for many grant competitions, failure to submit an NOI often disqualifies a subsequent submission.

Office of Research and Sponsored Programs This is an institutional office at a college or university whose role is to guide members of the faculty, as well as academic and administrative departments, in the procurement and management of sponsored project funding.

One Pager This is a one-page document, typically single sided, that gives a high-level overview of a topic. They are typically used as a proportional or persuasive tool and decision-makers or influencers are the most common audience.

Op-ed A commentary to a featured article. Typically, these are found in more mainstream publications and reach a broad segment of a given population.

Percentage of Effort This is a metric for identifying the amount of time that a scholar and other senior personnel will devote to a specific project. Typically, effort is based on the type of contract (12-month, academic year, academic term, per course affiliate) a person has with the organization. In grants, this metric is typically required.

Policy Brief A concise summary of a social problem that helps the reader understand an issue and make an informed decision. Policy briefs are usually targeted to politicians and policy makers.

Principal Investigator (PI) This person is responsible for the planning, writing, implementation, and administration of a grant, cooperative agreement, training or public service project, contract, or other types of sponsored/funded project. This person must act in, and is held accountable for, compliance with pertinent laws, regulations, and institutional policies controlling the management of funded projects.

Program Officer Within organizations, whether they are government entities, foundations, or nonprofits, typically an individual is identified as the person responsible for marshalling a grant opportunity from start (advertising and promotion) to finish (award).

Requests for Proposals (RFPs) Grant announcements which typically provide the requirements, deadlines, and logistics of applying for funding.

Routing An internal review process for all proposals that will be submitted to external sponsors as well as all proposals that include a commitment of faculty time. This includes foundation or other proposals that include faculty time or resource commitments made on behalf of the university or institution of higher education.

White Paper An authoritative report or guide that provides information on an issue. Although similar to op-eds and policy briefs, white papers typically reflect an issuing body, such as a unit or professional organization's views on an issue.

CRITICAL THINKING QUESTIONS————

- In addition to manuscripts such as journal articles and book chapters, what other kinds of academic proposal will leverage your work?

- What would be your first steps if you wanted to submit a book proposal?

- What foundations might fund your research?

- What institutional grants are aligned with your research agenda?

- What federal agencies issue or are issuing RFPs that would be compatible with your lines of research? What might be a future sabbatical?

- What public facing scholarship like op-eds, white papers, and policy briefs might be appropriate outlets for facets of your research?

ADDITIONAL REFERENCES AND RESOURCES

http://aroomofherownfoundation.org/awards/gift-of-freedom/gift-of-freedom-application/.

Grants Learning Center. https://www.grants.gov/web/grants/learn-grants.html.

This web portal is a growing compendium of resources on applying for grants. The Community Video Series and Grants 101 pages are excellent places to learn about the basic processes, procedures, and tips for applying for funding from the US government.

http://aroomofherownfoundation.org/awards/gift-of-freedom/gift-of-freedom-application/.

http://www.ncte.org/cccc/awards/researchinitiative.

https://mellon.org/grants/.

https://www.aauw.org/what-we-do/educational-funding-and-awards/career-development-grants/cdg-application/.

https://www.cies.org/program/fulbright-us-scholar-program.

https://www.neh.gov/grants/research/fellowships.

https://www.nsf.gov/.

https://www.spencer.org/.

https://www.spencer.org/lyle-spencer-research-awards.

WORKS CITED

Ellison, J., & Eatman, T. K. (2008). *Scholarship in public: Knowledge creation and tenure policy in the engaged university.* Syracuse, NY: Imagining America. Retrieved from https://imaginingamerica.org/wp-content/uploads/TTI_FINAL.pdf

Gürel, E., & Tat, M. (2017). SWOT analysis: A theoretical review. *Journal of International Social Research,* 10(51). doi:10.17719/jisr.2017.1832

Yapa, L. (2006). Public scholarship in the postmodern university. *New Directions for Teaching and Learning,* 2006(105), 73–83.

Next Steps

Conclusion

Purpose of Chapter

In this final chapter, we focus the readers' attention on creating and utilizing a research agenda, and we provide considerations regarding writing related to sustaining scholarly employment. Specifically, we provide advice on how to articulate and purposefully employ your research agenda across your career trajectory as well as writing for evaluation, promotion, and/or tenure. We also suggest ways to work harder and smarter as you build your scholarly career. Finally, the authors share their personal advice on achieving scholarly success in academia.

Learning Objectives

Several learning objectives that relate to utilizing and sustaining a research agenda frame this final chapter. Those objectives are:

1. Learning to create and utilize a cohesive research agenda

2. Learning to write for annual evaluation

3. Learning to write for promotion and/or tenure

4. Learning to work both hard and smart

Quick Write # 10

Source: iStock, georgeclerk

In this final quick write, we ask that you reflect on the picture above. As you reflect, visualize your future career.

- Specifically, what do you envision and imagine down the road or beyond the horizon for yourself?

- What are your goals and aspirations?

- What work would you like to be known for?

- What are some of the challenges, potholes, and forks in the road that you foresee?

- How can you be proactive in avoiding potholes, diversions, or wrong turns?

- What support do you think you might need in order to accomplish your goals and realize the future you envisioned for yourself?

Get out your preferred writing instruments and tools, set a timer for five minutes and reflect on your answer to these or related questions until the time ends. After your quick write, review your writing and reflect on the clarity of your desires. This Quick Write can be fashioned into a living document that can be both a guide and your roadmap to pursuing your research agenda.

Establishing and Utilizing a Cohesive Research Agenda

There are both external and internal rationales for establishing and utilizing a cohesive **research agenda** for your scholarly products and publications as early in your academic career as possible. From an external perspective, having a coherent research agenda assists you in getting and keeping a job in your field. Being able to articulate your research agenda during the job search and interview process demonstrates to your prospective employers that you can generate stimulating ideas and corresponding research questions to start and/or sustain your career at an institution as well as complement or supplement other researchers in the unit or department.

Also, by having a cohesive research agenda which focuses your scholarly products around a specific theme or topic, you can launch yourself as a serious scholar, become an individual with recognized expertise, and establish your reputation as a significant scholar in your area or field. As discussed in Chapter 8, after becoming a professional of note in your field, your citations typically increase, policy makers and professionals in your field will seek your opinion, and you become sought after to contribute to projects which further your work (and professional standing) (Ertmer & Glazewski, 2014). This expert recognition is also helpful as you apply for external funding, which is not a blinded process. Having a targeted focus with several publications in the topic of consideration can convince peer reviewers that you are a leader in the field and capable of driving new explorations in your area of study.

From an internal perspective, a cohesive research agenda allows you to set the purpose and establish a focus for your work. The research agenda should assist you in both contextualizing your work in your scholarly community and better articulating your contribution to the field and to your institution over the course of your career. Importantly, having a research agenda also allows you to identify what topics or research interests are _not_ your focus. In this way, your coherent and cohesive agenda allows you to turn down projects or tasks which distract or detract from your core research agenda. It is edifying when colleagues begin to seek you out as a collaborator; however, always determine if a venture will further your research interests. A focused and coherent research agenda can also assist you in framing difficult conversations with your supervisors or bosses who may try to influence your research agenda for their own or the unit's purposes, or perhaps, can help you articulate your agenda with superiors who lack sufficient background in your area of interest and research field.

Defining the Research Agenda

According to Ertmer and Glazewski (2014), "a research agenda can be viewed as both a noun and a verb" (p. 55). As such, the research agenda, both frames and contextualizes the work of an adept and proficient researcher and also provides the researcher with a guidepost to study a specific topic or content area from several approaches or perspectives. A research agenda should include a set of research questions, strands, purposes, or problems which all relate to common topic or content area and typically serve to guide your career trajectory in one-, three-, or six-year increments. This timeline depends on your institutional requirements for evaluation (more on that later in the chapter) and level of seniority in your career. Every institution has specific guidelines for productivity; however, research, teaching, and service are standard expectations across all institutions but to varying degrees.

For PhD candidates, new scholars, and novice researchers, it may help for you to think of a research agenda along the same vein of a "strategic plan" for an organization. Just as strategic plans help organizations document and shape the direction of their enterprise, your research agenda should align with your methodological toolkit, values, and vision for your long-term career. Developing a research agenda is a necessary exercise in terms of becoming a serious academic scholar.

To be effective, a research agenda must be grounded, focused, coherent, and strong. By grounded, we mean that it must be framed with a specific theoretical approach. According to Whetten (1989), there are four essential questions which must be addressed in a theoretical framework:

1. What factors are components of the phenomenon under inquiry?

2. How are the factors of the phenomenon related?

3. Why do these relationship(s) make sense?

4. Under what conditions or in what contexts would these representations not make sense or relationships not hold? (p. 60).

To better grasp the theoretical frames which undergird your specific topic, we recommend wide reading and exposure throughout your career. Read broadly in your discipline but also in related or allied disciplines. For example, Leah Katherine schedules time to read at least two new articles or book chapters weekly—one directly centered in her field/discipline and another in a related field or discipline approaching similar research questions. In this way, she is able to learn more about emerging theoretical frameworks in her own area as well as how the scholarly conversation is advancing and propagated in an interdisciplinary fashion. Similarly, when this same author attends professional research conferences, she attempts to split her time between presentations on topics which are consistently a part of her research agenda and presentations which offer new opportunities to engage in an allied topic or even learn about a new methodology.

As scholars, having a firm grasp of the theoretical framing of your field and its development means you are also better able to contextualize your own research agenda and corresponding questions in a focused manner. Ertmer and Glazewski (2014) identified a research agenda as too broad if it can be identified in a few words and too narrow if it can be addressed in just one study. A focused research agenda allows for multiple studies or strands (and corresponding research questions) where each study or question addresses a smaller component part of the larger agenda. The studies may use different methodologies to answer similar questions or may use nested or related questions and similar methodologies to explore a larger phenomenon. A focused and grounded approach to your scholarly work is a cornerstone of a strong research agenda.

However, a research agenda must be strong to have utility. While having a grounded and focused research agenda is necessary, it is not sufficient. A research agenda must be strong to support your claim as an expert in your field. If your topic is not novel to the scholarly conversation or is thought-provoking only to you, this will not prove your utility to the field or discipline. As Leah Katherine tells her graduate students, "mesearch," or a topic which is only germane to your specific questions and practice does not constitute strong, and, therefore, publishable research, that moves your field forward. As a developing academic, you have to be aware of your positionality in the field, existing literature, and the current trajectories of the larger scholarly exchange and development of new knowledge. This positionality cements a grounded and focused research trajectory as a strong scholarly agenda.

Identifying Your Research Agenda

Creating your personal research agenda is a mash-up of genre writing. Because a research agenda traverses different writing genres and styles, this makes them particularly difficult writing tasks. As an informative or explanatory genre, a research agenda's central purpose is to inform or explain the topic or topics you hold at the center of all of your inquiries. Further, as your research agenda should position you as an/the expert on your topic, there are elements of the persuasive genre of writing to consider. Finally, your positionality and personal experiences, or **researcher's lens**, certainly shape your research agenda. This is a feature of the narrative genre of writing.

In the activity below, an opportunity for you to brainstorm, develop, extend, and/or hone your research agenda is provided.

Step 3: Drafting a Research Agenda

Based on your Quick Write and observations, attempt to fill in the writing frame below.

I am becoming an expert in (specific component of discipline). My research agenda is (topic) and is grounded in (name) theor(ies) using (name) methodologies. My research agenda attempts to address (number) of strands/questions including (list).

We emphasize that this is simply a draft. You will continue to revise and hone this agenda prior to any academic appointments and at designated times throughout your career. Specifically, we encourage researchers to revisit their research agenda every three to six years at minimum as well as especially during any institutionally designated evaluation markers, such as promotion and/or tenure. Consider how you might graphically represent your research agenda, using the sample graphics in the previous section.

Writing Activity 11.1

Step 1: Utilizing the Quick Write from the beginning of the chapter, we would like you to reflect on the following questions:

- Identify what topics you wish to become an expert in or would like to know more about. Why these topics?

- Specifically, spend time reflecting on how these topics do or do not relate to one another?

- Which are you most passionate about? Why?

- What is your lens on this work?

- What are the theoretical frames which undergird these topics?

- How do these topics add to the scholarly conversation?

- Is there an audience for these topics beyond yourself? Why or why not?

As you answer these and any related wonderings you have, attempt to establish a more singular focus that is broad enough to cover multiple strands or research topics. A singular focus should be identified where there is overlap across your interests. If overlap does not exist, we suggest that you cull your interests until you can identify where there is overlap. This type of cohesiveness is necessary as you carve out your research agenda and identity yourself as an expert. As exemplars, each of the authors of this text has carved a research agenda that is coherent and includes multiple strands and sub-strands.

Step 2: Review the research agenda descriptions and graphic representations below. As you review the exemplars, below, consider:

- How are they similar/different?

- How are they informative?

- How are they persuasive?

- How are they narrative?

- How can you represent your burgeoning research agenda in writing and utilizing a graphic representation?

Social constructivism drives my research agenda which includes three strands focused on literacy in urban settings, specifically investigating the complexities of literacy leadership, examining service-learning as a pedagogical pathway to preparing pre-service teachers to teach literacy in urban environments, and exploring ways to provide access to literature, writing, and the arts (arts integration) in urban environs. I believe a central research question determines design. Traversing the fields of literacy research and educational leadership, as a qualitative researcher, typically, I employ case study design, ethnography, and most recently, autoethnography as a stance to understand complex issues in PK-12 educational settings.

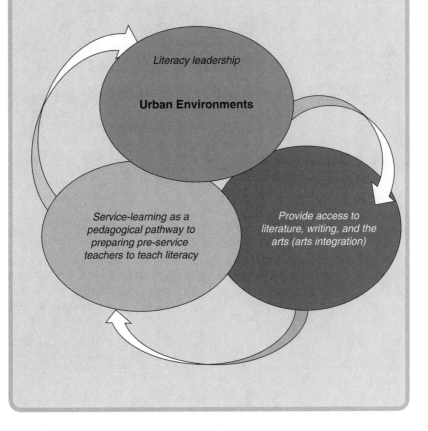

Exemplar 11.2 Dr. Saal's Research Agenda and Graphic Representation

My engaged scholarly agenda focuses on the intersectionality of literacy and social justice with a community literacy lens. Community literacy is fraught with complexities and encompassing of multiple and evolving dimensions of diversity. As a mixed methodologist, I use quantitative and qualitative methods and a Freirean pedagogical stance to attempt to rigorously answer complex questions. My research includes two dovetailing strands. In the first strand of my research, I focus on the literacy skills and practices of adults and older students in and out of school settings. In my second strand of research, I investigate the preparation and support of literacy educator-leaders to work for social justice.

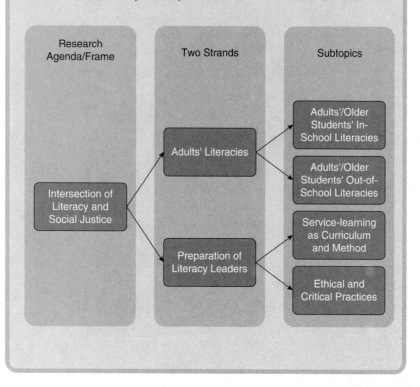

My work as an early intervention practitioner has shaped my research agenda. My research focuses on interventions to improve outcomes for young children and clarification and innovations in recommended practices in early childhood. Within my work, I frequently use single case research design within the quantitative paradigm to measure the effectiveness of teachers' use of interventions with young children, which has also led to the investigation of practices used in the field. I am committed to mentoring undergraduate and graduate students through this process via coursework and cocurricular programming.

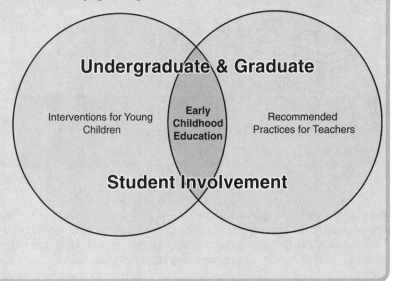

Utilizing Your Research Agenda to Drive Productivity and Publishing

Each research question, study, and corresponding manuscript you produce should align to your research agenda. Prior to the onset of any new research, you should always ask yourself, "Does this research question or project directly align to my research agenda? If so, how?". Considering these central questions proactively and only moving forward with projects you can answer in the affirmative and in detail will move your productivity and, ultimately, reputation as a scholar

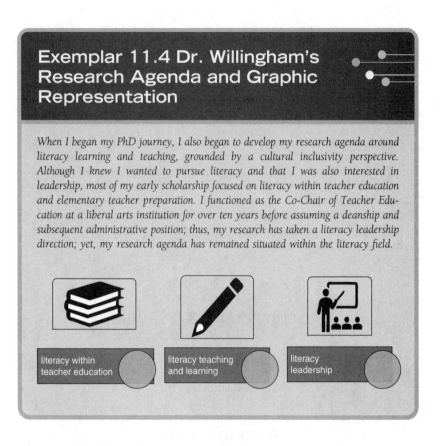

Exemplar 11.4 Dr. Willingham's Research Agenda and Graphic Representation

When I began my PhD journey, I also began to develop my research agenda around literacy learning and teaching, grounded by a cultural inclusivity perspective. Although I knew I wanted to pursue literacy and that I was also interested in leadership, most of my early scholarship focused on literacy within teacher education and elementary teacher preparation. I functioned as the Co-Chair of Teacher Education at a liberal arts institution for over ten years before assuming a deanship and subsequent administrative position; thus, my research has taken a literacy leadership direction; yet, my research agenda has remained situated within the literacy field.

literacy within teacher education

literacy teaching and learning

literacy leadership

forward. For most of us in the academy, our scholarship is the one area of our employment which is our sole responsibility to drive and articulate. Therefore, we must be attentive in developing both our agenda and corresponding standing in our fields. This extends to professional organizations where we showcase our work, what we publish and where, what grant funding we pursue, and how we craft service opportunities to interface with scholarly productivity and teaching. Our agenda and standing within our fields also may determine with whom we collaborate on projects, from research to publications to grant work.

Each author of this text can trace every scholarly contribution they have made from their time as advanced graduate students to senior scholars to a component part of their former or current research agenda. As careers progress, so does your research agenda, but typically not in dramatic ways. After all, you have spent your time in training and in service honing your skill as an expert. Typically, over time, your area of expertise may broaden in scale to having policy impact or may narrow in scope as your inquiries drive further, more specialized investigations. Regardless, a colleague, your supervisor, or a peer reviewer should be able to cold-categorize, without further assistance from you, the component items on your CV into one of your articulated strands or research areas within your research agenda.

Therefore, as your career advances and you are invited to participate in collaborative scholarship, be advised to consider your personal research agenda first. If the project does not directly align with your agenda, you should not accept the invitation. The project will not advance your agenda, and, worse, will siphon valuable research time from those studies which do. This kind of situation can present a conundrum: while you want to remain viable and productive, you don't want publications at the cost of scattering and diluting your research agenda. As experts in our field, in many ways, one of the worst critiques we could receive from those evaluating our productivity and impact is that we are "a jack of all trades and a master of none."

Writing for Purpose of Annual Review or Evaluation

Many, although not all, institutions of higher learning have a process and procedure for annual review, tenure, and promotion. A successful annual evaluation should always be the first goal on the horizon. And while the process may appear somewhat similar, every institution is different. Typically, you will be evaluated on three characteristic areas of scholarship—research productivity, teaching expertise, and meaningful service to the profession. It is a scholar's responsibility to locate, know, and understand the institutional policies and their applicability for annual review/evaluation, promotion, and tenure. This understanding also extends to knowing the percentage of your contract that you are expected to devote to each of these areas. In institutions of higher learning, within these policies, faculty expectations regarding research and publishing productivity are discussed, along with teaching load and service requirements. Most policies are comprehensive in that they detail loads per **rank**. Institutional expectations vary.

For example, at research intensive institutions in the US, often referred to as an R1 institution, you will probably encounter an expectation of at least two to three peer-reviewed, higher tier publications annually. Research will likely be 40% of your work load. At a regional institution, you can expect to produce less peer-reviewed publications annually than an R1, but you can also anticipate an increased teaching load, perhaps 40–50%. Many liberal arts institutions are mission-driven so scholarship and teaching are tightly woven into service as well. Expectations may shift slightly from the ranks of assistant to associate. Your job as an emerging scholar is to know these expectations. Don't be afraid to ask colleagues at varied rank and across disciplines to describe the expectations to ensure clarity, read your contract, and the university documents governing promotion and tenure.

While there is an institutional policy, oftentimes, colleges with the institution, and units within the college also have policy. Typically, but not always, an institutional policy supersedes college and unit policy in that the college or unit cannot exceed an institution's policy, yet these policies can differ. Annual reviews are conducted by unit directors and heads, and sometimes, in conjunction with faculty at or above the rank of the individual being evaluated. Annual reviews are important for continuation of contracts, and, therefore, you should carefully consider corresponding feedback. We recommend that scholars take feedback from their first annual review and in consideration of both review feedback and any associated promotion and or tenure guidelines, create a checklist of targets. Carefully consider effort in terms of percentages across the components of research, teaching, and service. Scholars should determine "what counts" for each component and ascertain quality indicators for each component as a helpful way to navigate these documents.

One area to pay particular attention to are what is understood by **top tier**, second tier, etc. journals and publication houses. Oftentimes, units and colleges will specify this information while an institutional policy may not—as they are broader documents. This is important as annual evaluations may contain advice to consider such as seeking more single or first author publications and an annual evaluation may also specify what tier level should be sought. In addition, annual evaluations may also contain information such as seeking publication in regional, national, and interventional venues or converting more conference presentations to publications.

Reviewing Policy Documents for Annual Review or Evaluation

We recommend that graduate students investigate their degree-granting institution's policies to familiarize themselves with publishing and research expectations as a means to gain a sense of institutional expectations. For new scholars and novice researchers, we suggest you discuss scholarly mentorship while interviewing for positions. Is there a formal mentorship process or program for new faculty? Is mentorship and/or training of new faculty approached with a laissez-faire attitude? Find an early career faculty member (off your itinerary) to ask about their experience with onboarding. We argue that this information should be considered in your decision-making about potential positions as a new scholar or novice researcher by allowing you to glimpse what support is available within your potential department or college.

If not provided, new scholars and novice researchers should expressly request a mentor upon hire. State that you seek a mentor who can guide you through the institution's annual review, promotion, and (where appropriate) tenure process. In addition, it is an excellent idea to set meetings with your direct supervisor in the beginning of annual review cycle to clarify any confusion or ask questions regarding their expectations of your teaching, research, and service. Request rubrics or whatever checklists may exist in addition to narrative criteria. It is important to know what the expectations are so that you can make and implement a plan to directly address them. In terms of publishing specifically, you should note: both the acceptable number of publications as well as the caliber of publications, expectations for single-authored publications, and how coauthored publications and order of authorship are valued. If possible, new scholars and novice researchers can request at least the template to be used, or, request an exemplar of an acceptable annual evaluation, name redacted, of course, to consider as a model.

Research	Teaching	Service	Policy Specifications	Indicators
1				
2				
3				
4				
5				

Now take the time to add what your institutions state as policy in the fourth column. Finally, consider what artifacts you can include that support your writing. These are your targets.

Once a scholar has completed an initial annual review, they can create a personal checklist of annual evaluation feedback and consider feedback in terms of setting publishing targets. At this point, it is assistive to return to your personal research agenda (step 3 of writing activity 9.1) and compare the checklist with the agenda. There should be alignment.

Writing Clearly and Persuasively to Your Targets

At some universities, a personal statement or statement of philosophy accompanies the annual evaluation. The focus of this document should be to highlight your work through the lens of your research agenda and the guidelines outlined by your institution. The purpose is to explain how you have met the requirements of your institution within the year, with accompanying documentation. It is important to know who you are writing this for—such as the unit director or dean or a committee of peers. Again, we suggest you request a sample of an exemplar. Take your time to prepare this document, edit, and review thoroughly prior to submission. This is not something you should put off as a "have to task." Think of this activity as an extension of your hiring process. An annual review or evaluation is like an annual job interview and opportunity to sell yourself again to your institution—explaining how your work is novel, important, and supports the institution.

Writing for the Purpose of Promotion and/or Tenure

If you are lucky enough to have the opportunity to earn promotion or tenure, taking the time to draft components of your promotion or tenure dossier early in your career will yield dividends as you begin the process of preparing for your initial review by your peers. Part of the review process requires you to write a statement (or set of statements) that summarizes your productivity across research, teaching and service. Soliciting feedback at your previous annual reviews, in addition to working closely with a mentor, serves to help you "course correct" if necessary, so that your work is in alignment with standards within your program, department, college, and/or university.

Your statement(s) should begin by stating the terms of your appointment (i.e., 50% scholarship, 40% teaching, 10% service) and your hire date (or start date at this rank), and provide the reader with an overall summary of your productivity since starting at the institution (or at this rank) across the areas of scholarship, teaching, and service, highlighting noteworthy details that are not communicated on your CV. For some, administrative load is also part of the equation and will need to be considered and written toward. In some institutions, this is considered service, whereas in others this is a separate area to consider and write toward. The body of the statement(s) should be divided across the three or four major areas and provide additional detail.

Specifically, within the area of scholarship, state your research agenda to include major and minor areas. Note not only recent publications, but work in various stages of development (e.g., revise and resubmit, manuscript preparation, data analysis, data collection) and collaborative partnerships with other agencies or departments. Summarize grant or external funding including funded, unfunded (demonstrates effort), and those in preparation. Note your presentations at local, state, national, and international conferences. You might consider adding a graphic representation of your research agenda from Writing Activity 11.1 for your scholarship section.

Within the area of teaching, be sure to note both quantitative and qualitative information, noting consistencies and inconsistencies. Note any additional responsibilities, such as the development of or major revisions to courses, and mentoring of graduate students. Be sure to include any service-learning partnerships with outside agencies (which could become research partners).

Within the area of service, be sure to note department, college, university, professional, and related community service, including offices held (i.e., officer, chair). These can be ongoing commitments (e.g., Secretary of your professional organization for two years) or discrete activities (e.g., guest reviewer for a journal or serving on a local board related to your area of study).

If you have an administrative load which is part of your contract and separate from your service obligations, note all of your primary responsibilities and the time and effort you have allocated to these tasks—per week, per semester or academic term, and per academic year. This way, your evaluators can get an accurate accounting for how your administrative load really "looks" in the context of your contract and responsibilities.

The personal statement should close with a summarizing section that demonstrates the scholars' trajectory for success based on the stated performance across each area. Use the summary statement to guide readers to consider your research agenda. This is not just a simple exercise; rather, it is a very useful exercise. **It is important to note that external reviewers or external evaluators**, persons within your field but not at your institution, may also review your application for promotion or dossier and render an opinion of your work. It is never too early to begin considering who in your field may be an ideal colleague to review and speak to the merits of your scholarly work.

Reviewing Policy Documents for Promotion and/or Tenure

Higher education institutions often have policies and corresponding processes for promotion and/or tenure. As stated previously, typically, the institution has one committee, often a college or school has one committee, and usually, a unit, department, or program has one committee. In many instances, the institution's promotion and/or tenure document typically supersedes a college's or school's, and a unit's, department's, or program's tenure and promotion document. These documents outline both a process, including timelines, and as well as what a scholar needs to produce for tenure in terms of documentation. Some units and colleges have metrics that need to be met. Most units and colleges also have committee structures whose members evaluate materials and make recommendations to unit and college leaders. Knowing your institution's policies and procedures is paramount. Three or four areas are assessed: scholarly productivity or research, teaching, service, and, sometimes, administration.

Along with the specifications that institution, college/school, and unit/department documents contain, it is important to understand how tenure and promotion documents are assessed and evaluated. Many institutions, for example, require **external letters** of evaluation. Processes differ but frequently follow a similar pattern. Scholars going up for a next step in the promotion or tenure process prepare materials and also provide a list of external evaluators in their field who can submit letters that support a tenure and promotion bid. It is very important to take the process of preparing this list very seriously; these reviewers will judge your work and contribute to the decision on your tenure. Be careful to choose reviewers who have a similar background and understand your work. In some cases, the identity of the letter writer is masked, and the process is blind. The scholar going up for tenure and promotion does not know who submits letters, even if the scholar generates an initial list to be considered.

Writing Clearly and Persuasively to Your Targets

Similar to your annual review, a statement typically accompanies your promotion and/or tenure materials. The focus of this document should be to highlight your work since your arrival at the university (or your last change in rank) through the lens of your research agenda and the guidelines outlined by your institution. The purpose is to explain how you have met the requirements of your institution since your hire (or last change in rank), with accompanying documentation. It is important to know the review process, so that you are able to write to not only the guidelines of your unit or department but also your college and the university. It is especially critical that you are careful to explain nuances, as your work will be reviewed by those outside of your area and outside of your discipline. It is imperative that your promotion and/or tenure materials are very clearly written. Again, ask for an exemplar which received a successful outcome, take your time, and edit judiciously.

Working Hard *and* Smart

Achieving a continued academic contract, promotion, or tenure is strenuous work; it takes mental acuity, discipline, continuous energy, and determination. Achieving promotion and/or tenure is cumulative and labor intensive. Given the effort involved, it is important to work hard but also work smart toward these goals—where applicable. Understanding your institution's process is paramount and an important first step. Knowing that you won't be provided a second chance can be sobering but is a realistic perspective. Hence, concentrated, strategic effort is needed.

Early chapters in this text adequately addressed the discipline needed to be productive and publish at a steady rate. The authors of this text have compiled useful information about a variety of elements that produce productivity. Here we offer two strategies which have been discussed in previous chapters but that epitomize the notion of working hard and smart with these goals in mind.

Mining Collected Data. There are many opportunities that can yield usable data. These opportunities can come from your teaching, novel practices, presentations, or other research projects, given some planning and consideration.

One of the authors of this text, Cyndi, regularly teaches an undergraduate assessment course within the program area of Early Childhood. As part of the course competencies, students learn how to design assessments to measure child progress. As the course instructor, she designs a project she is interested in studying to meet the requirements of the course and teaches the students in the course to collect the data, imparting to them critical research design and measurement skills within the data collection project.

Although it can take a little longer to amass the data, they are data she wouldn't have if she hadn't integrated the project into her course. As a side benefit, her students are less intimidated by the research process. This has resulted in many undergrads pursuing undergraduate research, and some going on to pursue graduate school. This practice has a four-fold purpose: incorporate a high-impact practice, stimulate interest in undergraduate research, collecting useful data—mining data, and by piquing the interest of undergrads in the research process, also functioning as a recruiting strategy for advanced studies in early childhood.

Margaret-Mary, another author, has used her teaching as a mechanism for data collection as well. Earlier in her career, as she was expanding her service-learning scholarship, she combined teaching and service with a research opportunity. She incorporated service-learning opportunities in establishing community gardens at a partnering school site into a required undergraduate literacy course while teaching at her first academic job at a regional university in Mississippi. Her IRB focused on students' dispositional shifts, an important consideration in the fields of teacher education and literacy. This resulted in her first service-learning publication. In the years immediately after Hurricane Katrina decimated the New Orleans metroplex, including schools and public libraries, she strategically embedded a service project around creating classroom libraries in a required grades 1–5 undergraduate literacy course. Margaret-Mary had moved to a large RI institution at this point in her career. There, her undergraduate students explored the efficacy of classroom libraries and the notion of access to literature, especially in a post-Katrina environment. She created a classroom library service project and collected data on students' dispositions toward access and classroom libraries. This resulted in several publications in her service-learning research area as well as her access research area, both under the umbrella of literacy in urban environments.

Tynisha, also a service-learning scholar, created an intensive service project while she was a teacher education faculty member at a small Catholic liberal arts institution. Tynisha crafted a unique credit-bearing special topics course over the winter intercession wherein elementary education candidates traveled to New Orleans post-Katrina and experienced both a community charter school as a site for field work and the issues associated with accessing education in a challenging urban environment. Her students all stayed at a local community worker house, used only public transportation, and created community meals for each other in an effort to emulate the experiences of access and economics while also witnessing firsthand, the creation of a community charter school in the post-Katrina environment.

Selected publications of the authors Cyndi, Leah Katherine, Margaret-Mary, and Tynisha are included in the Additional References and Resource section of this chapter as examples of both data collection within teaching and as examples of how a strong agenda plays out in publishing opportunities. Note the strands of each authors" agenda exemplified through publications. Each author was very careful to file IRBs and follow strict protocols as well as to acknowledge their positionality and situatedness within such research.

Data can also be mined from novel practices. One semester, Cyndi unexpectedly had an overload of students that needed supervision. Due to competing priorities and the geographic locations of the field sites, she opted to do (pre-pandemic) "virtual" supervision. She took this as an opportunity to collect data on both the effectiveness of this virtual model (good) and also the social satisfaction (not so good). Information from this pilot data served the program well when circumstances necessitated making this shift with the entire program. She had data that supported how to move forward with this model of supervision.

Collaborative partnerships are also great opportunities to collect data. During a conversation with a community partner of Cyndi's, the partner voiced a concern related to parent/family training and infant care. As the university partner, she designed a study to meet the needs of the parent through parent training within the context of the research design that yielded a publishable product. She involved a graduate student and supported in the design of a research project that ultimately became the graduate student's thesis. This rich experience exposed the graduate student to the work of collaborating with community partners, as well as the research and publication process, while also providing the community partner with insight on parent training and infant care.

In another instance of opportune data collection, Margaret-Mary was working with two research and writing partners, all of whom were investigating the emerging subfield of literacy leadership. After an exhaustive literature review where they isolated the content knowledge, literacy pedagogical knowledge, and supervisory and management skills associated with literacy leadership, the three researchers created a framework for elementary literacy leadership. Then they attended several literacy and educational leadership conferences over the course of three academic semesters, presenting on their framework. They invited approximately 140 attendees to critique the framework, eliciting critical feedback from scholars in the fields of educational leadership and literacy. The critique was used to revise and strengthen the framework, which yielded publications as well. Although these publications were published in 2010 and 2012, a doctoral candidate at another institution reached out to Margaret-Mary in the spring of 2021, seeking permission to use the framework in her proposed dissertation study. Not only is this an example of being established within a field and recognized, but also of how to mine data.

This brings us to a final, but important point. Always collect more data than you think you need.

- Are there any secondary (or tertiary) questions related to your main focus? Include them in your data collection.

- Do you have a colleague who is collecting data on a population of interest? Ask if you can add a few questions.

These data points can help you in your trajectory career focus in establishing yourself as an expert in your area.

Considering Projects That Will Produce Publications Quickly and Will Still Move Your Research Agenda Forward in the Long Term

One strategy that can effectively advance your publication record is to ensure that you write companion practitioner or policy articles to accompany research articles. We have addressed this practice previously, but it bears repeating in this final chapter as well. The process to crafting these manuscripts is relatively straightforward. Consider the findings of your research study and specifically, focus exclusively on what recommendations come from this work—what should be done differently as a result of your findings? Combining supporting literature from your research study, your intervention methods, and findings provide the structure for your practitioner- or policy-focused manuscript. Choosing practitioner- or policy-focused publication outlets also involves strategy. In this arena, consider the readership of the publication outlet, as well as any affiliation to a professional or policymaking or evaluating organization.

An extension of submitting your research to a practitioner or policy publication outlet would be to also *present* your work to practitioners or policy makers. There are several professional and policy-focused organizations that hold annual conferences for their state, regional, national, and international membership. Presenting your work in these forums provides visibility to both you and your research, helping you to establish yourself as an expert in your topic area. This exposure could lead to consulting work or collaborative relationships.

Other Longer-Term Recommendations

We assume the competence and expertise of every reader of this text. In this book, we hoped to demystify the processes required for productivity and publication, so that you can "show what you know." We take this explicit asset perspective and assume that all of our readers will be successful in their pursuits of publishing productivity. That said, when you are, know that there may be some changes to what others perceive as your commitment and responsibility to academia. As we have mentioned previously, your expertise may place you in increased demand by scholars in your field and funding agencies. You may be asked to take on a larger mentorship or leadership role in your field or at your intuition. We mention these to note that while flattering, where possible, do not let these "opportunities" distract you from your research agenda and goals for your career. Continuing to control and balance your time using the strategies already articulated in this book in order to establish a continuous publishing record is key. For your continued career viability and advancement, inside and, most important, outside of your current institution, it is important to maintain your objectivity and ability to say "no" to projects which do not fall within your research agenda or interests. While your job is to serve the needs of the institution or field, your academic and scholarly career is your own. You must continue to steer the ship. Balancing these sometimes-competing priorities as a senior scholar requires laser focus and clarity in communication. We know you will be up to the challenge.

Mentor Reflections

In this section, the authors of this text offer final advice on publishing and productivity, as distant mentors-on-the-page to readers. Culled from their experiences in academia, each author has traveled a different path to success. These are our final thoughts and strategies that have contributed to successful productivity and publishing.

Margaret-Mary's Strategies for Success

My three strategies for success include developing a clear focus for a research agenda, utilizing professional organizations and leveraging my service with them, and developing both reading and writing discipline. I was a high school English teacher, taught middle school English for eight years, and then ended my career as a public school teacher as a Title 1 literacy specialist. I love literacy, and that has been my chosen field and area of interest, broadly, since pursuing both my bachelor's and master's degree and earning my PhD in 1999. I knew this about myself and strategically parleyed my keen interest in literacy, language, and culture into the foundation for my research agenda. In addition to literacy, I have always been drawn to teaching and learning and now, leadership, in urban settings.

Early in my career, I chose to steep myself in the literacy field and to immerse myself in urban research. I carefully selected several major professional organizations as my academic "homes" and concentrated on knowing my field through these organizations. This included volunteering for committees, serving as a reviewer for manuscripts and proposals, and coming into contact with pillars in the literacy field. This helped when I pursued tenure as an associate professor and as a full professor in terms of securing external evaluators. I have been particularly influenced by the work of Richard Milner and Kofi Lomotey (2012, 2014), and in understanding the difference between the concepts of urban characteristic, urban emergent, and urban intensive. I am committed to staying current, and I have done so by regularly reading journal articles and books. The leap to access issues and literacy leadership seemed natural to me, and again, I exploited the structures available to me through professional organizations to further my agenda.

Finally, I carved out "sacred" writing and reading time, first dedicating large portions of days twice a week, then three days a week, and now, almost daily. I wake up at 4:30 a.m. almost every day, a holdover from my PhD days. I cook and eat breakfast with my husband, and after he departs our home at 5:30 a.m., I set goals for the day (think Chapter 2), tidy up my house to avoid any potential task avoidance behaviors, and write from 6:00 a.m. until noon most days. I take small breaks, employing the Pomodoro Technique, but stick to this schedule on average, five days per week. This acquired discipline has resulted in a respectable publishing record and continual productivity. Knowing my interests, shaping my interests into a research agenda, accessing professional organizations, and developing strong and sustaining reading and writing habits are strategies that have benefitted my professional career.

Leah Katherine's Strategies for Success

As an engaged scholar focused on adult and community literacies, I have two specific recommendations for strategies that I have used to be more productive in publishing. First, I sought employment at an institution which had an explicit mission and history aligned with my research agenda. When I was on the job market, I looked purposely for urban institutions with not only an overt commitment to engaged scholarship but who also *put their money where their mouth/PR was*. In other words, that the stated institutional commitment to engaged scholarship was clearly prioritized with institutional supports like a large, staffed department dedicated to community service, service-learning, and engaged scholarship and endowed internal/institutional funding unequivocally devoted to this type of work. As a result, I was supported in my entrée into my communities of practice at my new institution and locale, as well as in my quest to align my teaching, service, and research. In the same way, you should carefully choose a publication outlet that fits your work, where possible. I recommend being highly selective and purposeful about where you work.

Second, I recommend, where possible, to continue to maintain some form of connection to current practice in your field. For example, a great deal of my scholarship continues to be informed by my ongoing volunteer experiences teaching with and learning from families, adults, and communities in and out of school settings in the greater Baltimore-Washington DC metroplex. A personal understanding of the issues and concerns, wants, and needs of these communities is necessary for me to address authentic questions of policy and practice. Ultimately, I hope this prevents my research and corresponding publications from spiraling into "mesearch."

Neither of these suggestions may be germane to you or your interests, and that is okay. These are merely strategies I have found that push me forward to maintain productivity in my scholarship.

Cyndi's Strategies for Success

As a practitioner and action researcher, I worked directly with young children with disabilities in home, center, and community-based child care environments for 10 years prior to joining academia full time. In my practice, I sought to determine the best course of action to maximize student learning and worked with teachers on delivering meaningful instruction to help children reach developmental milestones. My research and writing are drawn from my work as a practitioner, and as extension of this work, as well as my desire to help other practitioners work successfully with young children and make a difference in their lives.

My writing style may not appear organized, but it is very deliberate. I believe that to be effective at what you do, you have to know yourself, strengths and needs, very well. I work best in the morning and in long spurts. I often work on several projects at once and always with a variety of different writing partners, who are most often action researchers. I find the collaborative process energizing, and for me, collaboration keeps the process motivating.

Tynisha's Strategies for Success

My success has depended on two attributes—patience and perseverance. Because I developed a clear focus for a research agenda early in my career, wrote to that agenda, and developed both reading and writing discipline, I was successful. I also drew upon seminal teaching experience as a part of my research agenda. I was a Teach for America (TFA) Corps member from 2002 to 2004, teaching in both the Rio Grande Valley in Texas and in the Baltimore City Public Schools in Maryland. As an educator, that experience was life changing. Since that time, I served in several administrative and instructional support roles for TFA's summer institute. As a former charter school founder, a curriculum coordinator, and curriculum specialist for TFA, my signature focus was the need for in-depth literacy knowledge as well as leadership capacity, which I view as integral to supporting novice teachers as well as school leaders. Thus, my experiences prior to becoming a faculty member or having a role in the academy shaped my research agenda, and while it has expanded, keeping my focus contributed to my success.

I write when I can, meaning I have three children so their needs and schedules must come first in my life. However, this has not handicapped me; rather, I have learned to carve out time and to set regular time to write when they are involved in school work, sports, and sleeping. I love late-night writing time. As a mother, I am at peace with knowing my children are steps away, sleeping, their lunches have been packed, their school clothes selected, and they are safe under my roof. While not always writing for long periods of time, my late-night writing time allows me to continue productivity while not interfering with either parenting or my job as a senior academic administrator.

SUMMARY

In this final chapter, the authors focus readers' attention on thinking through how to craft a viable **research agenda**. In addition, the issues surrounding unit-level, college-level, and institutional level considerations regarding successful writing and publishing with the ultimate goal of achieving continued employment and career advancement, including but not limited to tenure and promotion, were presented. We ended this final chapter with personal reflection, positioning ourselves as mentors-on-the page for readers.

KEY TERMS

External Letters As part of a tenure review, many institutions require a set number of external letters from scholars above or at the same level as the person pursuing tenure who share interest and work in a field of study or one that is closely related. Intuitions have their own requirements but generally, external letters are written blind so that the reviewer knows the individual's name who is seeking tenure, but the individual may not know who wrote an external letter. Usually, there is no personal relationship involved but you may have worked in a professional capacity with someone who asks you to write an external letter of review. Typically, they carry a great deal of weight in a tenure review process.

External Reviewers/External Evaluators Scholars above or at the same level as the person pursuing tenure who share interest and work in a field of study or one that is closely related are external reviewers. These are individuals within your field or closely related field who can evaluate your work against your institution's expectations for tenure and promotion. Good consulates to consider external reviewers/external evaluators as are those with whom you may have worked in a professional capacity such as editors for whom you have reviewed, committee chairs of professional organization's standing committees. The perspectives of external reviewers/external evaluators carry substantial weight in a tenure review process.

Rank Rank refers to the positions with academic hierarchy that reflect faculty titles. For example, most US institutions of higher learning begin tenure-track positions with the assistant professor rank, then associate professor, and then the full professor. Outside the US, the term lecturer and senior lecturer may be used. Many institutions of higher learning also have nontenure track ranks such as instructor and senior instructor, as well as assistant, associate, and full professor of professional practice ranks.

Research Agenda A research agenda is a living, breathing document wherein a scholar determines the trajectory or trajectories they are pursuing in terms of the purpose and focus of their research. A research agenda frames and contextualizes the work of an expert researcher. A research agenda should include a set of research questions, strands, purposes, or problems which all relate to common topic or content area.

Researcher's Lens The view taken by the researcher when approaching an issue. This can be epistemological or theoretical.

Top Tier Journal Refers to journals that have a high rate of rejection, only publishing the top 10% of submitted manuscripts.

CRITICAL THINKING QUESTIONS

1. What is the singular focus and purpose of your research agenda?

2. What issues/problems frame and contextualize your research agenda?

3. What is your institution's policy on tenure and promotion?

4. Who are individuals in your field that could function as external reviewers?

ADDITIONAL REFERENCES AND RESOURCES

Bergen, D., Lee, L., DiCarlo, C., & Burnett, G. (2020). *Enhancing brain development in infants and young children: Strategies for caregivers and educators.* New York, NY: Teachers College Press.

Deris, A., & DiCarlo, C. F. (2021). *Making the DEC recommended practices "come to life": Using case method of instruction in early childhood special education.* Springfield, IL: Charles Thomas Publisher, LTD.

DiCarlo, C. F., Baumgartner, J., Ota, C., & Geary, K. (2016). Child sustained attention in preschool-aged children. *Journal of Research in Childhood Education*, 30(2), 143–152.

DiCarlo, C. F., Ota, C., & Deris, A. (2021). Ecobehavioral analysis of social behavior across learning contexts in kindergarten. *Early Childhood Education Journal*, 49, 657–668. doi:10.1007/s10643-020-01103-y

Hoewing, B., & Sulentic Dowell, M.-M. (2010). The elementary principal as chief literacy officer: Myth, legend, fairy tale or reality? *Journal of the Southern Regional Council of Educational Administration*, 63–73.

Horta, H., & Santos, J. M. (2016). An instrument to measure individuals' research agenda setting: The multi-dimensional research agendas inventory. *Scientometrics*, 108, 1243–1265.

King, S. (2000). *On writing: A memoir of the craft.* New York, NY: Simon & Shuster.

Lau, J., Meidl, T., & Sulentic Dowell, M.-M. (2019). *The literacy leadership guide for elementary principals: Reclaiming teacher autonomy and joy.* Landham, MD: Rowman and Littlefield.

Lutfiyya, M. N., Brandt, B., Delaney, C., Pechacek, J., & Cerra, F. (2016). Setting a research agenda for interprofessional education and collaborative practice in the context of United States health system reform. *Journal of Interprofessional Care*, 30(1), 7–14.

Meidl, T., & Baumann, B. (2015). Extreme make over: Disposition development of pre-service teachers. *Journal of Community Engagement and Scholarship*, 8(1), 10.

Meidl, T. D., Saal, L. K., & Dowell, M. M. S. (2018). A typology of conscious decision making for service-learning field experiences: Labeling practice and identifying praxis. In *Handbook of research on service-learning initiatives in teacher education programs* (pp. 504–513). Hershey, PA: IGI Global.

Meidl, T., & Sulentic Dowel, M.-M. (2018). *Handbook of service-learning initiatives in teacher education programs*. Hershey, PA: IGI Global.

Nasser, R. (2014). A methodological and scientific approach to developing a research agenda in education. *Journal of Applied Sciences*, 14(19), 2359–2366.

Saal, L. K. (2018). Exploring the impact of service-learning on literacy teachers' self-reported empathy. In T. Meidl, & M. -M. Sulentic Dowell (Eds.), *Handbook of research on service-learning initiatives in teacher education programs* (pp. 393–408). Hershey, PA: IGI Global.

Saal, L. K., & Minson, C. W. (2017). Working to learn together: Engaged scholarship addressing long-term unemployment. *Adult Learning*, 28(4), 167–170.

Saal, L. K., & Sulentic Dowell, M. M. (2014). A literacy lesson from an adult "burgeoning" reader. *Journal of Adolescent & Adult Literacy*, 58(2), 135–145.

Saal, L. K., Sulentic Dowell, M. M., & Meidl, T. D. (2019). Ethics of access: Provocative impacts of K-12 service-learning and civic engagement policy. *International Journal of Research on Service-Learning and Community Engagement*, 7(1), 11487.

Saal, L. K., Yamashita, T., Shaw, D. M., & Perry, K. H. (2020). An exploration of US adults' information processing skills and political efficacy. *Journal of Adult and Continuing Education*, 26(2), 178–202.

Santos, J. M., & Horta, H. (2018). The research agenda setting of higher education researchers. *Higher Education*, 76, 649–668.

Smutny, N. D., & Saal, L. K. (2021). A "good game" of readers responding. *The Reading Teacher*, 74(5), 517–525.

Sulentic Dowell, M.-M. (2008). Academic-service learning as pedagogy: An approach to preparing pre-service teachers for urban environments. *The Journal of Teaching and Learning*, 5, 1–21.

Sulentic Dowell, M.-M. (2009). Transformative opportunities for community engagement within teacher education: Creating opportunities for pre-service teachers for urban environments in post-katrina new Orleans. *Journal of Community Engagement and Higher Education*, 1(1), 1–10.

Sulentic Dowell, M.-M. (2011). Pre-service teachers' experience with classroom libraries: Urban teacher preparation in post-Katrina New Orleans. *Journal of Balanced Reading Instruction*, 18, 21–28.

Sulentic Dowell, M.-M. (2012). Addressing the complexities of literacy and urban teaching in the United States: Strategic professional development as intervention. *Teaching Education Journal*, 23(1), 40–49.

Sulentic Dowell, M.-M., Hoewing, B., & Bickmore, D. (2012). A framework for defining literacy leadership. *Journal of Reading Education*, 37(2), 7–15.

Sulentic Dowell, M.-M., & Meidl, T. (2021). Pedagogical approaches and models of service- learning in teacher preparation: An historical perspective and comparison. In *Research anthology on instilling social justice in the classroom*. (1st ed., pp. 222–237). Hershey, PA: IGI Global.

Sulentic Dowell, M.-M., & Meidl, T. (October, 2016) *Expanding elementary teacher education teacher education through service-learning: A handbook on extending literacy field experiences for 21st century teacher preparation.* Landham, MD: Rowman and Littlefield.

WORKS CITED

Ertmer, P. A., & Glazewski, K. D. (2014). Developing a research agenda: Contributing new knowledge via intent and focus. *Journal of Computing in Higher Education*, 26(1), 54–68. doi:10.1007/s12528-013-9076-4

Lomotey, K., & Milner, H. R. (2012). Inner-City education in times of transition: The journal, urban education, 46 years young. *Urban Education*, 47(2), 347–350.

Milner, H. R., & Lomotey, K. L. (2014). *Handbook of urban education.* New York, NY: Routledge.

Whetten, D. A. (1989). What constitutes a theoretical contribution? *Academy of Management Review*, 14, 490–495.

Additional Productivity and Publishing Activities

This appendix contains extension activities that further and expand upon each chapter's content. These activities are designed to support doctoral students, newly-minted PhDs, and novice researchers in becoming more deliberate and intentional with their time and provide direction in navigating a path to success in the academy. We know, from our experience, that the work of expanding productivity and publications only improves with practice. Therefore, we see this appendix as providing another opportunity to this end. That said, we hope readers also explore these offerings, engage with what they need or want, and feel free to leave the rest. Alternatively, for professors assigning this book, this appendix serves to provide further support for weekly or module-based activities around the content from each chapter.

Chapter 1 Getting Started With Your Writing

The purpose of Chapter 1 was to introduce strategic, targeted scholarly writing productivity supports specifically directed at doctoral students, newly-minted PhDs, and novice researchers, the audience for this text. Our goal in Chapter 1 was to provide a means for both focusing and advancing individual interests and ideas regarding research but also offering strategies for translating research ideas and subsequent research findings into practical, successful publications. This extension activity focuses on developing a CV. Specifically, this activity is designed to assist novice scholars in how to format their CV and use this document to help manage submissions.

Extension Activity 1.1

Every scholar needs a CV, and it is never too early to begin to assemble a CV. Using the following structure, create your CV if you do not have one. Please note to always list works in descending order, keeping the most recent first. As you develop your CV, we recommend asking a faculty mentor, supervisor, or senior colleague to review your CV for formatting. Some institutions have particular formats they require for CVs which are part of the annual review or evaluation process.

Name
Address
Email
Phone

Education

Employment History/Professional Experience (list in descending order)

Research (You may group together in descending order—newest to oldest; some scholars subgroup according to research agenda as discussed in Chapter 11. As an example, if public scholarship is part of your research agenda, you may want a specific subsection.)

Publications (list in descending order)

Presentations (list in descending order)

Grants (list in descending order)

Awards (list in descending order)

Journal Editing

Professional Service
   University Service
   College Service
   Unit Service

Professional Memberships (include any offices held)

Teaching Experience (include course name, not just number and semester in descending order)

Thesis/Committee Memberships (list in descending order)

References (We suggest you do not add anyone, rather, insert, Available upon request.)

If you already have a CV, update any new additions, for example, have you submitted a manuscript recently so you can list it as *in review*, or have you recently submitted a proposal for a conference that you can add as *proposal submitted*. Skim for formatting inconsistencies, including consistency of headings and subheadings, consistent punctuation, and spacing. Typically, your CV format will follow the reference conventions of your discipline's style guide. You can also use your CV to keep track of manuscript submissions by changing the manuscript status from *in review* to *in revision* to *in press*, noting the date at the end of the entry, until the manuscript is published. You can also address the status of proposal; for example, list that it was submitted as (proposal submitted) and once accepted, indicate that your proposal was accepted by deleting parenthetical information. Updating your CV at intervals (once monthly) is a great habit to acquire. The development of your CV should be ongoing. This is a living document. Add a CV update to your calendar once per month as a reoccurring appointment. By developing this habit early, you will facilitate the revising of the CV, particularly when it is called upon.

Finally, some scholars bold their names within their CV and indicate work with students or community members by underlining their names or noting them using an asterisk. This emphasis varies by institution; however, with the advent of promoting undergraduate research and some IHL's advocacy of actively working with and publishing with graduate students on publications, some mechanism for reporting is warranted. Again, let your institutional guidelines for annual review and/or promotion inform your decision-making on formatting such CV entries. Similarly, if you have published with others, also bold your name to highlight your collaborative work and order of authorship.

Chapter 2 Setting Goals and a Submission Schedule for Your Academic Writing

In Chapter 2, structures, methods, and tools for determining, expressing, and achieving goals and becoming more strategic in academic writing pursuits were introduced. This extension activity focuses on developing a work ethic. Specifically, this activity is designed to assist novice scholars in how to organize time around the three typical areas of evaluation—research, teaching, and service.

In the semester that you prepare to defend your dissertation study, address all suggested edits, and follow your institution's submission specifications, you are likely also seeking one of your first positions in the professorship. Looking for a job is a job in itself and demands careful consideration of what positions are available, what position announcements require, and where you are willing to relocate. This is time consuming and requires a considerable amount of effort. You will have to dedicate time to a job search, responding to announcements, and applying.

Extension Activity 2.1

Several publications and many professional organizations' listservs announce upcoming positions. While some position announcements are published in fall semesters for an August start date the following year, many are published early in a spring semester for the following August. Start with the *Chronicle of Higher Education* or navigate the faculty position announcements of an institution you admire; you can also examine your professional organization's websites for position announcements.

After you locate an announcement, the first thing you should do is determine if your qualifications fit the position announcement. Typically, the degree required is clearly indicated. Dissect the announcement, creating an outline of each specific qualification being sought. Then create a sentence or two, describing how your experience, expertise, and qualifications address each specification. If you meet all of the required qualifications, craft this list into a letter of application. Be sure you address the letter as per the announcement; sometimes that person is the chair of the committee; other times, a department's secretary gathers all application for a committee's review. Note that a CV is always required, as are references. Frequently, sample publications, teaching evaluations, and/or teaching philosophies are also required—depending on the type of institution to which you apply.

Once you have secured your new faculty position, you are no longer juggling perhaps a job and a doctoral degree. You are no longer writing a dissertation; rather, you have successfully defended, applied for your dream job or starter job, and have been hired as an academic. How will you structure your time?

Extension Activity 2.2

Create a daily and weekly schedule at the start of your position in the academy. Start with your morning nonnegotiables. When will you start your day?

What other considerations and circumstances need to be factored in to how you will schedule your day? For example, will you be commuting? Do you have to drop children off for school? Do you work out first thing in the morning? What time are your regular meal times?

Beginning with the time you either arrive at your on-campus office or arrive back home to work, what time will you dedicate to research and writing? Now plug in your dedicated writing time each day across a week. When will you plan for teaching? When do you teach? How much time and how often will you dedicate time to grading? When will you hold office hours? Do you have other responsibilities such as committee meetings or advising students? Many newly-minted PhDs initially struggle with time management once the demands of finishing and defending a dissertation have ended, and a job search has culminated in a first position in higher education.

One way to do this is to use an electronic calendar that syncs across all of your devices. Leah Katherine uses her electronic calendar to not only keep her organized, but she codes each entry by activity (teaching, research, service) when she places it on her calendar. In this way, at the end of the academic year, when she needs to write her annual evaluation, she can provide accurate accounting of her time. For example, as an engaged scholar, in 2019, she was able to document that she provided over 150 hours of volunteer-based consulting to local adult education providers in Baltimore, DC, and the greater DMV area. These kinds of "accounting" strategies can also help you to discern how much of your time is going to mentorship of students or other programmatic service which isn't always "counted" in the traditional metrics of scholarly evaluation.

Chapter 3 Avoiding the Blank Page: Starting From What You Know

Writing takes time to create and perfect, and developing writing as embedded scholarly productivity requires a great deal of ongoing practice. In Chapter 3, a strategy for avoiding the blank page was introduced to provide structured practice. This extension activity involves critiquing three articles in the most current journal issue of your choice. Specifically, this activity is designed to assist novice scholars learn how to gain additional information from the publication outlet on style and content expectations from the current editor(s).

Extension Activity 3.1

Begin by locating three articles in the most current issue of the journal of your choice in your field. Dissect each section of the article for structure. Record each article's bibliographic citation on a separate page (physical or electronic). As you begin your critique, count the number of headings and subheadings and note the actual number of paragraphs within sections and record this information. You may also want to identify the number of sentences per paragraph as well as how many tables and figures each article contains.

Now examine citations. Note the number of citations per section. Note the type of citations. Are the citations primarily from books or journals? What do you notice about the citations across the article's introduction, literature review, and conceptional or theoretical frame? Do you note citations in the conclusions or implications? Are there new citations throughout or all citations introduced in the literature review and carried through the article? What do you notice about the relevancy of the date of the citations and the publication date of the journal? Once you have this information for three articles, you can compare and contrast this information in order to have a better idea of what the current editors expect. While this information will (should) fit within the author's guidelines specified by the publication outlet, it is important to note that the current editors likely did not write those guidelines, and that each editor interprets guidelines in a slightly different manner. Dissecting three current articles helps you meet the current editors' expectations.

Chapter 4 Writing the Journal Article Step-By-Step

Chapter 4 provided a systematized framework for producing a typical research-based journal and/or research-based book chapter manuscript from beginning to end as a structured process for producing a publishable manuscript. This extension activity focuses on a journal's methodological guidelines for manuscripts. Specifically, this activity is designed to assist novice scholars in how to adhere to a journal's expectation for an article's methods as well as how to be a critical consumer of research methods.

Extension Activity 4.1

In recent issues of a journal in your field, locate two articles that report on an issue that fits your research agenda. They should be similar in terms of topic or related; if you locate a themed issue, this makes this activity work even better. Specifically, locate each article's method section and conduct a methodological check, using the following checklist. Write a descriptive sentence about each research element.

Methodological checklist

Research design

Research setting

Sampling techniques

Description of the sample (participants or subjects)

Data collection methods

Data analysis techniques

Methods of establishing validity, reliability, and/or trustworthiness

Limitations

Delimitations

Now take all of your one-sentence descriptions and craft them into a cohesive paragraph or two that includes author's name and publication date. Do this for each article. Finally, compare the two. In what ways are they similar or dissimilar in terms of research elements? This methodological check exercise can assist when writing a literature review, methods section, and corresponding findings. This exercise also requires a novice scholar to specifically focus on the research elements of a study for comparison purposes, a useful skill when either consuming research or comparing and contrasting sources selected for a literature review.

Chapter 5 Selecting an Appropriate Publishing Outlet

Chapter 5 focused on determining "fit" when selecting an appropriate publishing outlet. In this chapter, readers were invited to create lists through quick writes and activities. Readers were also invited to create a master list of potential journals. This extension activity focuses on finding the most appropriate outlet for your work. Specifically, this activity is designed to assist novice scholars in how to systematically review publication outlets in consideration of your current project. Return to that list, which if you continued with chapter activities, you had grouped categorically, methodologically, or according to some strategy for grouping journals together. For this extension activity, we suggest that readers label those groups.

Extension Activity 5.1

Read the following comprehensive list of literacy journals, partially labeled. Note how color codes were used as an initial grouping strategy.

Possible Literacy Journals

@ = ESL
* = only accepts qualitative studies
¶ = writing
$\sum$ = published outside the United States
Δ = early literacy
† = literature-based
‡ = secondary

1. *The Reading Teacher*

2. *Journal of Adolescent and Adult Literacy*[†]

3. *Reading Research Quarterly Online**

4. *Journal of Literacy Research*

5. *Literacy Innovations*

6. *Reading and Writing Quarterly*[¶]

7. *Teaching English as a Second and Foreign Language*[@]

8. *The Horn Book*[†]

9. *The Writing Instructor*[¶]

10. *Language Learning and Technology*

11. *Australian Journal of Language and Literacy*[Σ]

12. *Journal of Developmental Reading*

13. *Journal of Reading*

14. *Journal of Reading Behavior*

15. *Journal of Reading Education*

16. *Journal of Research in Reading (UK)*[Σ]

17. *Journal of the Reading Specialist*

18. *Language and Literacy (Canada)*[Σ]

19. *Literacy (UK)*[Σ]

20. *Literacy Research and Instruction*

21. *Literacy & Social Responsibility eJournal*

22. *Literacy Teaching and Learning: An International Journal of Early Reading and Writing*[Δ]

23. *Literacy Today*

24. *Reading Horizons*[Δ]

25. *Reading Improvement*

26. *Reading Psychology**

27. *Reading Research and Instruction*

28. *Scientific Studies of Reading**

29. *Summary of Investigations Related to Reading**

30. *Written Language and Literacy*¶

31. *Language Arts*

32. *Talking Points*

33. *Journal of Balanced Literacy*

34. *Voices from the Middle*†

35. *English Leadership Quarterly*†

36. *Research in the Teaching of English*†

37. *Journal of Early Childhood Literacy*Δ

38. *Reading Online*

39. *The Lion and the Unicorn*†

40. *The Looking Glass*†

41. *The Journal of Literacy and Technology*

42. *The ALAN Review*†

Create a fully developed, strategically identified list from what you began in Chapter 5. Use the coding strategy presented here or develop your own. Investigate three more journals in your field from one category. Using Table 5.1, investigate each publications' guidelines, locating and bulleting the following information. Specifically, we want you to better understand similarities and differences across the journals in this discrete category. What does the degree of uniformity say about your categories? Might you reconsider your classifications?

Table 5.1 Matrix of Journal Specifications to Determine Fit Graphic Organizer

Journal Name:

Editor(s) Name(s)

Provided Specifications	Notes from Journal	Fit? (Y/N)
About the Journal		
Access (Paid or Open)		
Frequency of Publication/Deadlines		

(Continued)

Table 5.1 (Continued)

Aims/Scope		
Readership		
Types of Manuscripts Considered		
Audience/Reach		
Peer Review Type/Time in Review		
Acceptance Rate		
Submission Guidelines *Make a note of each component below.*		
Collected Specifications	**Notes from Journal**	**Fit? (Y/N)**
Theoretical Perspectives		
Methodological Perspectives		
Length of Time Since Last Related Topic Published		
Editor and Editorial Review Board Positionality		

Chapter 6 An Editor's Perspective on Submitting Your Manuscript

Chapter 6 was written to help readers navigate the editorial process for manuscripts submitted for publication. We addressed the roles editors assume in the academic publication process as well as identifying guidelines for submission, considerations for, and specific considerations for addressing a call for papers for a themed issue. This extension activity focuses on communicating with an editor. Specifically, this activity is designed to assist novice scholars in how to craft initial communications to an editor and how to craft an accompanying letter for a resubmission. This activity serves as a model and demonstration of the kinds of communications that accompany manuscript submissions.

Extension Activity 6.1

For this extension activity you are going to read the following letters, germane to the field of Early Childhood, and craft a query to an editor and craft a submission letter.

Sample query:

Hello Dr. XXX,

I am writing to inquire if a study we just completed might be a good fit for the *Journal Name*. Thank you in advance for your time and consideration.

Our single case experimental design study was conducted across three prekindergarten classrooms. The purpose of the study was to identify leadership skills exhibited by children in a prekindergarten classroom and to determine if a teacher leadership prompting intervention would increase the observable leadership skills exhibited by children. Results revealed children initially displayed low levels of leadership skills but increased the frequency of leadership behaviors following the implementation of teacher leadership prompting.

Specifically, is this type of research readers of the *Journal Name* may find interesting?

Thank you for your time and consideration of our query.

Best,

Signature

Title

Sample initial submission letter:

Dear (Editor),

We are submitting the enclosed manuscript for your consideration to the *Name of Journal* entitled, Using Environmental Modification and Teacher Mediation to Increase Literacy Behaviors in Inclusive Preschool Settings. The purpose of the present study was to determine if an environmental modification (using the ELLCO) and teacher-mediated literacy intervention (invitation, modeling, encouragement and praise) would increase the literacy behaviors of 9 preschool children with identified special needs in an inclusive classroom. Results demonstrated that the intervention produced an average increase of 43 percentage points across all children in the sample. This is an original manuscript that has not been dual submitted elsewhere.

We believe the manuscript will be of interest to the readers of *Name of Journal* and look forward to your feedback.

Thank you in advance for your consideration.

Sincerely,

Signature

Title

Sample revision letter:

Dear Dr. XXX,

Attached is the revised manuscript (provide title). We want to thank both you and the reviewers for the very helpful feedback. We have incorporated the suggestions into the current manuscript. We feel that the result is stronger and more impactful as a result of the feedback and suggestions of the editor and reviewers.

Attached to this cover letter is a reconciliation chart that outlines the changes we have made and their location in the manuscript. As per your query, there are no conflicts of interest (grants, employment by, consultancy for, shared ownership in, or any close relationship with, an organization whose interests, financial or otherwise) to disclose in the Methods section.

The second author collected the data under the supervision of the first author. The first author takes responsibility for the accuracy of the data analysis.

Thank you so much for the detailed feedback. While we have taken great care to respond to the concerns, if there is something that is not clearly addressed, we would appreciate the opportunity to respond again. We hope you will agree that this manuscript reflects material that would be of great interest to the readers of *Name of Journal*.

Sincerely,
Signature
Title

While these sample letters come from the Early Childhood field, as indicated, they can easily be adapted to any field or discipline. The goal is to create at least one for your files so you will be ready to query an editor, submit, or resubmit; then you will have boiler plate language for such future letters as your publishing and productivity increase.

Chapter 7 Working With and From Manuscript Reviews: Revising and Resubmitting Your Manuscript

Chapter 7 addressed learning how to accept rejection, as well as how to systematically capture advice from reviewers and revise and then resubmit a manuscript. Being intentional about the amount of revision needed between acceptance and rejection is an important skill set to master. This extension activity focuses on responding to requests to revise and resubmit. Specifically, this activity is designed to assist novice scholars in how to format reviews from a submission in order to systematically address these reviews prior to resubmission.

Extension Activity 7.1

For this activity, carefully read reviewers' suggestions and scrutinize how the Early Childhood authorship team responded.

Reviewer # 1:	
Authors should consider placing the social expectations and norms within cultural norms to situate the paper. Kindergarten is not universal in design and expectation, so knowing that the authors have centered US kindergarten	We have added language, making it clear that this study was conducted in the United States and also have referenced ACEI's organizational *Global Guidelines for the Education and Care*

(Continued)

(Continued)

formats is critical to understanding the context.
Likewise, social expectations and norms are culture-based. Discussing these expectations and norms in context is critical to situating the study. The resources provided are all national to the United States. Consider adding international organizations and resources given that *ECEJ* is an international journal with readers from across the globe.

of Young Children to demonstrate the global implications of social skills.

The research question poses some issues. It would be clearer to describe what types of social behaviors the researchers are looking for in the learning contexts studied.

We agree; however, our anecdotal observations of kindergarten classrooms found that many classrooms did not provide opportunities for social interactions, which is why we initiated this study. This information has been added before the research question.

The setting descriptions are not clear. It appears that all school sites have been aggregated to provide data; however, it would be better to present data (e.g., demographic data) by school site for transparency. Also, "diversity" is not the same as ethnic or racial demographics. Additional data should be considered, such as socioeconomic data for the school sites, how long children had been in school (e.g., did participants attend preschool or daycare prior to entering kindergarten?), actual ages of the participants.
Clarify that the longitudinal aspect of this study is across different groups of participants, not across the same group for multiple years (while this is eventually discussed, providing this in the description of the participants would add transparency). This information could be presented in a table format.

We have referred to ethnic/race information as "ethnic composition" rather than "diversity."
A table has been added that includes the enrollment and grade levels per school and information that is available on SES to clarify.
We do not have information on if the child attended PreK or childcare prior to grade K.
We do not have actual ages of children, only that they turned 5 prior to the Sept 30 date to be eligible for grade K.

In the methods, it is not clear how variability across classrooms and teachers were accounted for given the

We have clarified that data were analyzed separately across years and deepened discussion.

(Continued)

(Continued)

study occurred across multiple school sites. While the ecobehavioral framework is discussed, perhaps a more in-depth discussion is needed.

The discussion, like the introduction, should view social behaviors and the early childhood setting with a more global view. The implications should provide clearer "to-dos" for practitioners seeking to increase social behaviors and skills with their own learners. More discussion should be considered for the implications.	Although we do have a clinical implications section within the Discussion section, many strategies are embedded within the context-specific headings (whole group, small group, center time, recess, and lunch).

Reviewer # 2:

More grounding is needed on the nature of "ecobehavioral." On p. 7, it feels like there is a big jump from simple behaviorism to ecobehaviorism.	More language has been added to this section to better explain ecobehavioral analysis and to clarify between terms.
The authors state: "Kindergarten classrooms move through a variety of different learning contexts throughout the day...." This seems like an unusual statement. The meaning is not clear here. Likewise, the wording of the following sentence ("Five learning contexts that typically occur in early childhood classrooms were selected for study that were a combination of adult-led and child-initiated") seems awkward.	We have reworded this sentence within the manuscript for clarity. Additionally, we have added the learning context in parentheses after the "Five learning context..." sentence for additional clarity.
A lot of statistics are presented here. This is fine, but I also found myself wanting to have more grounded "takeaways" from the manuscript. *ECEJ* has a broad audience of readers, many of whom are practitioners. Thus, if included, statistical findings should be clearly unpacked and strongly linked to implications for practice.	We have embedded suggestions in the discussion section under the discussion of each learning context and provided a clinical implications section. We are happy to display these in a table format, if the editor agrees.
The conclusions section is in need of much stronger development.	We have expanded the concluding paragraph to strengthen it.

(Continued)

(Continued)

Although the authors write in a straightforward manner, there are many writing style issues throughout (singular vs plural, verb tense, short cuts on wording, grammatical errors, etc.).	We have carefully reviewed the manuscript for grammatical and style issues and had our university's *Center for Excellence in Scholarship and Research (CEFR)* review.
Since *ECEJ* has such an international audience, it would be great to articulate global connections and implications more clearly.	A statement on the global perspective on social behavior has been added to the discussion section.

Specifically, what do you notice about their tone, word choice? Specificity? How does this compare for responses to a suggestion the team agrees with and takes versus responses to a suggestion the team does not take?

Chapter 8 Beyond Impact Factor: Understanding Scholarly Metrics and Increasing Exposure

Citation metrics were the focus of Chapter 8. Given that the measurement of research impact has surfaced as a major consideration when deciding where to publish as well as having evolved as a measure of productivity, the chapter explored the interconnectivity of research impact and research exposure or visibility of one's research. This extension activity focuses on using publications metrics to guide your publication decisions. Specifically, this activity is designed to assist novice scholars in how to interpret publication metrics from different outlets and use this information to guide your submissions.

Extension Activity 8.1

Using the list of possible publication venues and outlets you created previously, visit the website of the journals you are considering, survey, and select two; then populate this table:

Publication	Impact Factor	5-Year Impact Factor	Almetrics	Eigenfactor

Extension Activity 8.2

For this activity, you are going to scrutinize the website of Cabell's, which is a comprehensive source for journal information, evaluation metrics, and submission details for universities of any size. Open the link, register, and begin by reading about Dr. David Cabell's background. Then investigate the practice of Journalistics. https://www2.cabells.com/.

Chapter 9 Considerations for Productive Collaborative Relationships for Writing

Chapter 9 provided information and considerations regarding a range of collaboration configurations. While it may have read as a cautionary tale, various elements of collaborating warrant careful thought and deliberate action. This extension activity focuses on maximizing your effort through collaborative partnerships. Specifically, this activity is designed to assist novice scholars in identifying coauthors for their writing projects.

Extension Activity 9.1

As readers consider their nearing completion or completed dissertation, one way to optimize productivity is to think of the possible articles you might cull from a dissertation study. With whom might you collaborate on certain parts? Could Chapter 1 provide an issues paper? Could Chapter 2 yield a meta-analysis of research reviewed or a literature review around an issue? Will you distill a 20- to 25-page article from your study, or did you structure your dissertation as a three-article dissertation? Think of a system that works for you and plot out whom might collaborate (if anyone); include potential target dates and also try to align manuscripts with publication venues. When thinking through the potential collaborators think strategically as to what collaboration means for your project. Does the collaborator's current research align with your study? Is the collaborator able to serve as a methodologist? Is the collaborator a community member that will allow for a research focus that is research in action or for a practitioner-based audience where they are able to provide implications that aren't specific to extending the research but applying strategies within the field?

Current Projects (Research or Practice)	Potential Collaborators	Expertise/ Potential Contribution	Inside/ External to Institution	Potential Publication Outlet

Chapter 10 Leveraging Your Scholarship: Lagniappe Considerations

....

Being productive means a scholar is aware of the status of their work and recognizes that they may have several pieces in various states simultaneously. Being productive also means that a scholar considers different kinds of productivity, including grant proposals, fellowships, and book proposals as well as op-eds, white papers, and policy briefs. As projects are coming to fruition, savvy scholars should consider how they can increase the exposure of their work. This extension activity focuses on maximizing your work through a grant proposal and op-eds. Grants can extend your work by providing additional data from expanded or alternative samples or participants as well as by expanding your reputation as a scholar. Typically, grants also require some larger purpose, grand challenge, or explicit public good produced. Specifically, this activity is designed to assist novice scholars in learning more about the grant process—especially how to identify appropriate funding outlets for their future projects. In the op-ed activity, we focus on expanding your awareness of the several projects for accessing and creating public scholarship.

Extension Activity 10.1

For this extension activity, particularly for US scholars, we recommend "taking" the Grants 101 minicourse in the Grants Learning Center under the "learn grants" tab of the Grants.gov website. This website houses all grant opportunities with dollars that flow through the federal government. This section of the website also provides information on the grant "lifecycle" as well as information on policies, eligibility, terms, participating agencies, systems, programs, careers, reporting, and fraud. Subsequently, we also recommend perusing the Grants.gov Community Blog. Before meeting with your Office of Research and Sponsored Programs (or similar office) to seek assistance, we recommend reviewing these two resources, at a minimum. Finally, there are also excellent Community Videos in the Introduction to Grants Video Series within the Grants Learning Center. While we know that not all scholars wish or will apply for US federal grants, many of the concepts expertly outlined here apply across funding agencies or opportunities in other locales.

https://www.grants.gov/web/grants/learn-grants/grants-101.html

https://grantsgovprod.wordpress.com/category/learngrants/what-is-a-grant/

https://www.youtube.com/playlist?list=PLNSNGxQE7NWlPcYxVJsglJbRc6c PcfC8X

As a novice scholar, given the continued expansion of public scholarship and op-eds, we would encourage bringing the Op-ed project to your campus. This workshop strategically focuses on supporting scholars in translating their scholarship to a broader audience.

Extension Activity 10.2

We encourage readers to peruse the Op Ed website to gain an understanding of other avenues that can extend your productivity; see https://www.theopedproject.org/. Many scholars find themselves writing op-eds for the *Chronicle of Higher Education, Ed Week*, or *Inside Higher Education*. This extension activity can be used to determine a possible op-ed, and it is not designed to supersede the robust development the Op-ed Project can provide to scholars.

Scholarly Topic (Derived From Your Current Work)	Timeliness (What About Your Work Is Important in This Moment)	What Is the Issue/ Argument?	What Is the Counterissue?

Chapter 11 Next Steps: Conclusion

In Chapter 11, we asked readers to consider and spend time reflecting on how research topics do or do not relate to one another, interface, and possibly overlap. We focused the readers' attention on creating and utilizing a research agenda, and we provided basic considerations regarding writing related to sustaining scholarly employment. This extension activity focuses on creating a visual representation of your research trajectory. Specifically, this activity is designed to assist novice scholars in visualizing the relationship between their areas of study.

Extension Activity 11.1

For this extension exercise, create a visual display of your research agenda indicating connections, where topics comingle, and possibly overlap. We suggest creating a Jamboard with digital sticky notes, using a white board or even large post-it note paper.

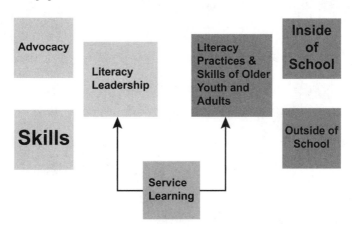

Extension Activity 11.2

Investigate your dream job and corresponding dream institution's policies to familiarize yourself with publishing and research expectations as a means of gaining a sense of institutional expectations. For public institutions, this information is public and typically found in the faculty handbook. For private institutions, this information is typically not public and will require some networking and delicate questioning of colleagues. If the information is not readily available in your search review the faculty profiles in your disciplinary area. If a CV is available, download and review and compare the types of publications, publication outlets, and time from hire to promotion. This will give you a sense of the expectations.

After you have a clear idea around these metrics, create a schedule of what is expected unit-wise and institutionally. This extension activity focuses on developing a clear path for professional growth and development. Specifically, this activity is designed to assist novice scholars in how to be planful in designing and seeking out ongoing professional growth to develop the skills they need to have the career they imagine.

Time-Frame	Publications	Presentations	Conference Attendance	External Professional Development	Internal Professional Development
By the end of first-year review					
By the end of third-year review					
By the time of application for promotion (associate/tenure)					

Index